RECORD OF
GRANCREST
— WAR —

2

Original Story by **Ryo Mizuno**
Story & Art by **Makoto Yotsuba**
Character Design by **Miyuu**

Story

In a world where chaos is the most powerful force,
the people are terrified of the threat it poses. They live under the
protection of lords, who are the only ones capable
of wielding crests that can quell chaos.

However, the lords use their crests to
fight each other in petty battles over territory, and the
continent has been plunged into a war-torn era.

Siluca Meletes, the talented mage whose abilities were on
display at the Grand Hall Tragedy, catches the attention of the
lecherous Count Villar and is ordered to enter a contract with
him. On her way to his domain, Siluca is attacked by Villar's
enemies and eventually defended by the wandering Lord Theo.
Siluca sees in Theo the potential to become the ideal lord she's
been seeking, so she enters a contract with him instead.

The two defeat the feudal lord that attacked Siluca, and Theo
soon becomes the lord of that territory. Lassic David,
the ambitious lord of the neighboring domain, sees an
opportunity to absorb the territory by challenging
the newly-crowned Lord Theo.

With her old friend, the Artist Aishela, on their side,
Siluca prepares for battle.

Key

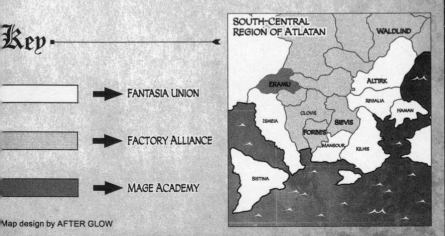

➡ FANTASIA UNION

➡ FACTORY ALLIANCE

➡ MAGE ACADEMY

SOUTH-CENTRAL
REGION OF ATLATAN

WALDLIND

ERAMU

ALTIRK

REGALIA

HAMAN

CLOVIS

ISMEIA

SIEVIS

FORBES

MANSOUR

KILHIS

SISTINA

Map design by AFTER GLOW

Characters

Theo

A wandering lord who hopes to one day free his village from tyranny. He enters a contract with Siluca.

Siluca Meletes

A mage thought at school to be a genius. She believes that Theo could be an ideal lord and decides to serve him.

Irvin

A brilliant Artist who used to serve an Archduke. Seeing potential in Siluca due to her ability to "treat him roughly," he chooses to serve her.

Aishela

A female warrior and Artist who loves Siluca very much. She is distrustful of Theo. Her skill with pole weapons is both beautiful and deadly.

Lassic David

An independent lord of Savis. Full of ambition, he invades Theo's territory.

Moreno Dortous

A mage who serves Lassic. He believes Lassic to have the makings of an emperor and advises him with that in mind.

Contents

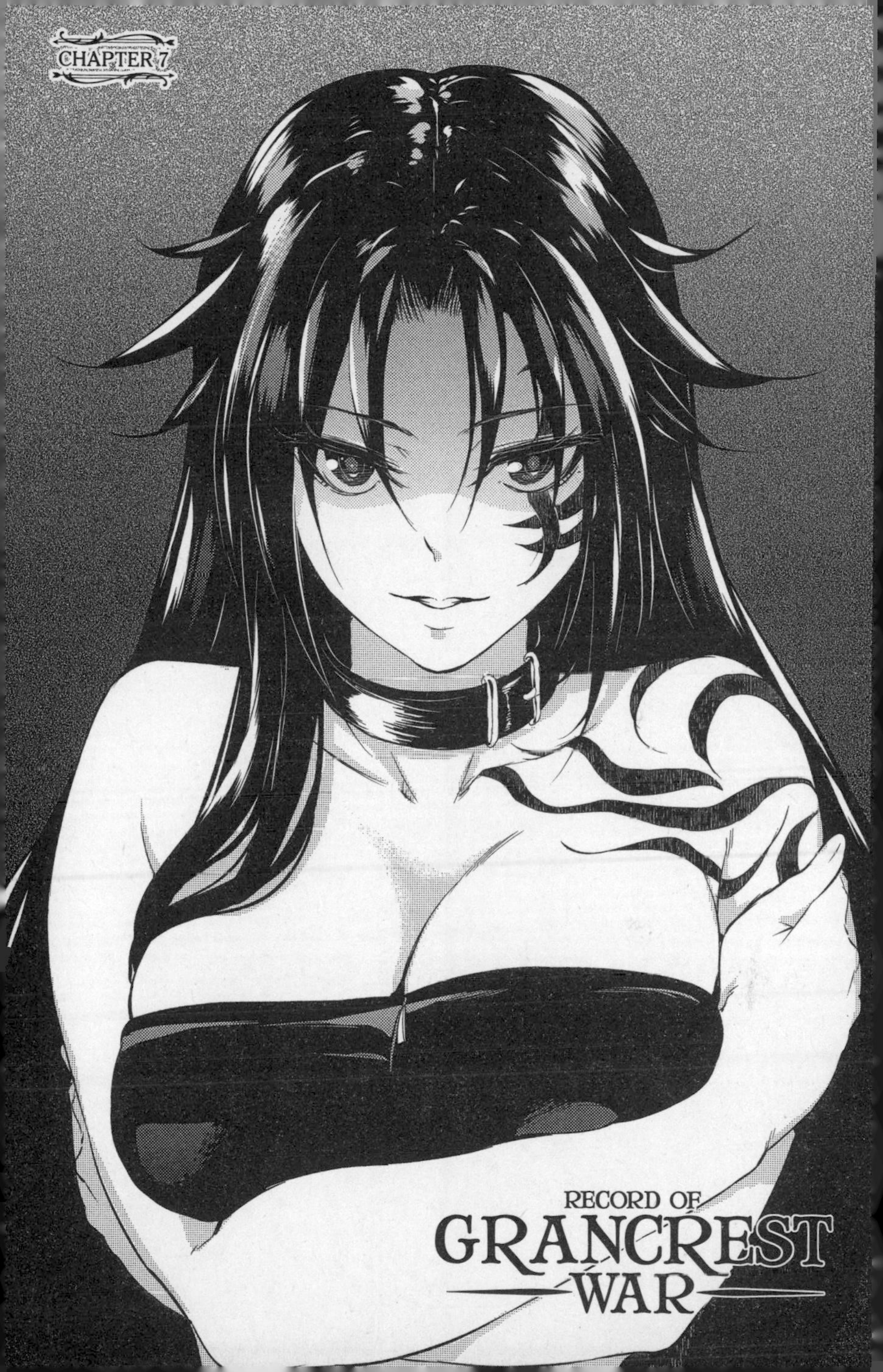
CHAPTER 7
RECORD OF
GRANCREST
WAR

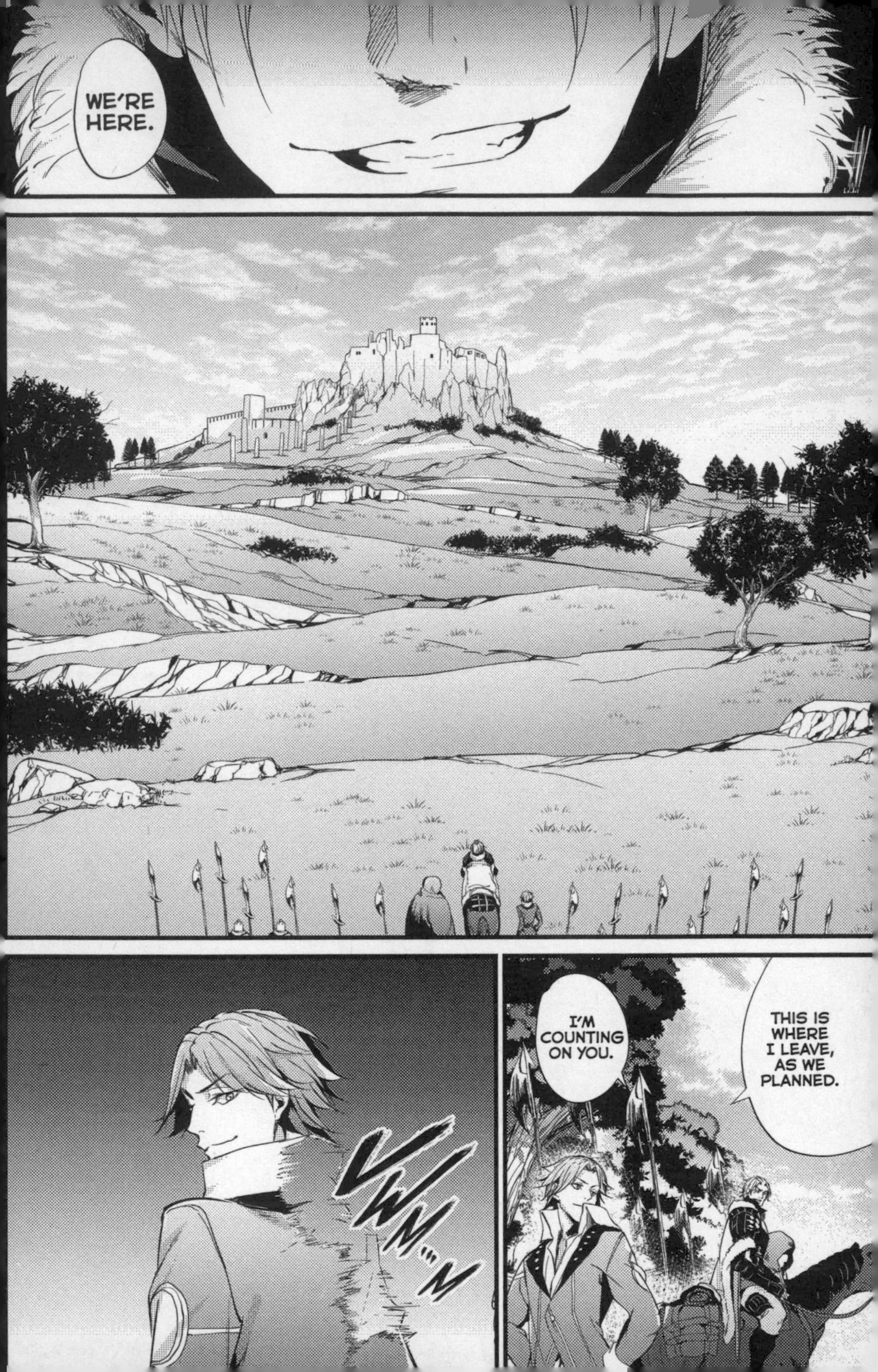
WE'RE HERE.
THIS IS WHERE I LEAVE, AS WE PLANNED.
I'M COUNTING ON YOU.

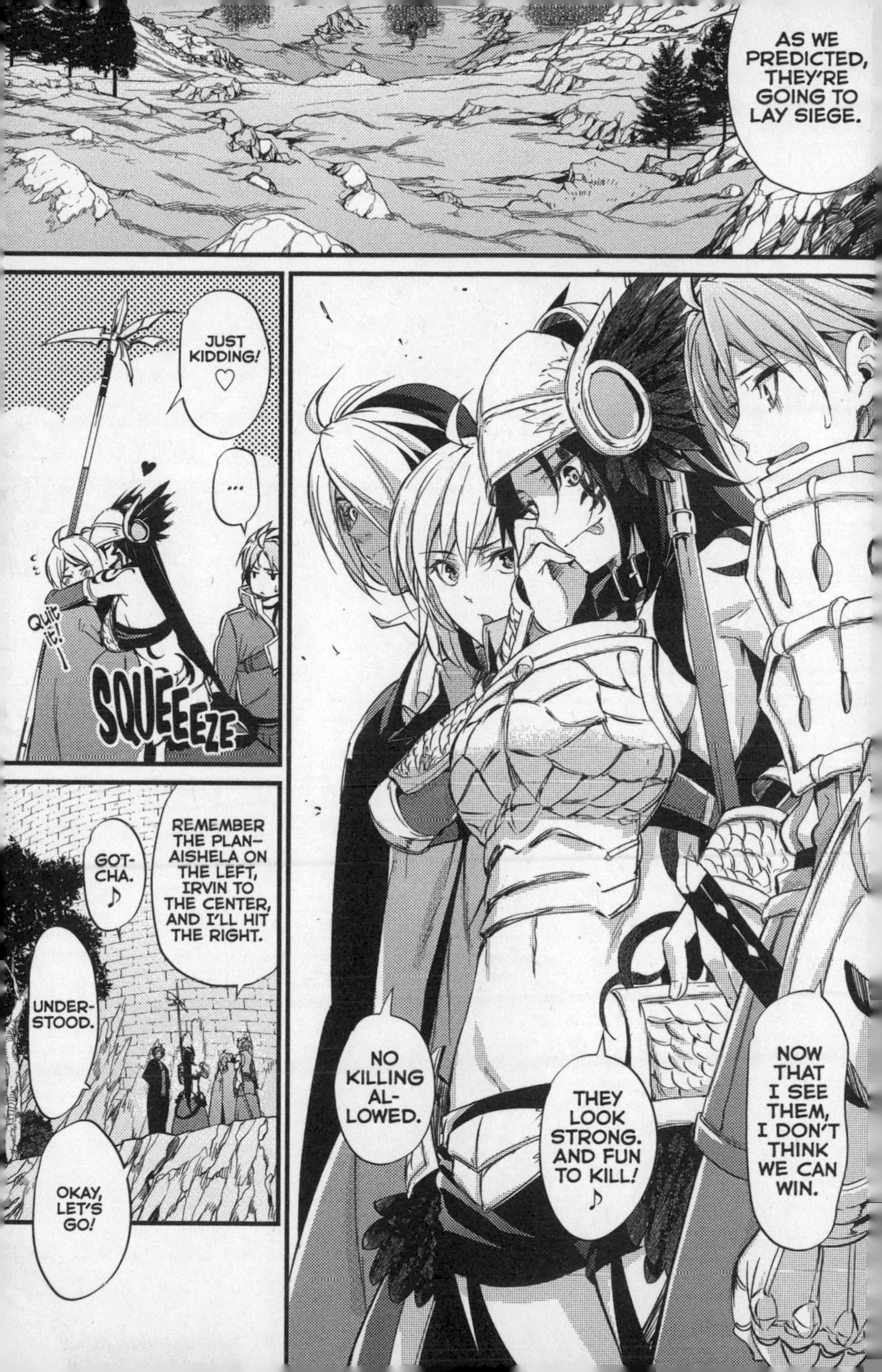
AS WE PREDICTED, THEY'RE GOING TO LAY SIEGE.
NOW THAT I SEE THEM, I DON'T THINK WE CAN WIN.
THEY LOOK STRONG. AND FUN TO KILL! ♪
NO KILLING AL-LOWED.
JUST KIDDING! ♡
...
Quit it!
SQUEEEEZE
REMEMBER THE PLAN—AISHELA ON THE LEFT, IRVIN TO THE CENTER, AND I'LL HIT THE RIGHT.
GOT-CHA. ♪
UNDERSTOOD.
OKAY, LET'S GO!

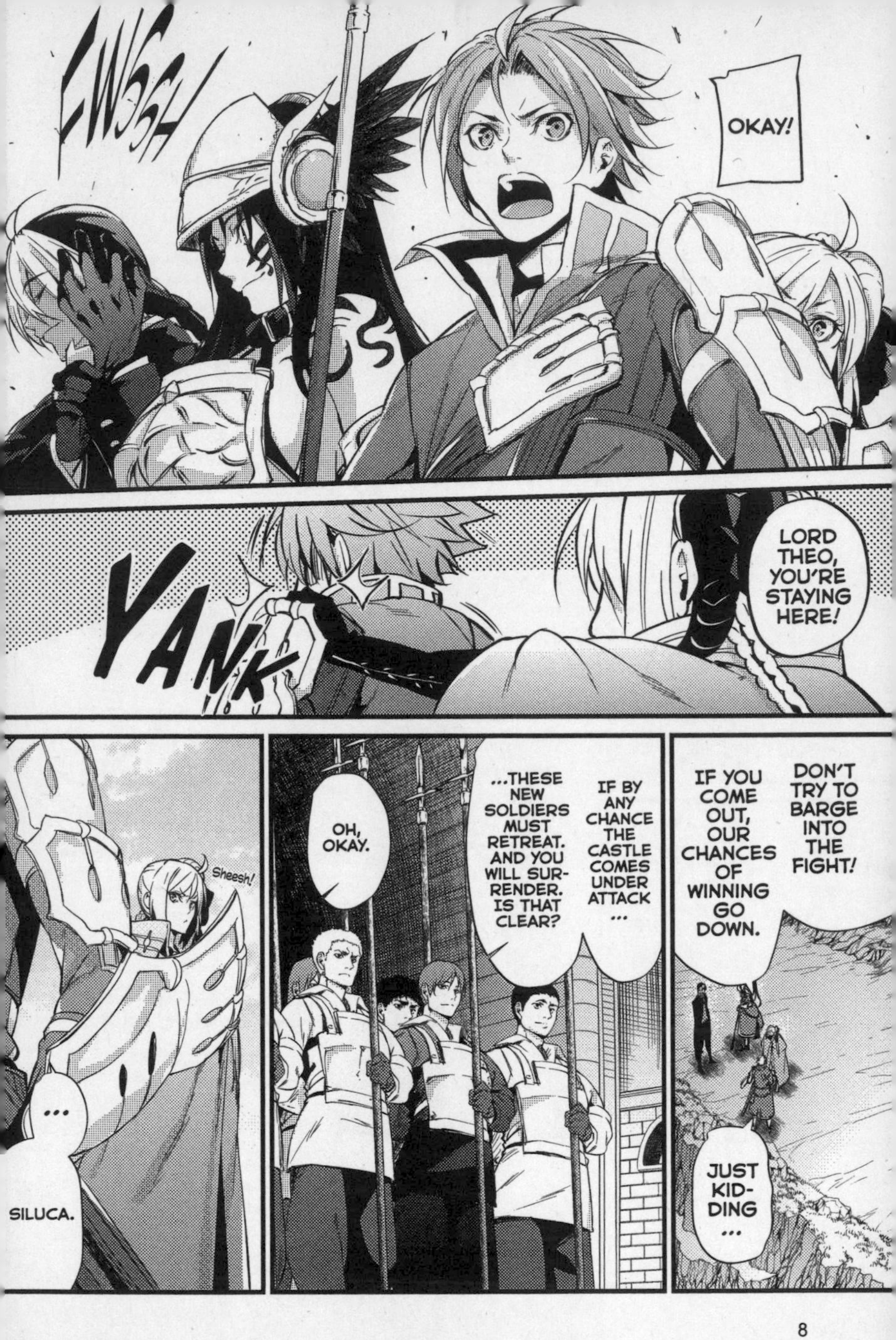
OKAY!
FWSSH
LORD THEO, YOU'RE STAYING HERE!
YANK
DON'T TRY TO BARGE INTO THE FIGHT!
IF YOU COME OUT, OUR CHANCES OF WINNING GO DOWN.
JUST KID-DING ...
IF BY ANY CHANCE THE CASTLE COMES UNDER ATTACK ...
...THESE NEW SOLDIERS MUST RETREAT. AND YOU WILL SUR-RENDER. IS THAT CLEAR?
OH, OKAY.
Sheesh!
...
SILUCA.

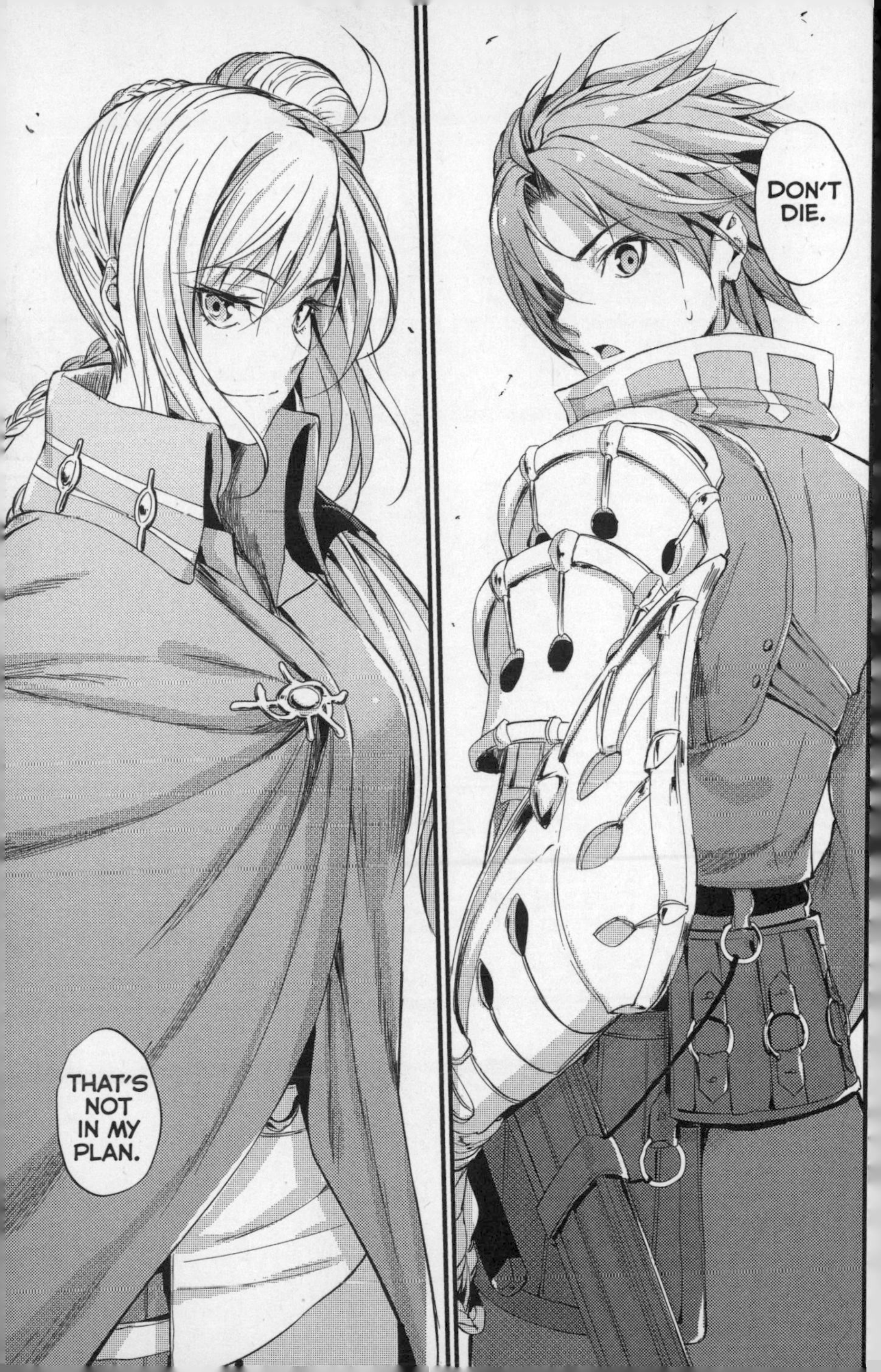
DON'T DIE.
THAT'S NOT IN MY PLAN.

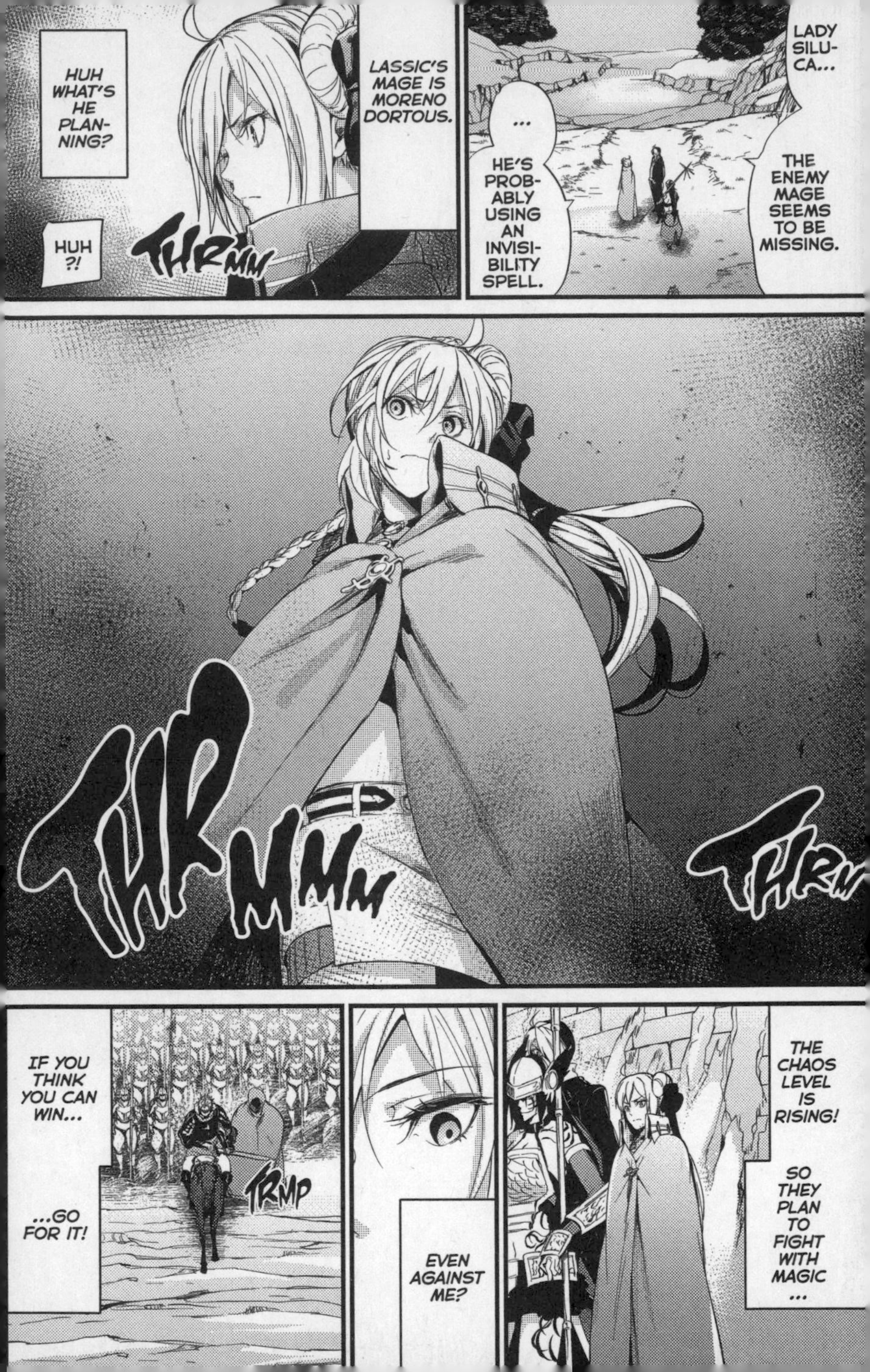
LADY SILUCA...
THE ENEMY MAGE SEEMS TO BE MISSING.
...
HE'S PROBABLY USING AN INVISIBILITY SPELL.
LASSIC'S MAGE IS MORENO DORTOUS.
HUH WHAT'S HE PLANNING?
THRMM
HUH ?!
THRM
THRMMM
THE CHAOS LEVEL IS RISING!
SO THEY PLAN TO FIGHT WITH MAGIC...
EVEN AGAINST ME?
IF YOU THINK YOU CAN WIN...
TRMP
...GO FOR IT!

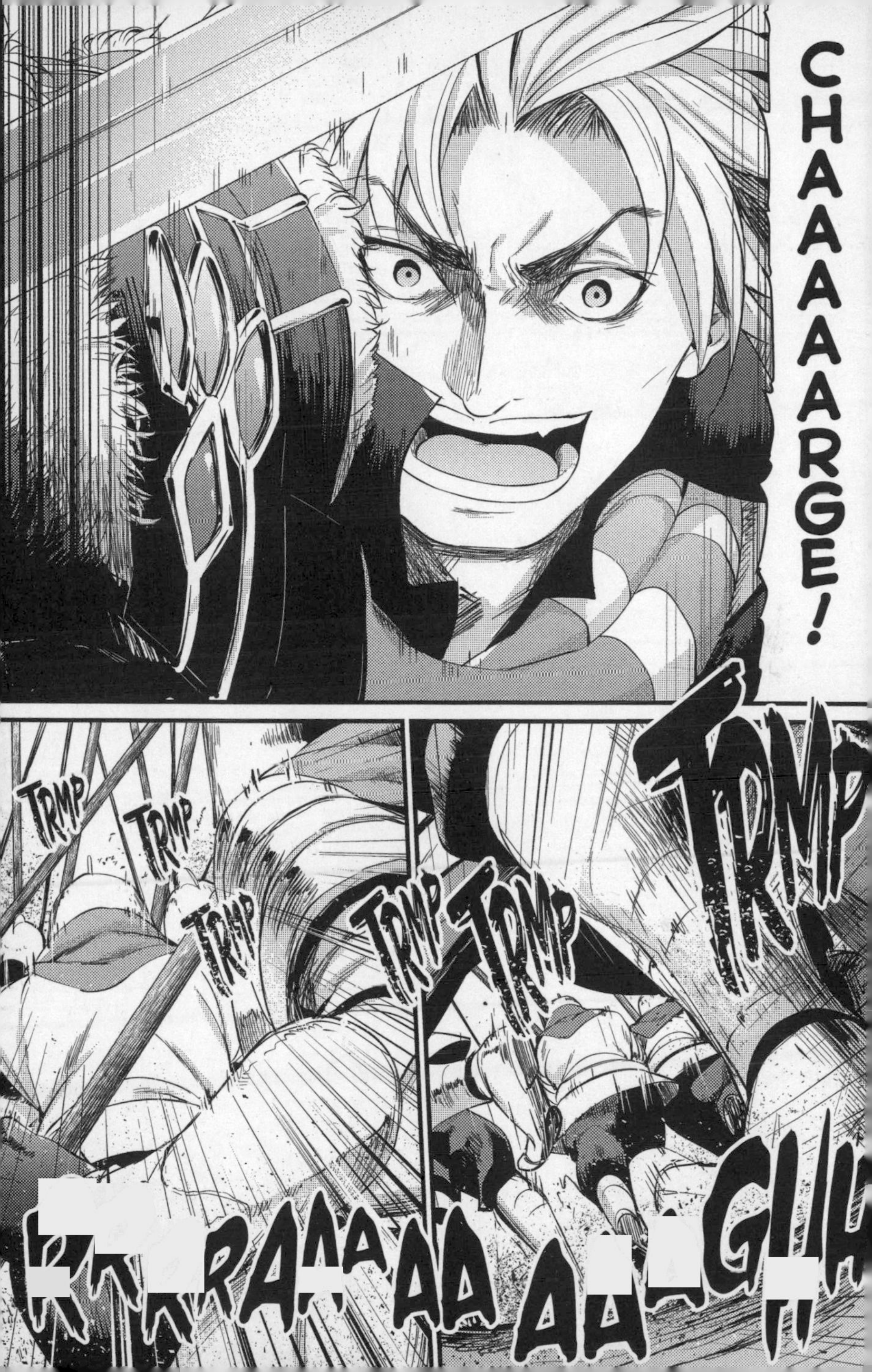
CHAAAARGE!
TRMP
TRMP
TRMP
TRMP
TRMP
TRMP

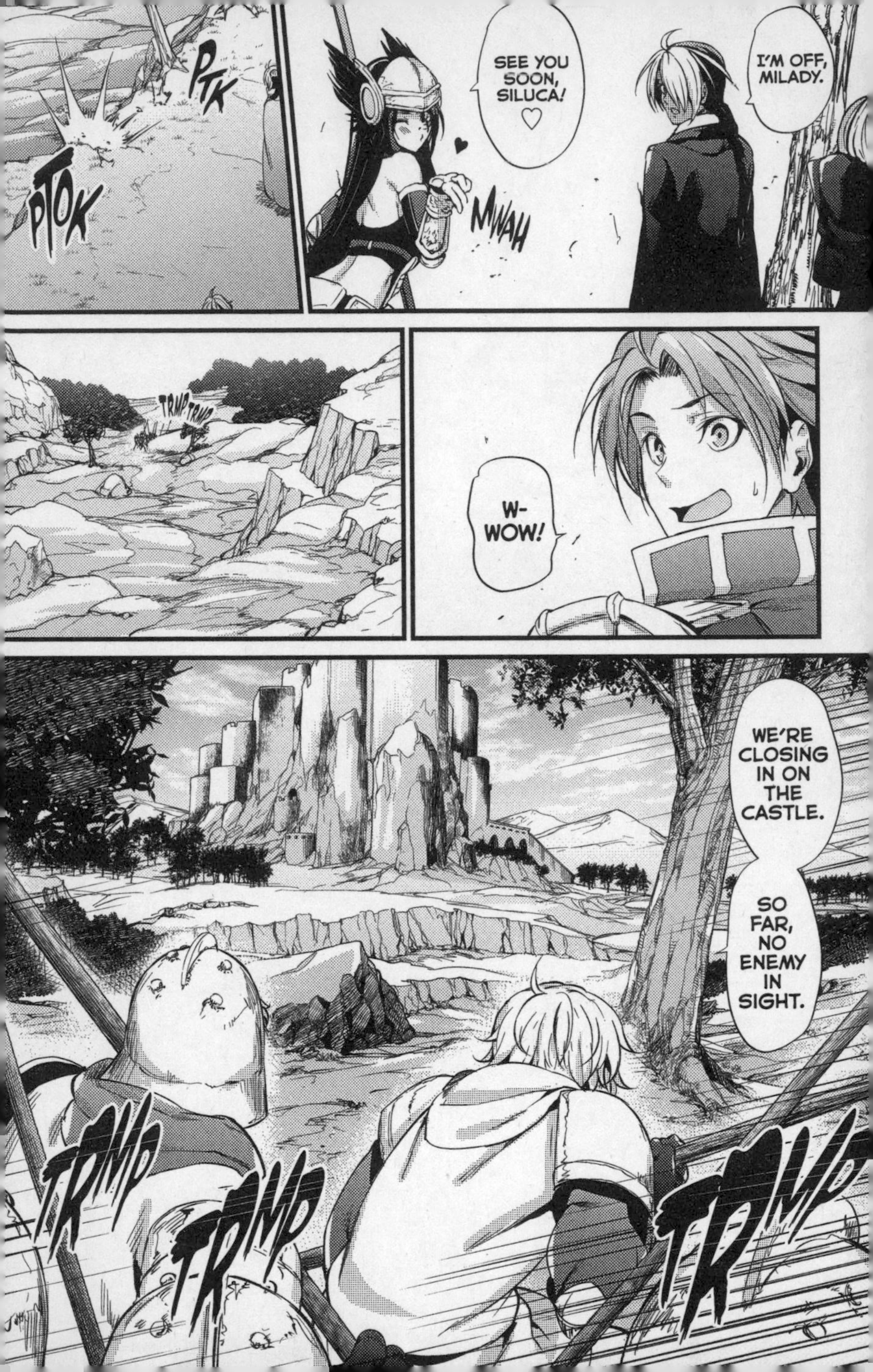
I'M OFF, MILADY.
SEE YOU SOON, SILUCA! ♡
MWAH
PTK
PTOK
W-WOW!
TRMP TRMP
WE'RE CLOSING IN ON THE CASTLE.
SO FAR, NO ENEMY IN SIGHT.
TRMP
TRMP
TRMP

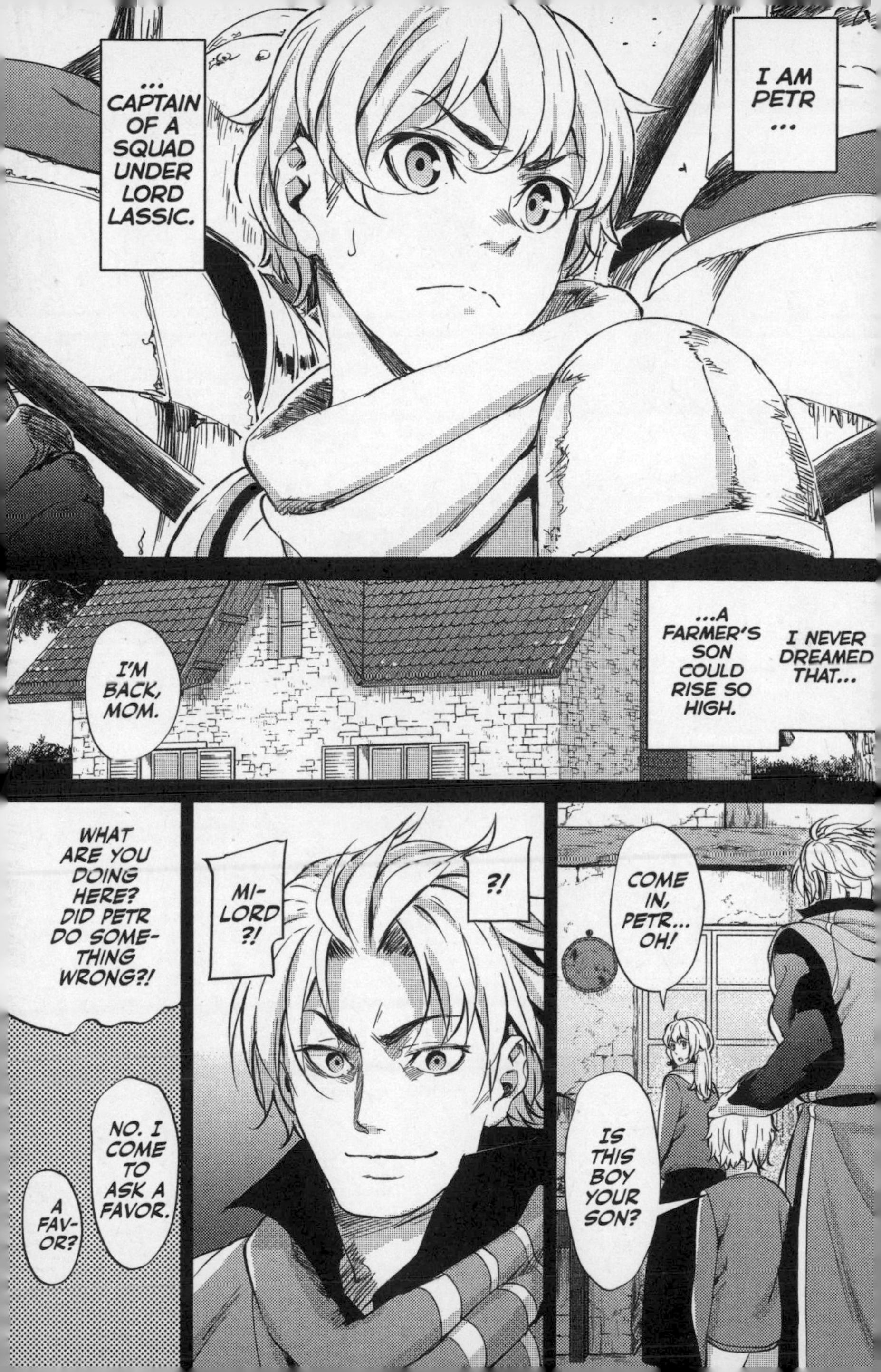
I AM PETR ...
... CAPTAIN OF A SQUAD UNDER LORD LASSIC.
I NEVER DREAMED THAT...
...A FARMER'S SON COULD RISE SO HIGH.
I'M BACK, MOM.
COME IN, PETR... OH!
IS THIS BOY YOUR SON?
?!
MI-LORD?!
WHAT ARE YOU DOING HERE? DID PETR DO SOME-THING WRONG?!
NO. I COME TO ASK A FAVOR.
A FAV-OR?

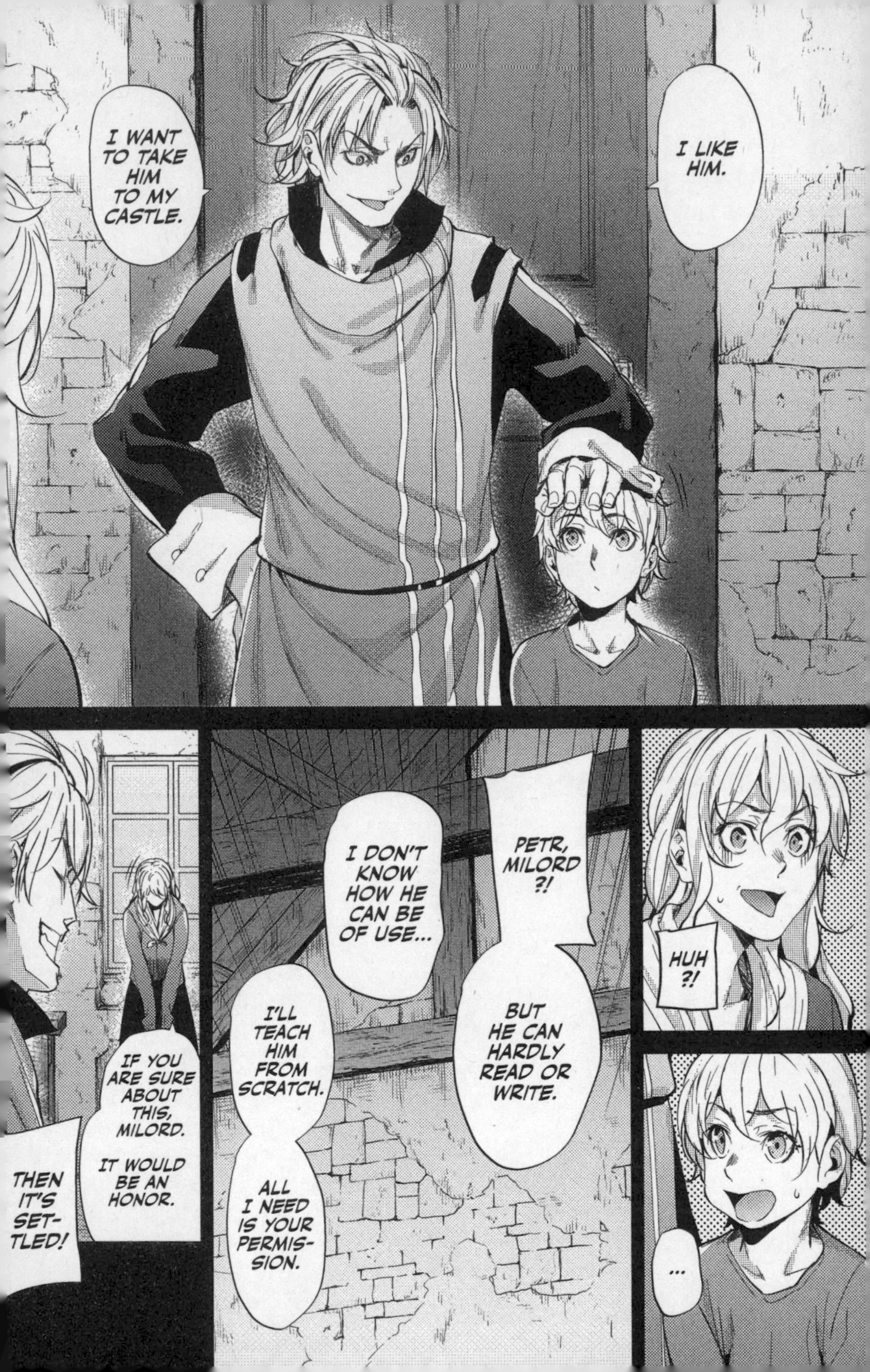
I LIKE HIM.
I WANT TO TAKE HIM TO MY CASTLE.
HUH ?!
...
PETR, MILORD ?!
I DON'T KNOW HOW HE CAN BE OF USE...
BUT HE CAN HARDLY READ OR WRITE.
I'LL TEACH HIM FROM SCRATCH.
ALL I NEED IS YOUR PERMIS-SION.
IF YOU ARE SURE ABOUT THIS, MILORD.
IT WOULD BE AN HONOR.
THEN IT'S SET-TLED!

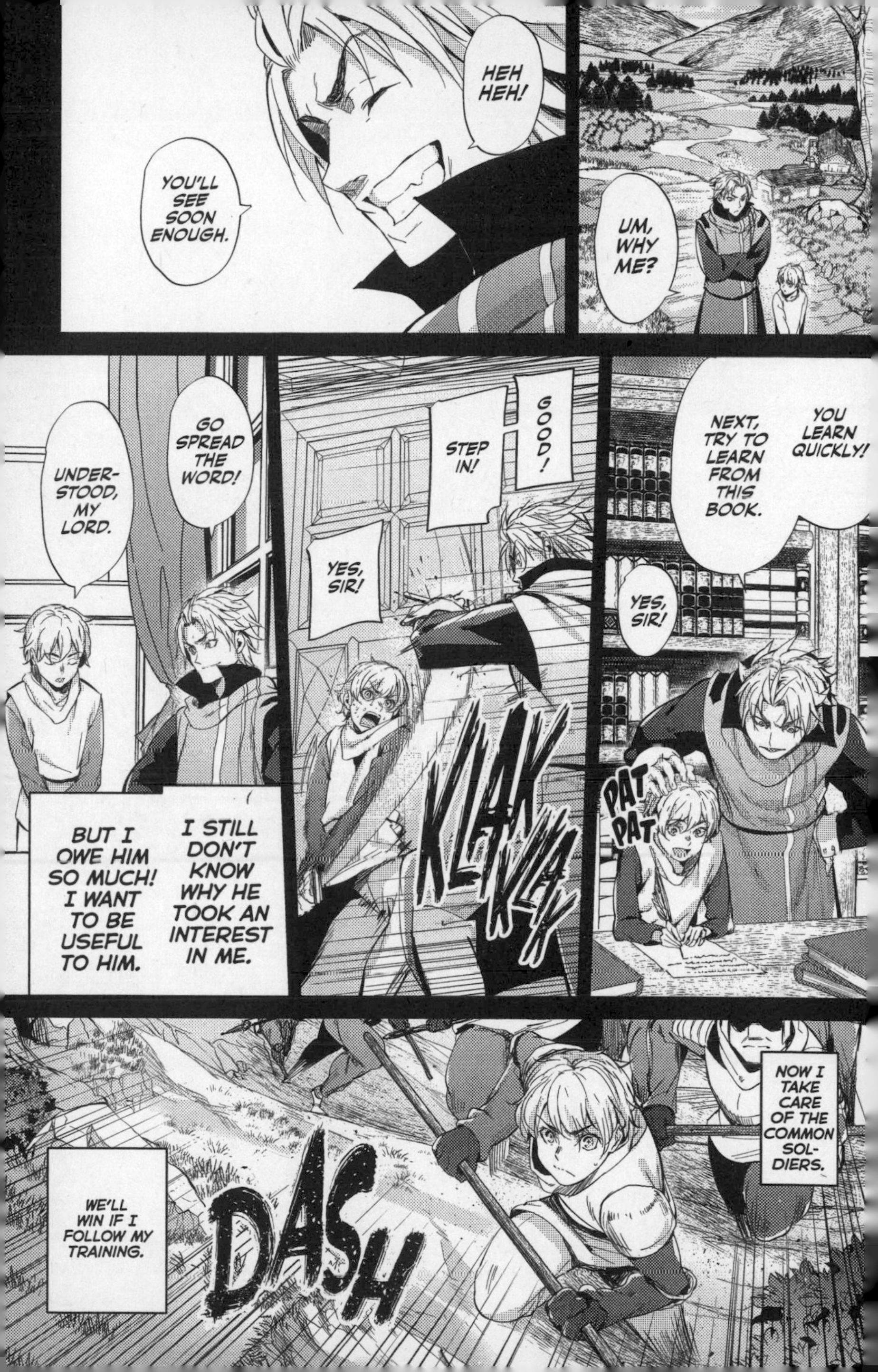
UM, WHY ME?
HEH HEH!
YOU'LL SEE SOON ENOUGH.
YOU LEARN QUICKLY!
NEXT, TRY TO LEARN FROM THIS BOOK.
YES, SIR!
PAT PAT
GOOD!
STEP IN!
YES, SIR!
KLAK KLAK
GO SPREAD THE WORD!
UNDER-STOOD, MY LORD.
I STILL DON'T KNOW WHY HE TOOK AN INTEREST IN ME.
BUT I OWE HIM SO MUCH! I WANT TO BE USEFUL TO HIM.
NOW I TAKE CARE OF THE COMMON SOL-DIERS.
DASH
WE'LL WIN IF I FOLLOW MY TRAINING.

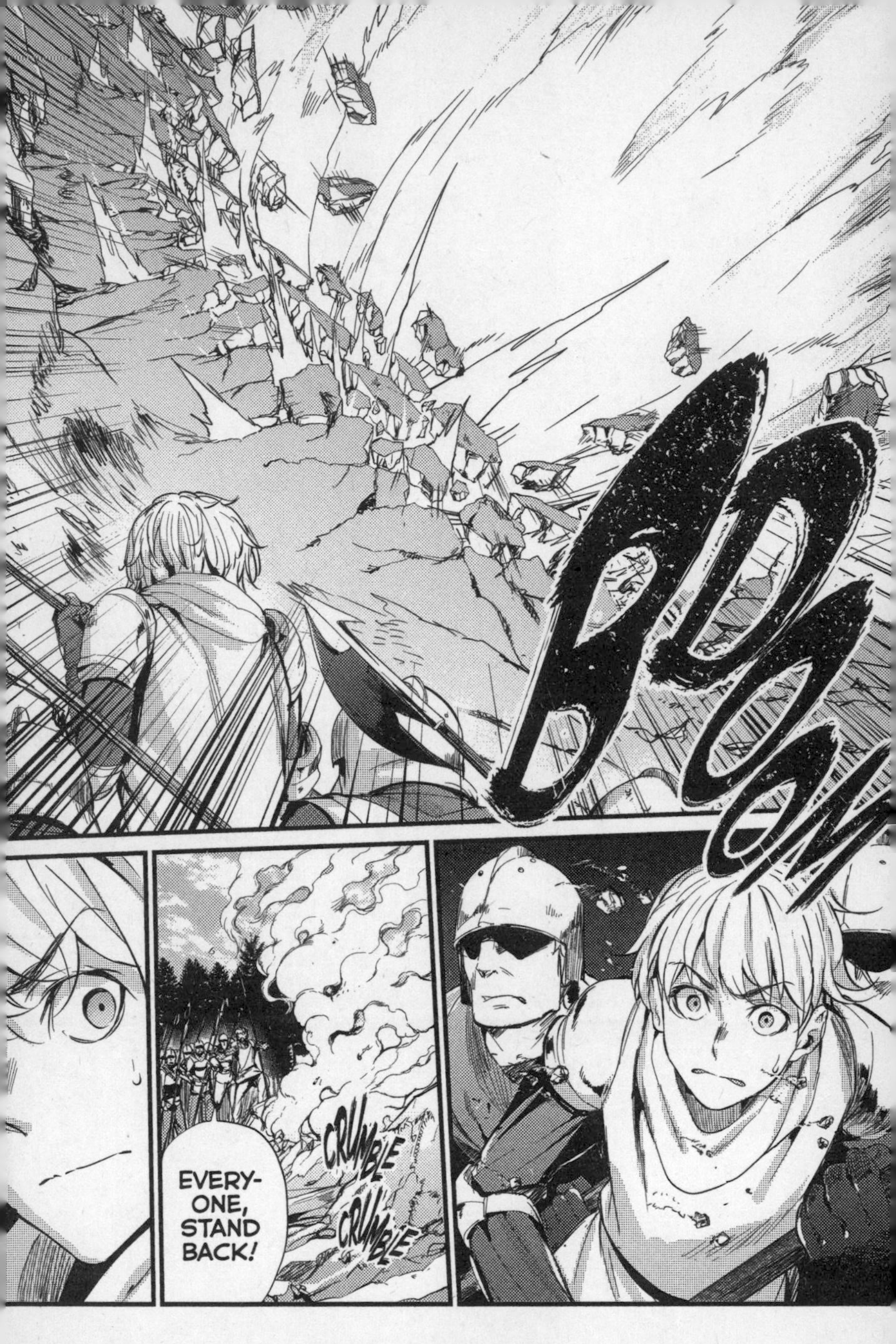
BOOM
EVERY-ONE, STAND BACK!
CRUMBLE
CRUMBLE

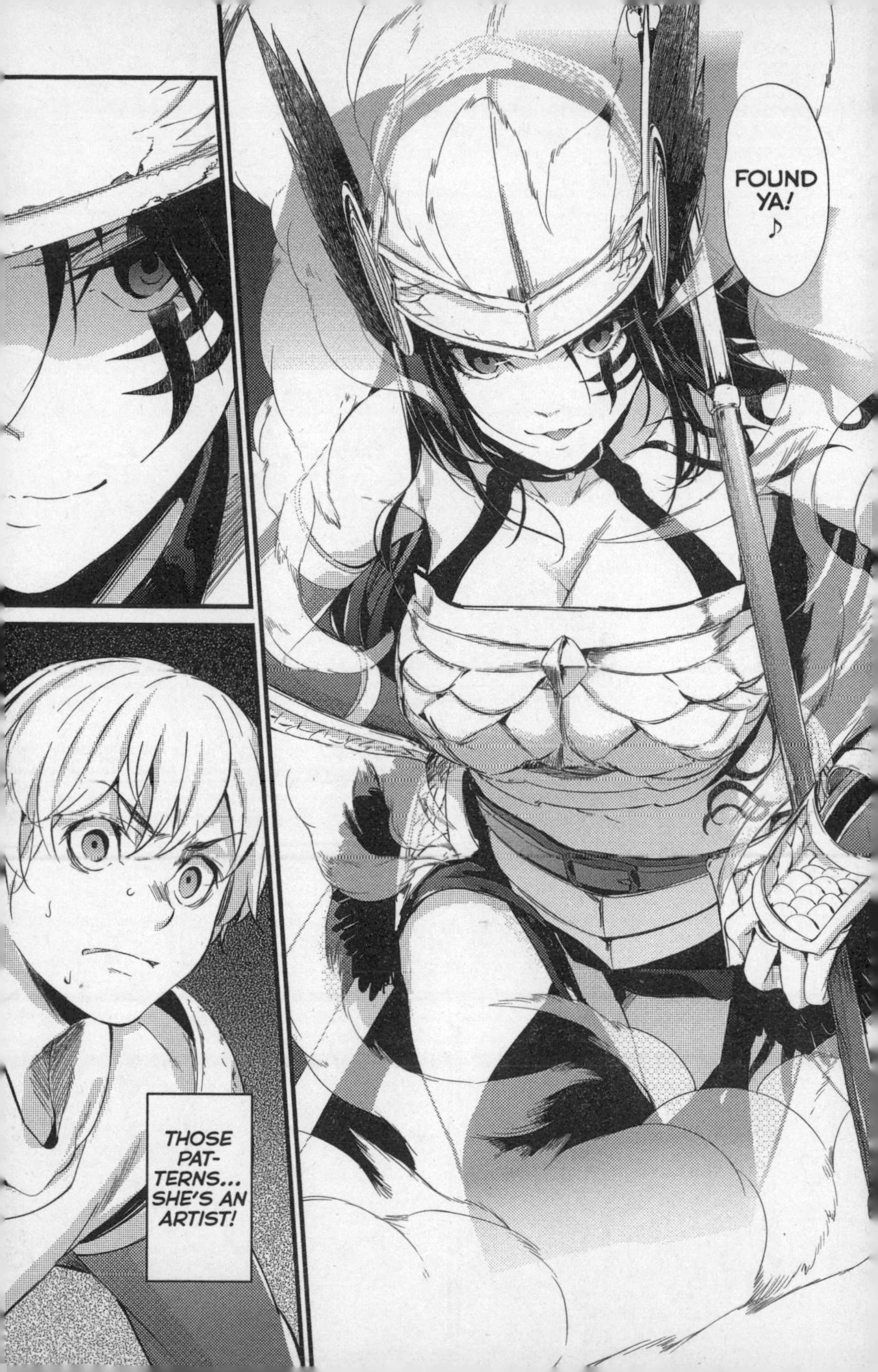
FOUND YA! ♪
THOSE PATTERNS... SHE'S AN ARTIST!

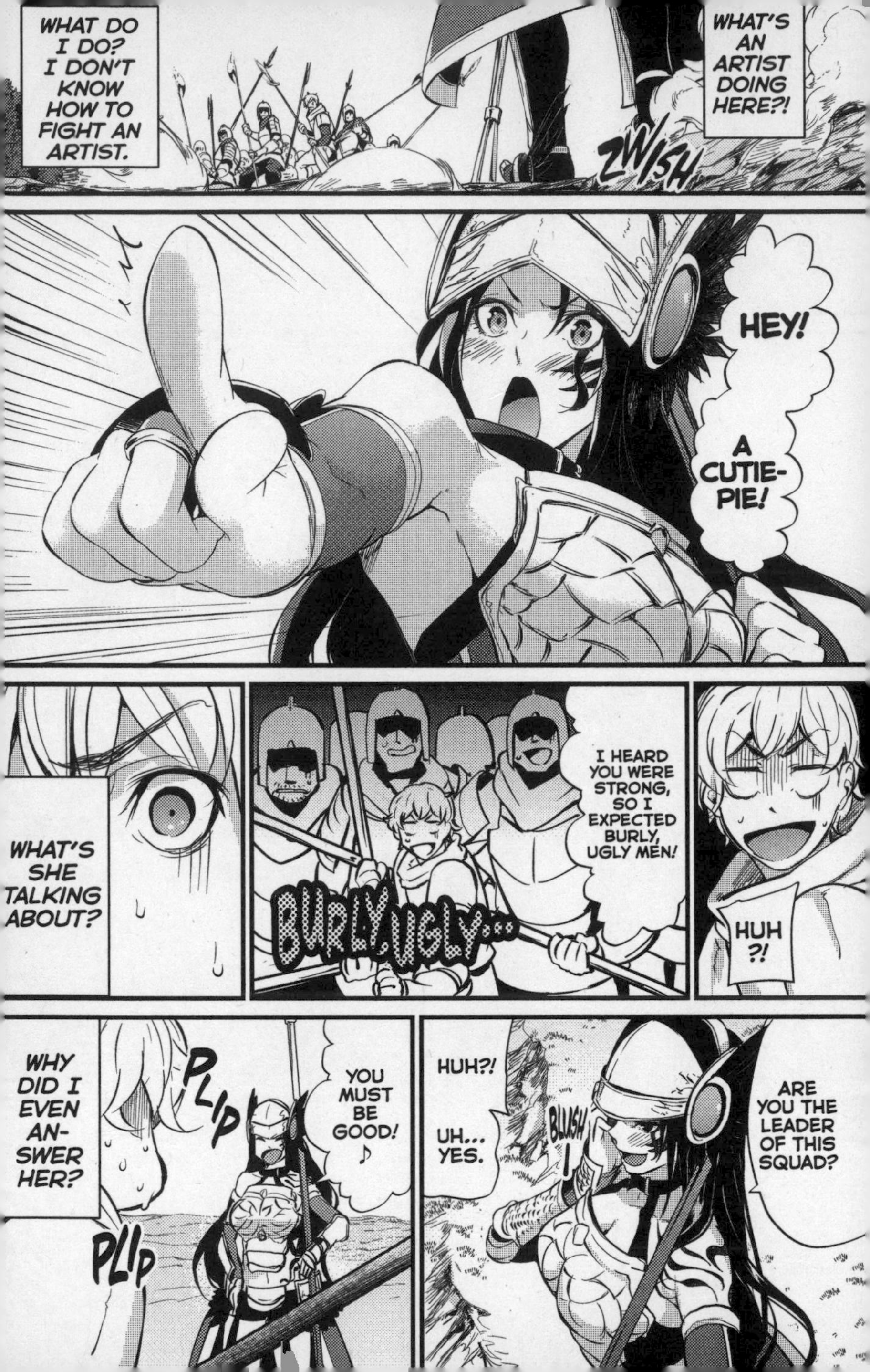
WHAT'S AN ARTIST DOING HERE?!
ZWISH
WHAT DO I DO? I DON'T KNOW HOW TO FIGHT AN ARTIST.
HEY!
A CUTIE-PIE!
HUH ?!
I HEARD YOU WERE STRONG, SO I EXPECTED BURLY, UGLY MEN!
BURLY, UGLY...
WHAT'S SHE TALKING ABOUT?
ARE YOU THE LEADER OF THIS SQUAD?
BLUSH
HUH?!
UH... YES.
YOU MUST BE GOOD! ♪
PLIP
WHY DID I EVEN AN-SWER HER?
PLIP

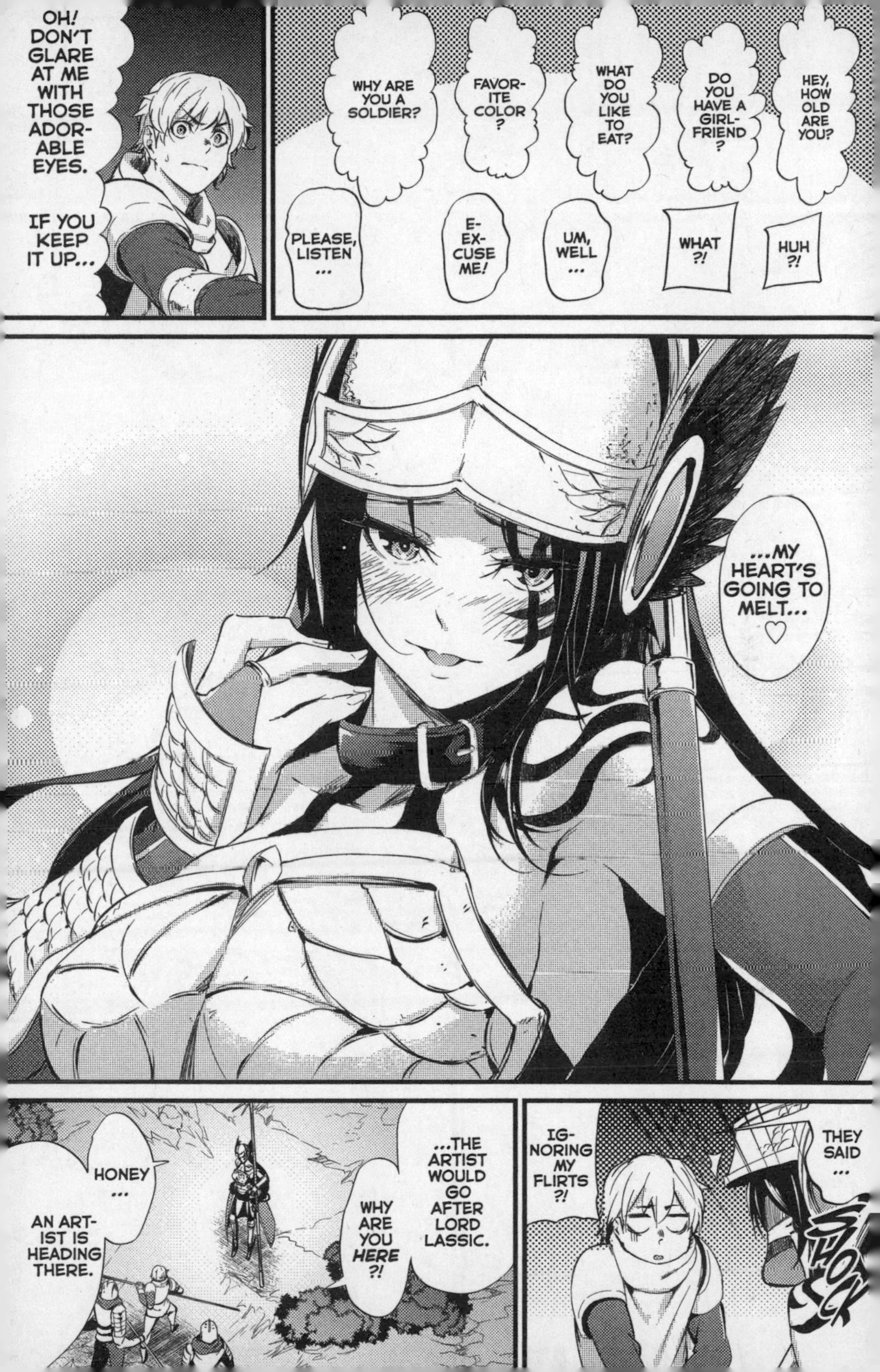
HEY, HOW OLD ARE YOU?
HUH ?!
DO YOU HAVE A GIRL-FRIEND ?
WHAT ?!
WHAT DO YOU LIKE TO EAT?
UM, WELL ...
FAVOR-ITE COLOR ?
E-EX-CUSE ME!
WHY ARE YOU A SOLDIER?
PLEASE, LISTEN ...
OH! DON'T GLARE AT ME WITH THOSE ADOR-ABLE EYES.
IF YOU KEEP IT UP...
...MY HEART'S GOING TO MELT... ♡
THEY SAID ...
SHOCK
IG-NORING MY FLIRTS ?!
...THE ARTIST WOULD GO AFTER LORD LASSIC.
WHY ARE YOU *HERE* ?!
HONEY ...
AN ART-IST IS HEADING THERE.

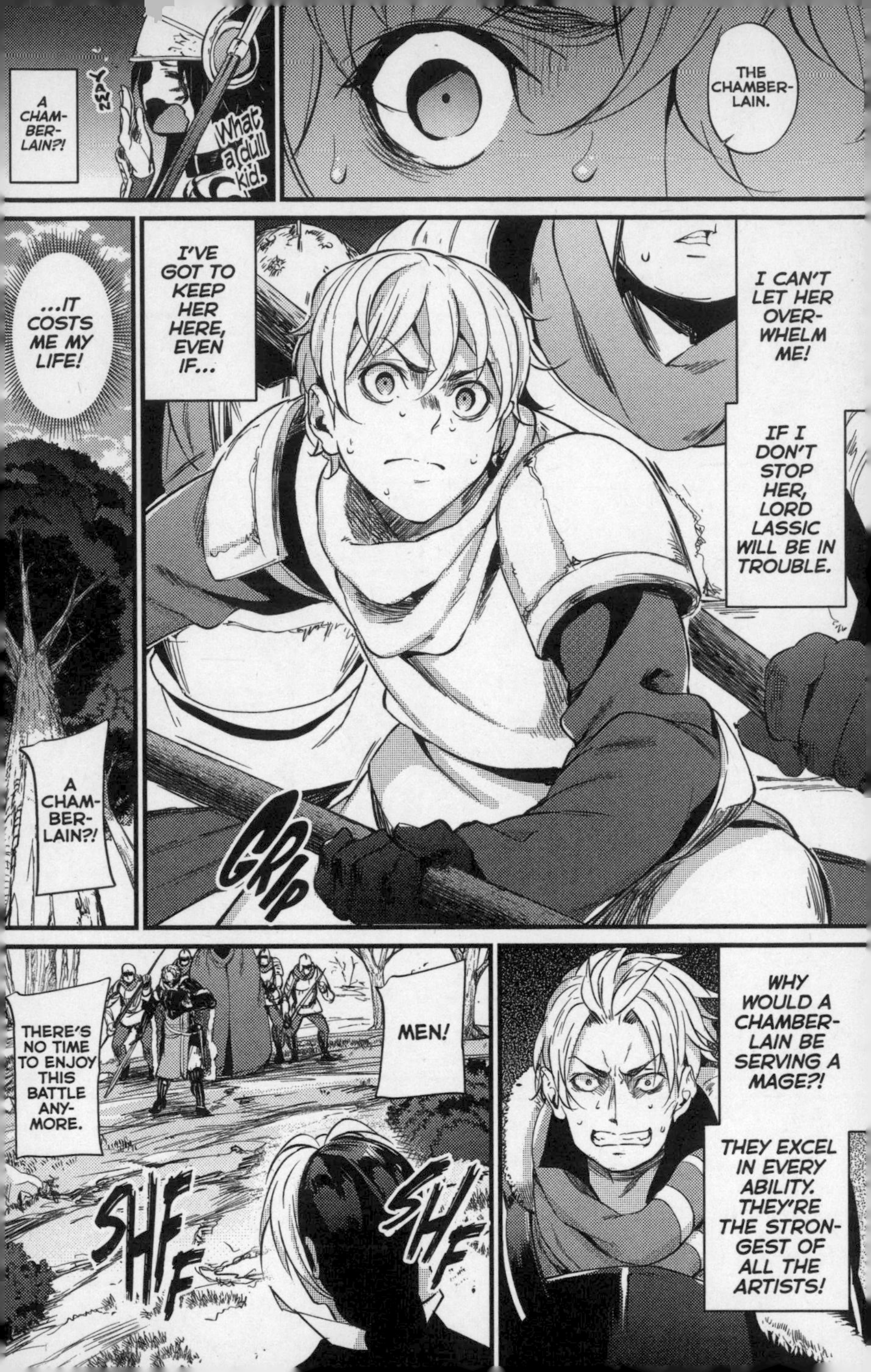
THE CHAMBERLAIN.
What a dull kid.
YAWN
A CHAMBERLAIN?!
I CAN'T LET HER OVERWHELM ME!
IF I DON'T STOP HER, LORD LASSIC WILL BE IN TROUBLE.
I'VE GOT TO KEEP HER HERE, EVEN IF...
GRIP
...IT COSTS ME MY LIFE!
A CHAMBERLAIN?!
WHY WOULD A CHAMBERLAIN BE SERVING A MAGE?!
THEY EXCEL IN EVERY ABILITY. THEY'RE THE STRONGEST OF ALL THE ARTISTS!
MEN!
THERE'S NO TIME TO ENJOY THIS BATTLE ANYMORE.
SHF
SHF
SHF
SHF

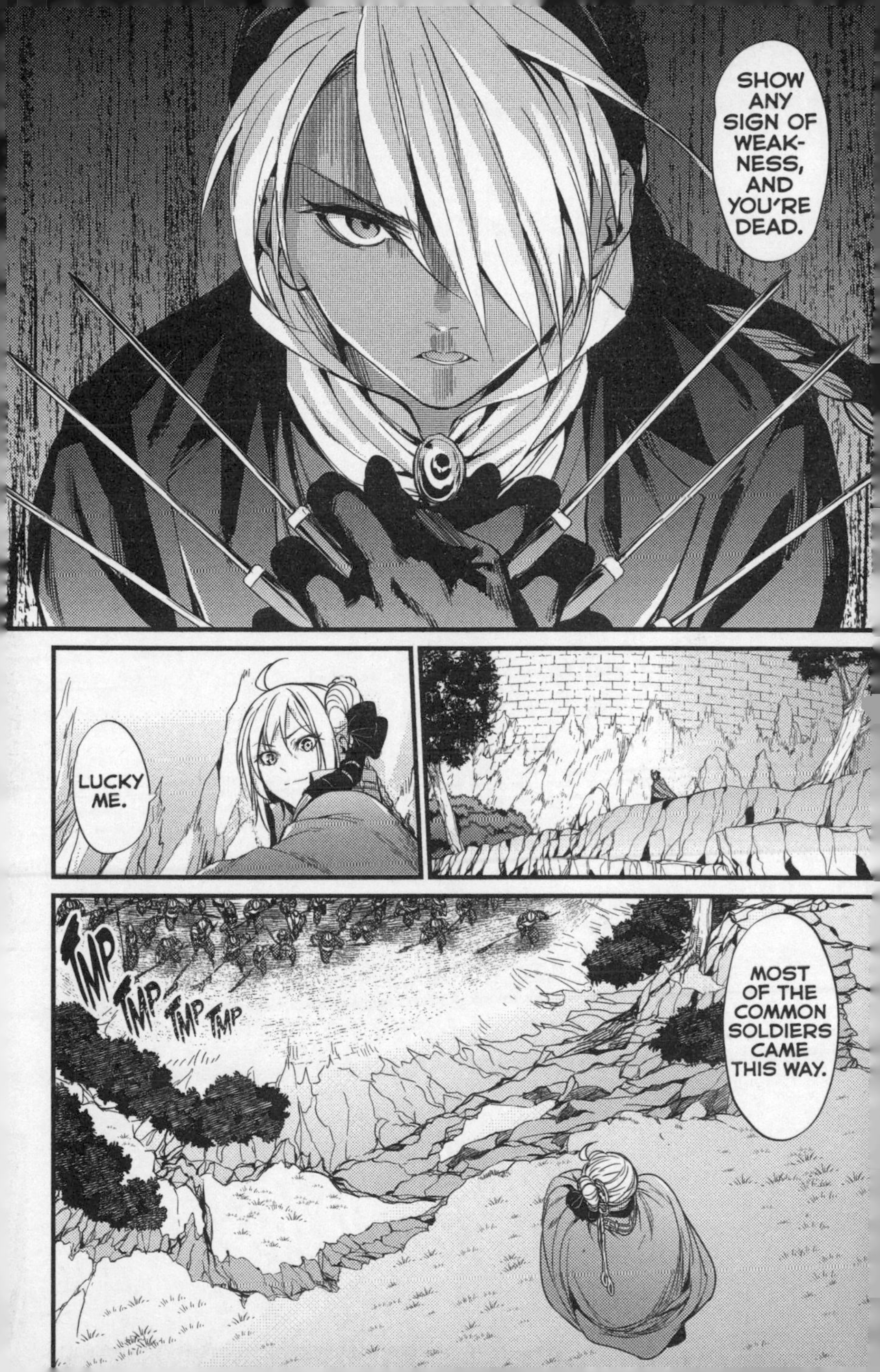
SHOW ANY SIGN OF WEAK-NESS, AND YOU'RE DEAD.
LUCKY ME.
MOST OF THE COMMON SOLDIERS CAME THIS WAY.
TMP TMP TMP TMP

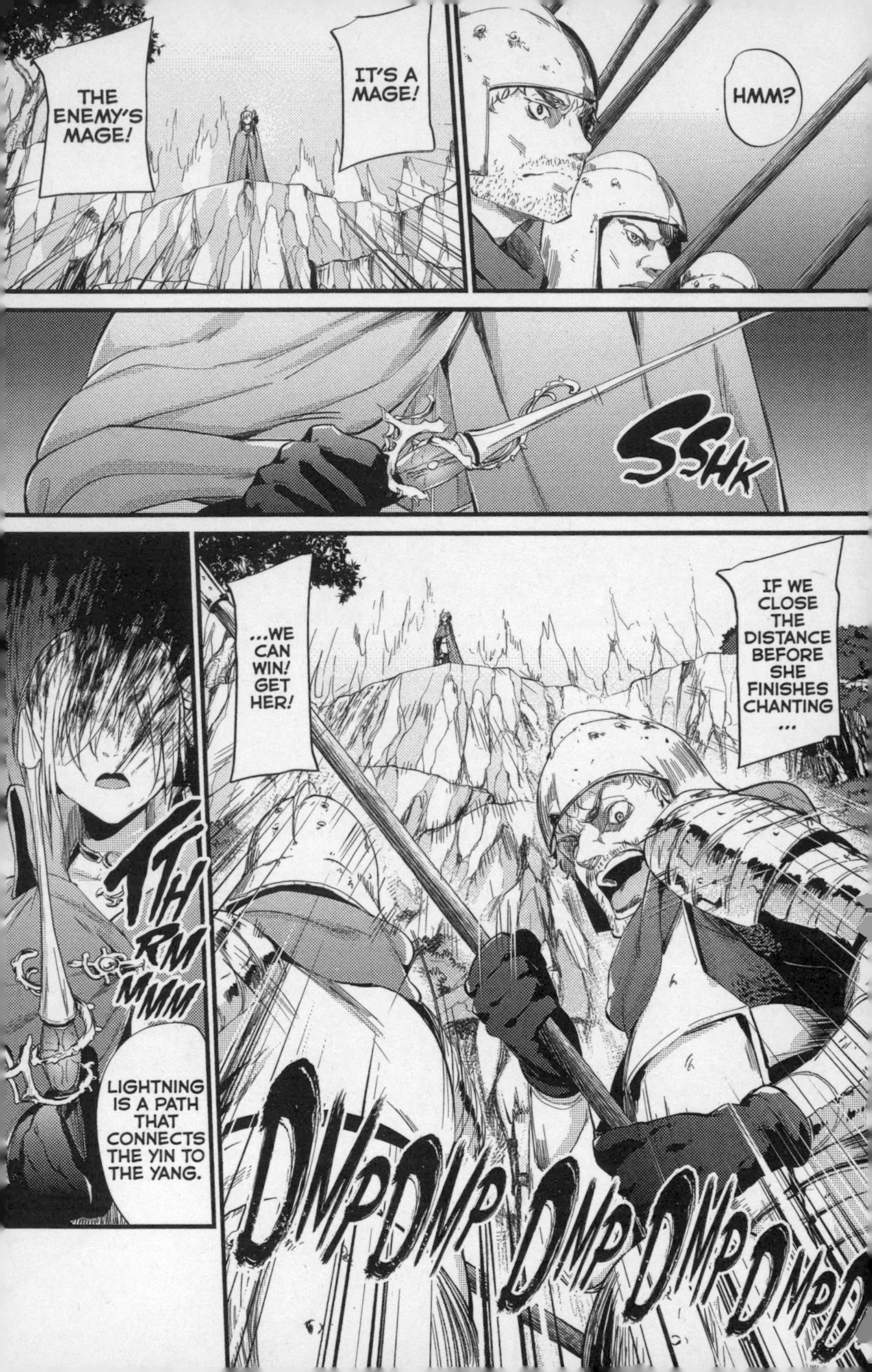
HMM?
IT'S A MAGE!
THE ENEMY'S MAGE!
SSHK
IF WE CLOSE THE DISTANCE BEFORE SHE FINISHES CHANTING...
...WE CAN WIN! GET HER!
DMP DMP DMP DMP DMP DMP DMP DMP
TTHRMMMM
LIGHTNING IS A PATH THAT CONNECTS THE YIN TO THE YANG.

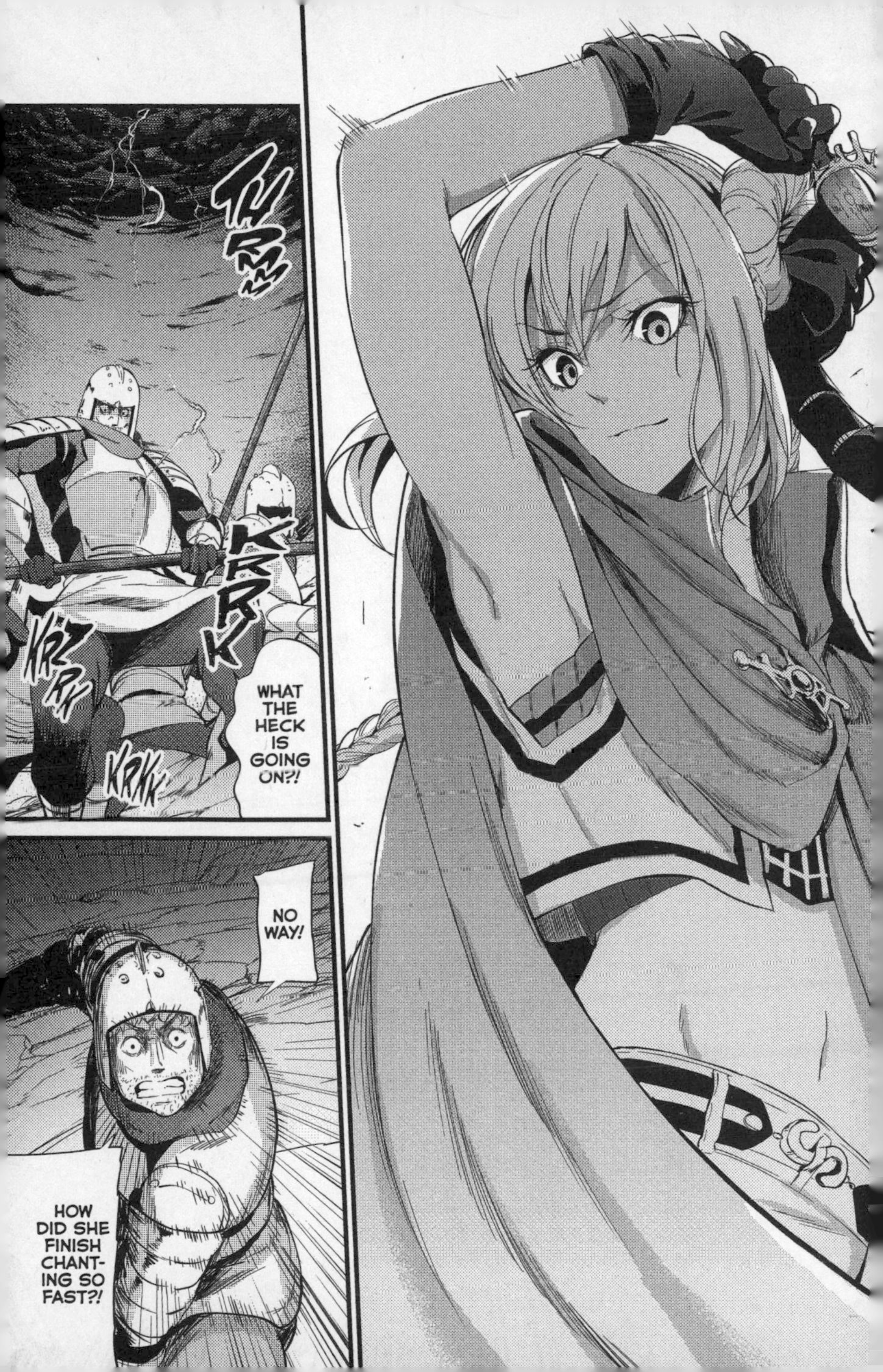
THRMMM
KRRK
KRZRK
KRKK
WHAT THE HECK IS GOING ON?!
NO WAY!
HOW DID SHE FINISH CHANTING SO FAST?!

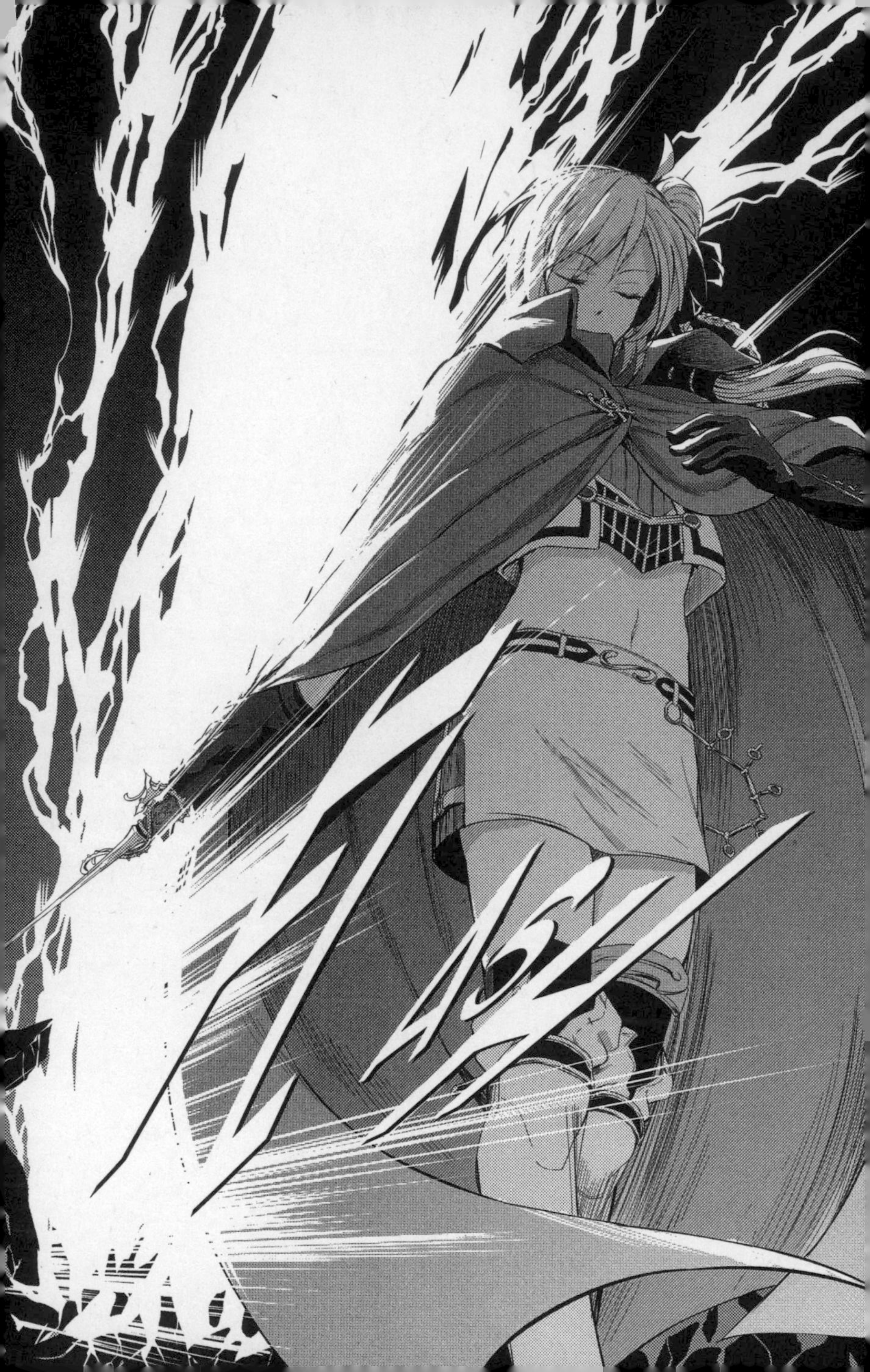

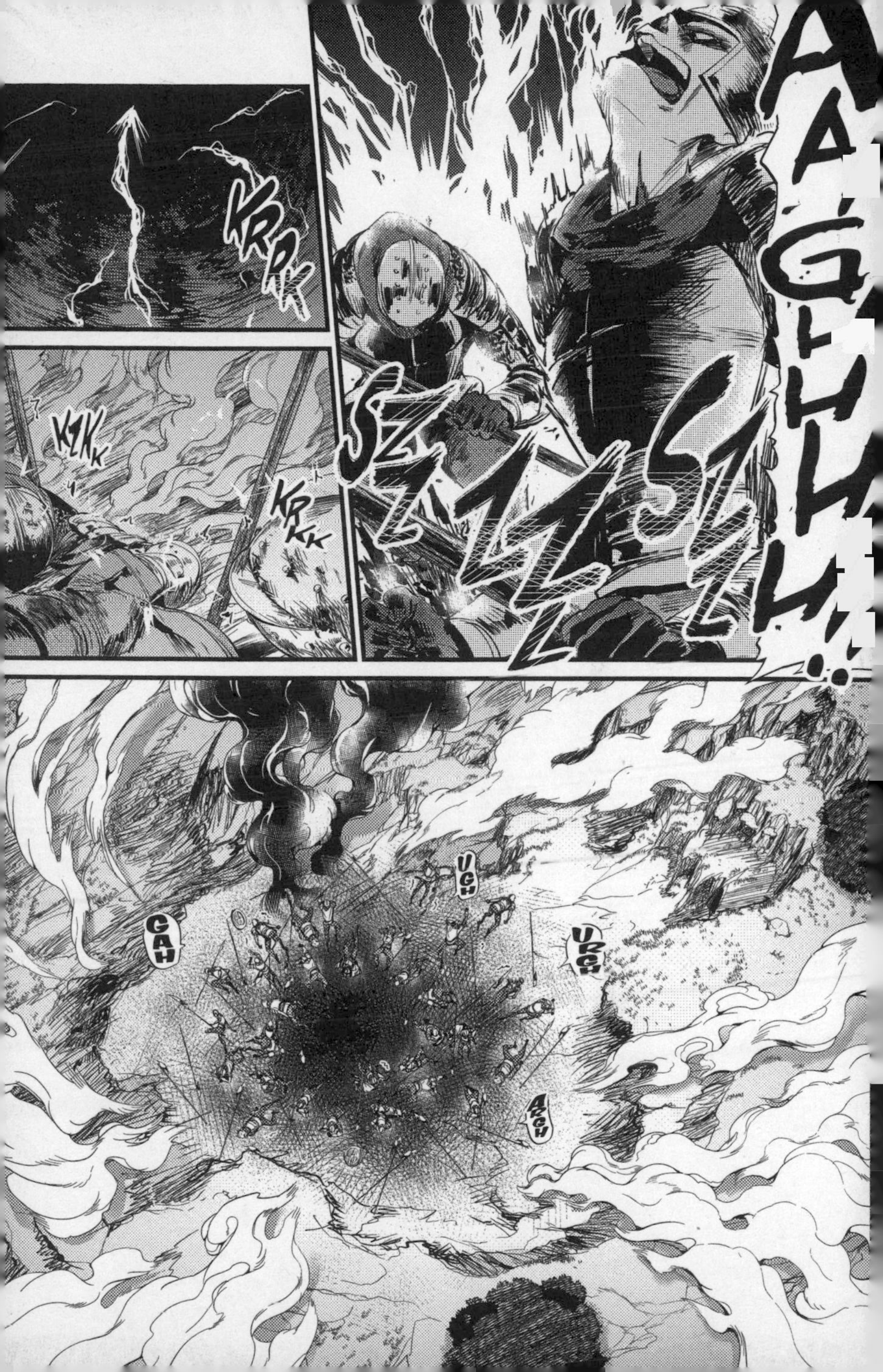
AAGHHH!!
SZZZ
SZZZ
KRRK
KZKK
KRKKK
UGH
URGH
GAH
ARGH

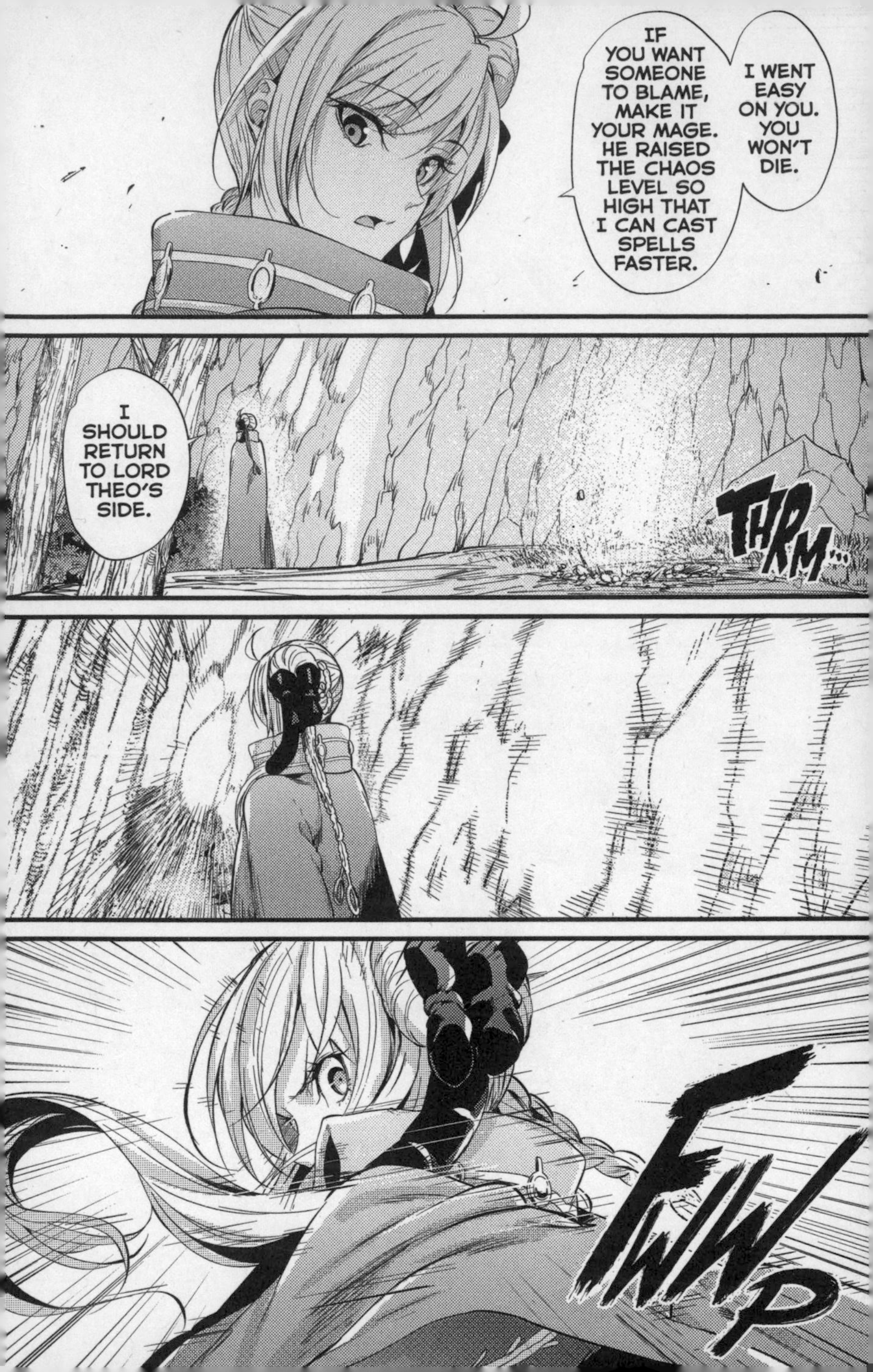
I WENT EASY ON YOU. YOU WON'T DIE.
IF YOU WANT SOMEONE TO BLAME, MAKE IT YOUR MAGE. HE RAISED THE CHAOS LEVEL SO HIGH THAT I CAN CAST SPELLS FASTER.
THRM...
I SHOULD RETURN TO LORD THEO'S SIDE.

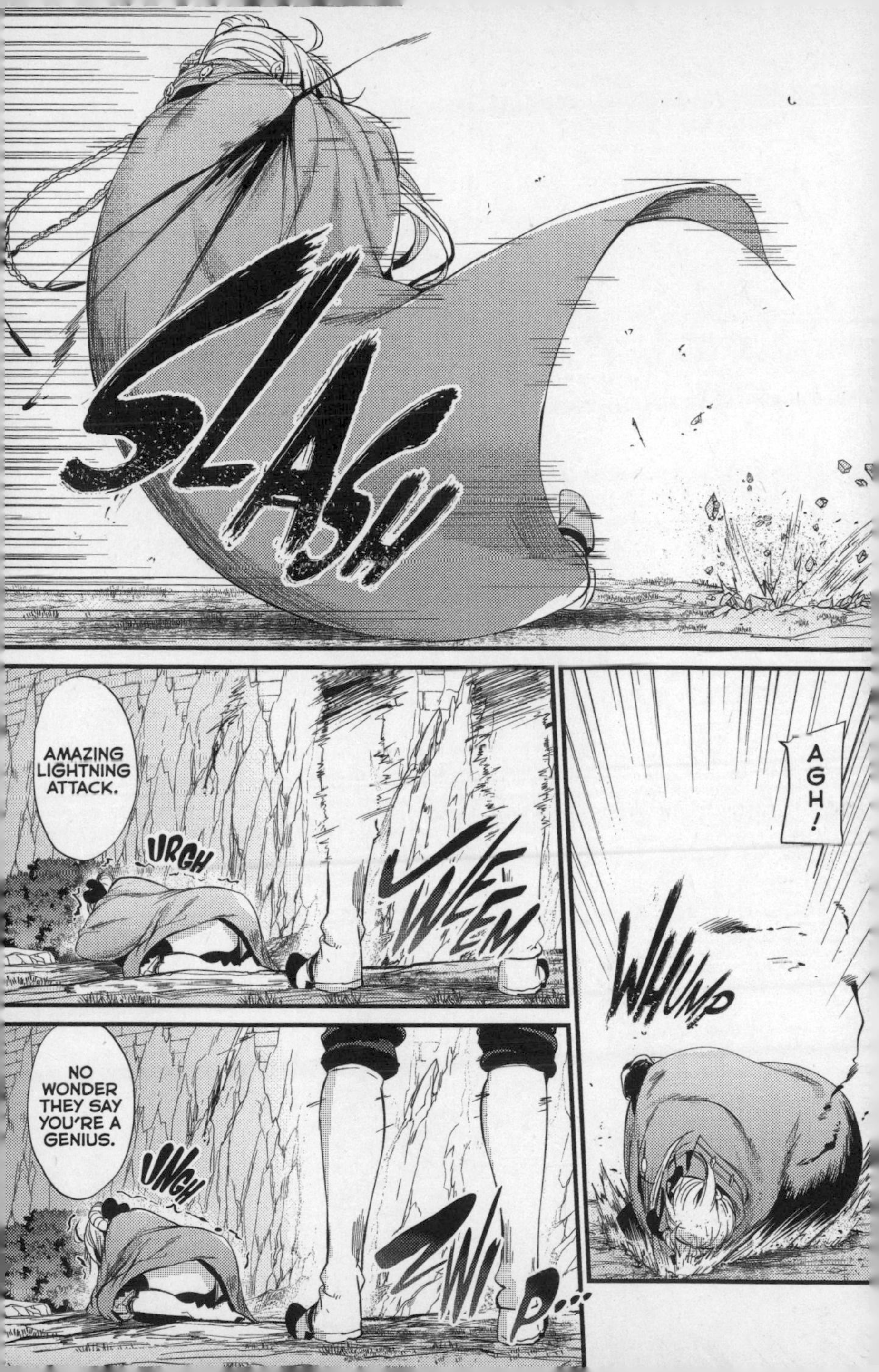
SLASH
AGH!
WHUMP
AMAZING LIGHTNING ATTACK.
URGH
VWEM
NO WONDER THEY SAY YOU'RE A GENIUS.
UNGH
ZWIP..

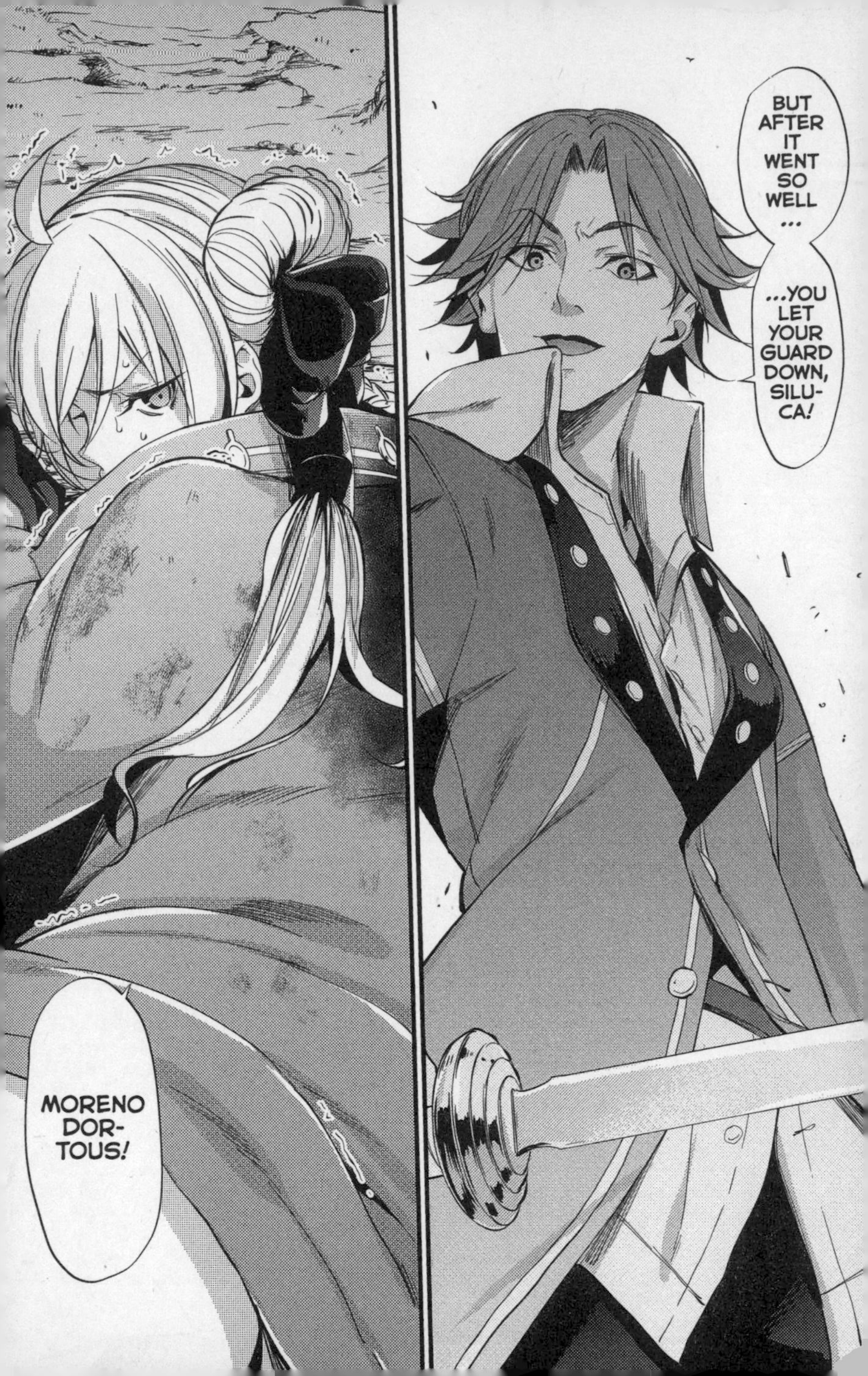
BUT AFTER IT WENT SO WELL...
...YOU LET YOUR GUARD DOWN, SILU-CA!
MORENO DOR-TOUS!

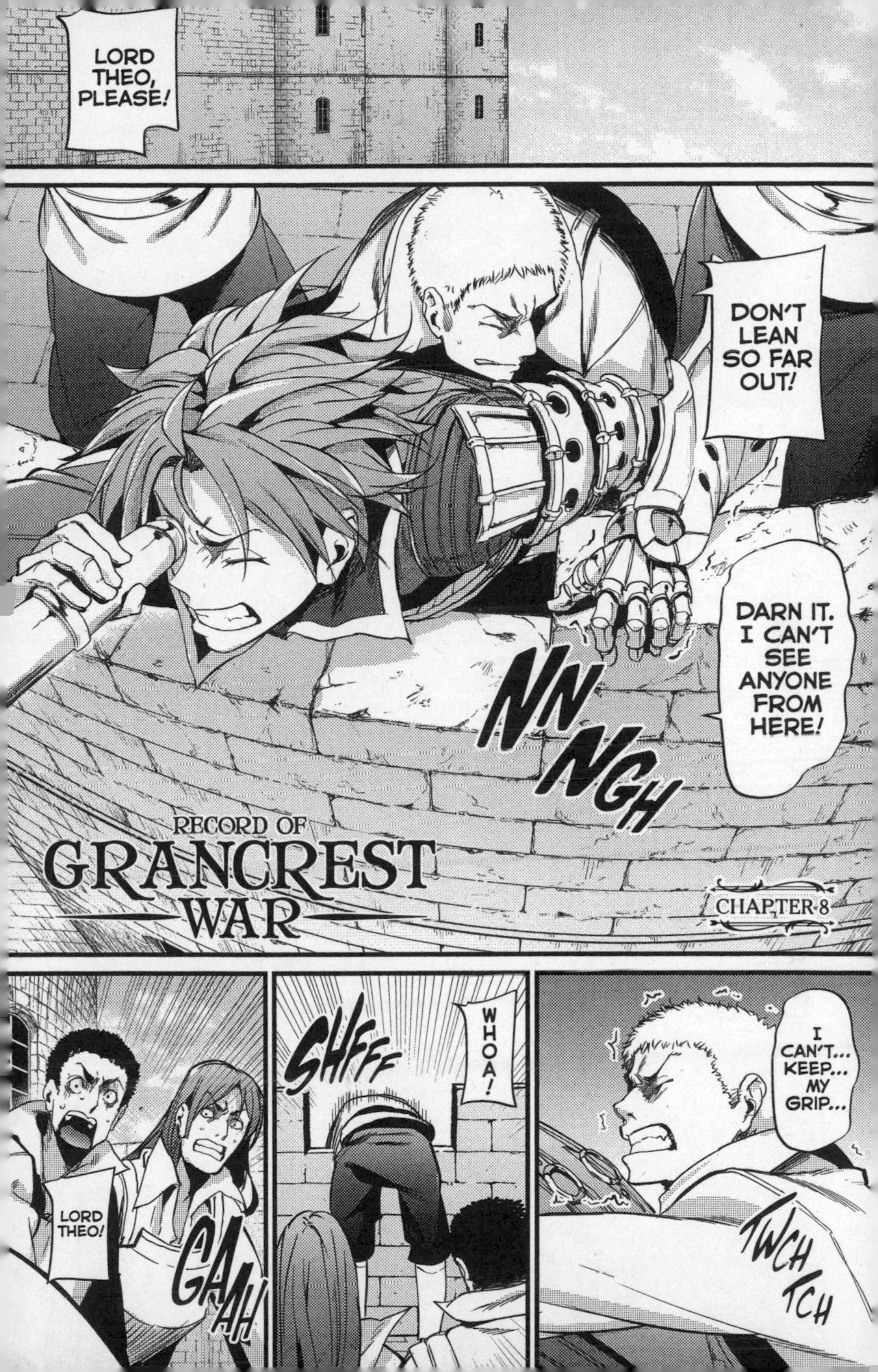
LORD THEO, PLEASE!
DON'T LEAN SO FAR OUT!
DARN IT. I CAN'T SEE ANYONE FROM HERE!
NNNGH
RECORD OF GRANCREST WAR
CHAPTER 8
I CAN'T... KEEP... MY GRIP...
TWCH TCH
WHOA!
SHFFF
LORD THEO!
GAAH

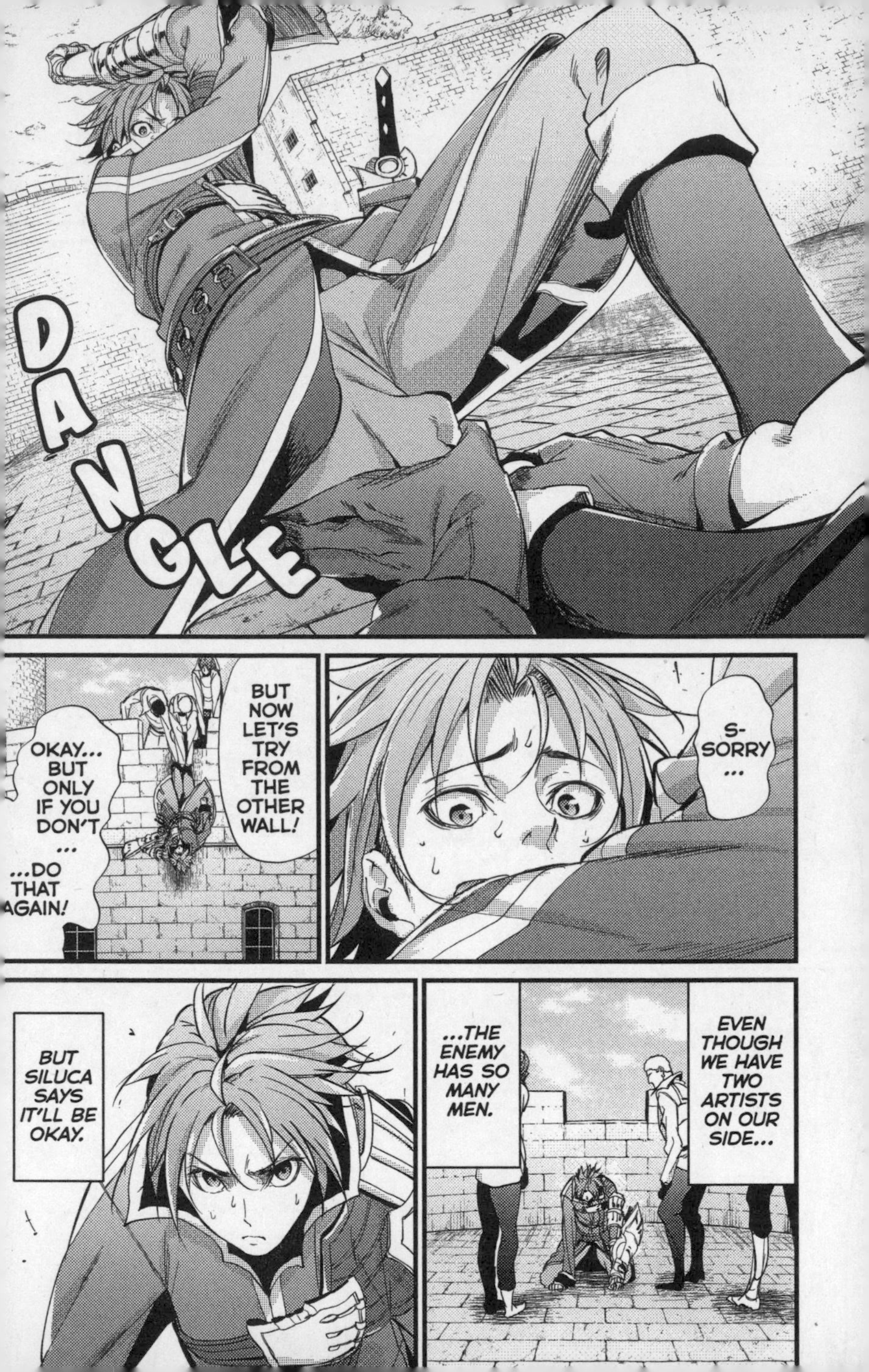
DANGLE
S-SORRY...
BUT NOW LET'S TRY FROM THE OTHER WALL!
OKAY... BUT ONLY IF YOU DON'T... ...DO THAT AGAIN!
EVEN THOUGH WE HAVE TWO ARTISTS ON OUR SIDE...
...THE ENEMY HAS SO MANY MEN.
BUT SILUCA SAYS IT'LL BE OKAY.

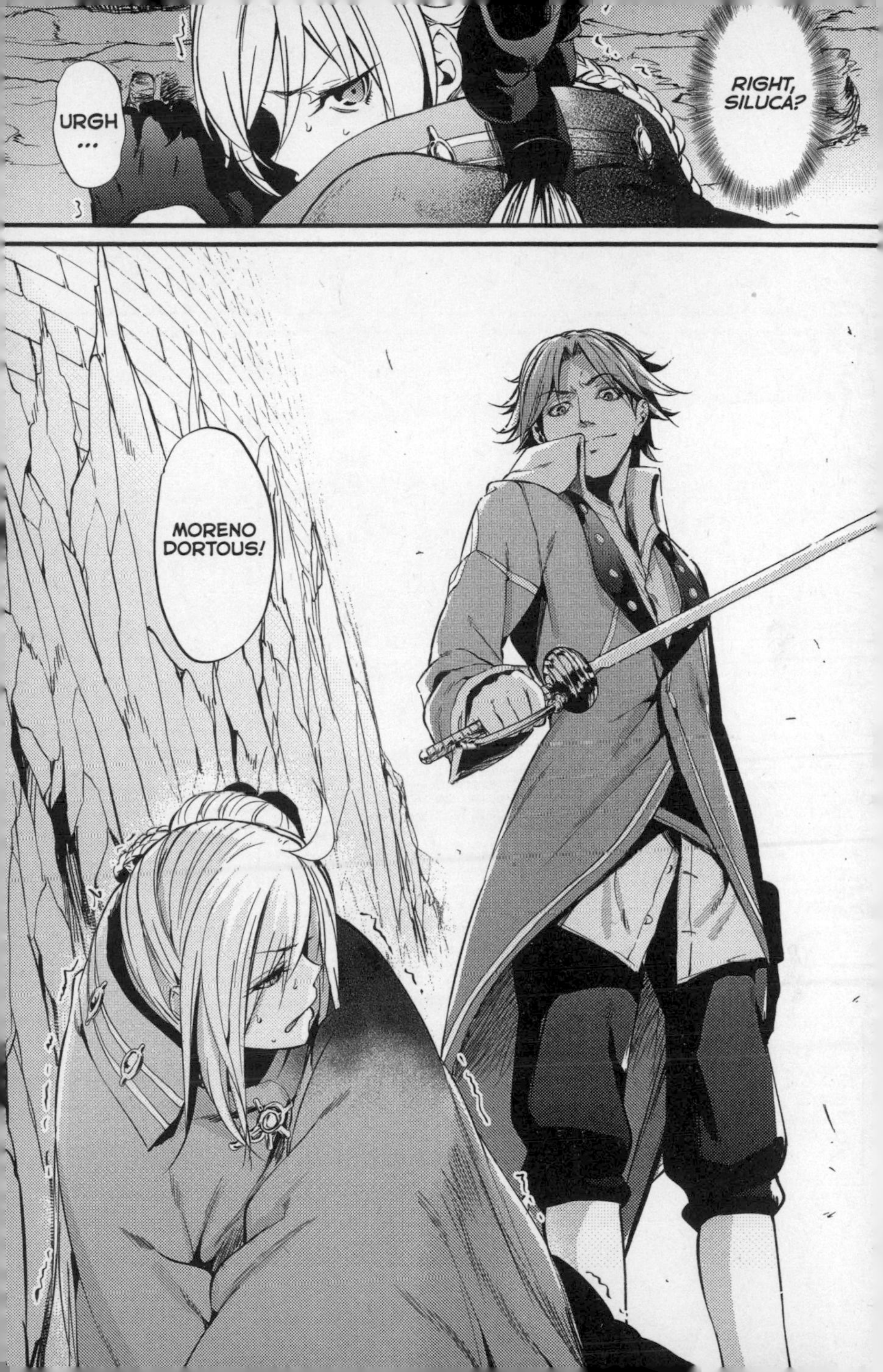
RIGHT, SILUCA?
URGH...
MORENO DORTOUS!

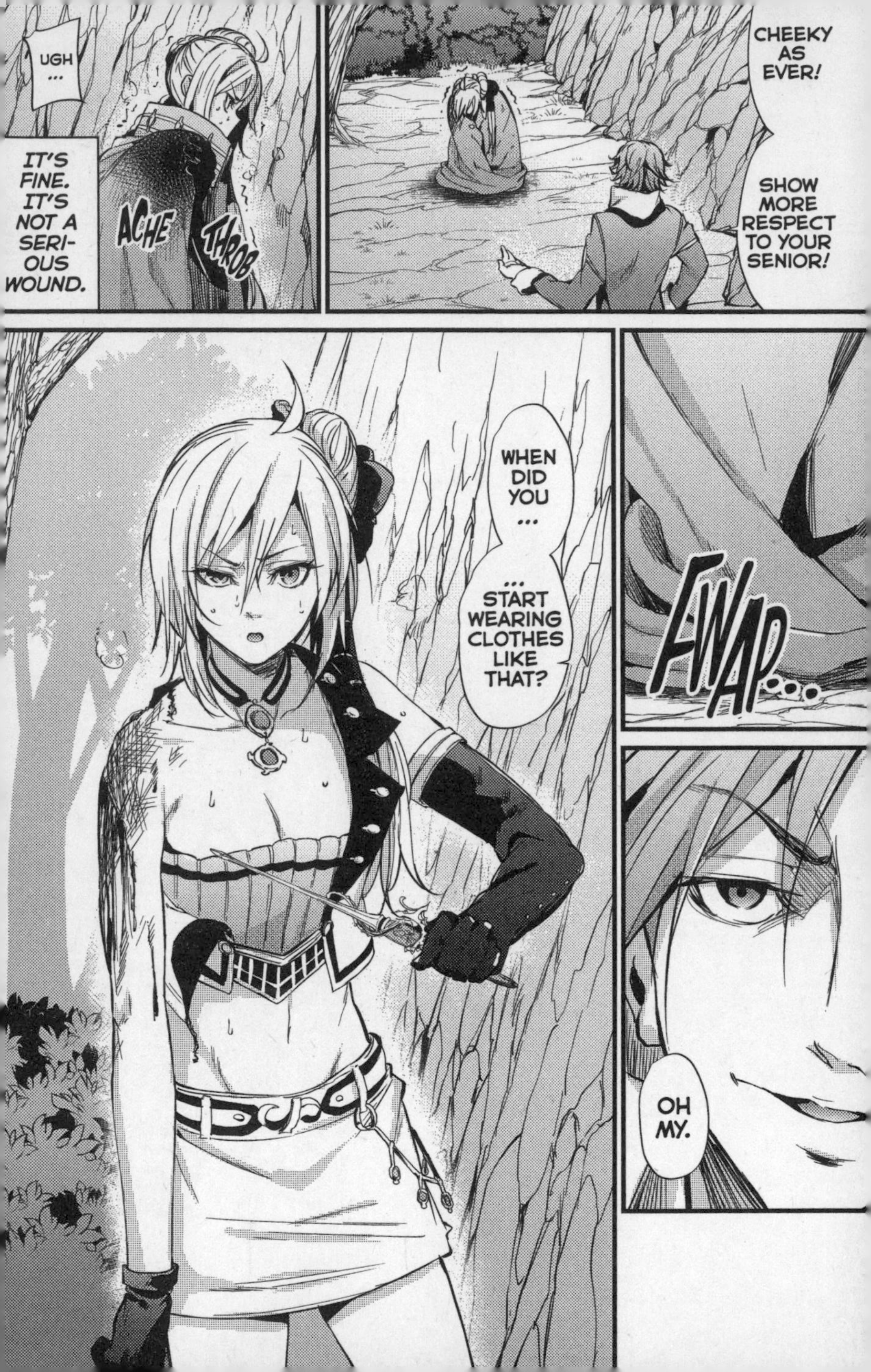
CHEEKY AS EVER!
SHOW MORE RESPECT TO YOUR SENIOR!
UGH ...
IT'S FINE. IT'S NOT A SERI-OUS WOUND.
ACHE
THROB
FWAP...
OH MY.
WHEN DID YOU ...
... START WEARING CLOTHES LIKE THAT?

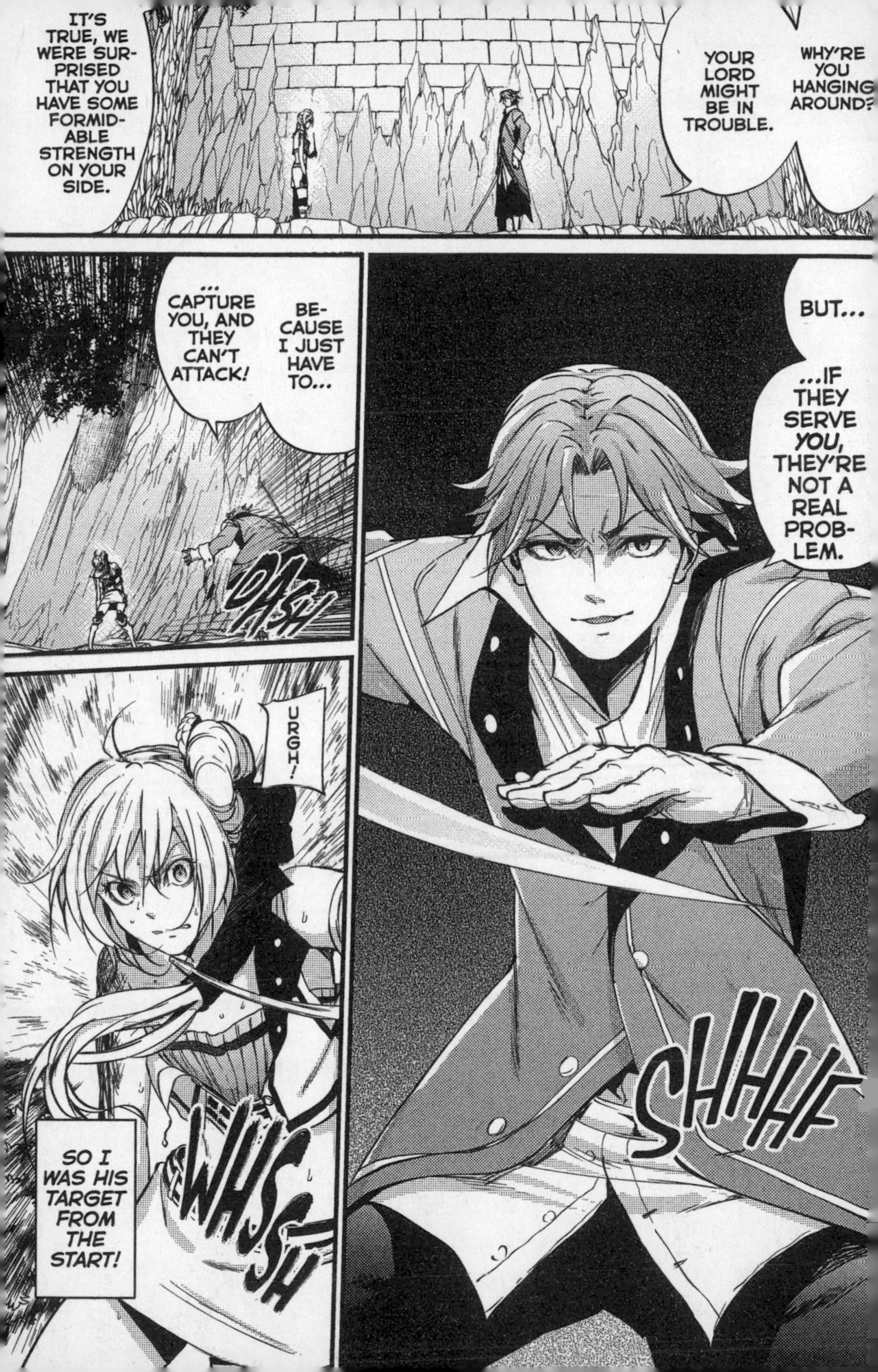
WHY'RE YOU HANGING AROUND?
YOUR LORD MIGHT BE IN TROUBLE.
IT'S TRUE, WE WERE SUR-PRISED THAT YOU HAVE SOME FORMID-ABLE STRENGTH ON YOUR SIDE.
BUT...
...IF THEY SERVE *YOU*, THEY'RE NOT A REAL PROB-LEM.
SHHF
BE-CAUSE I JUST HAVE TO...
...CAPTURE YOU, AND THEY CAN'T ATTACK!
DASH
URGH!
WHSSH
SO I WAS HIS TARGET FROM THE START!

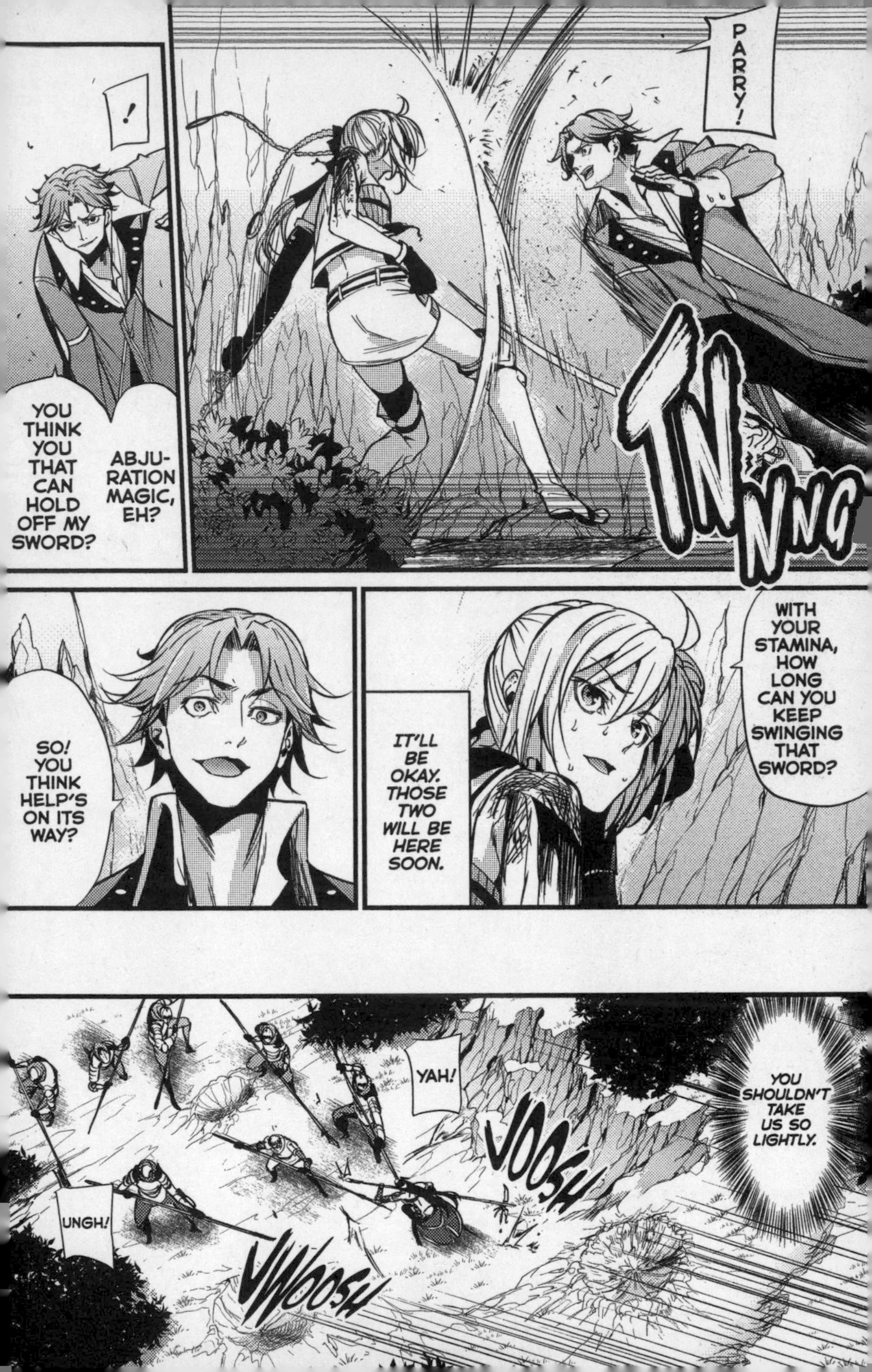
PARRY!
TINNNG
!
ABJU-RATION MAGIC, EH?
YOU THINK YOU THAT CAN HOLD OFF MY SWORD?
WITH YOUR STAMINA, HOW LONG CAN YOU KEEP SWINGING THAT SWORD?
IT'LL BE OKAY. THOSE TWO WILL BE HERE SOON.
SO! YOU THINK HELP'S ON ITS WAY?
YOU SHOULDN'T TAKE US SO LIGHTLY.
YAH!
VOOSH
UNGH!
VWOOSH

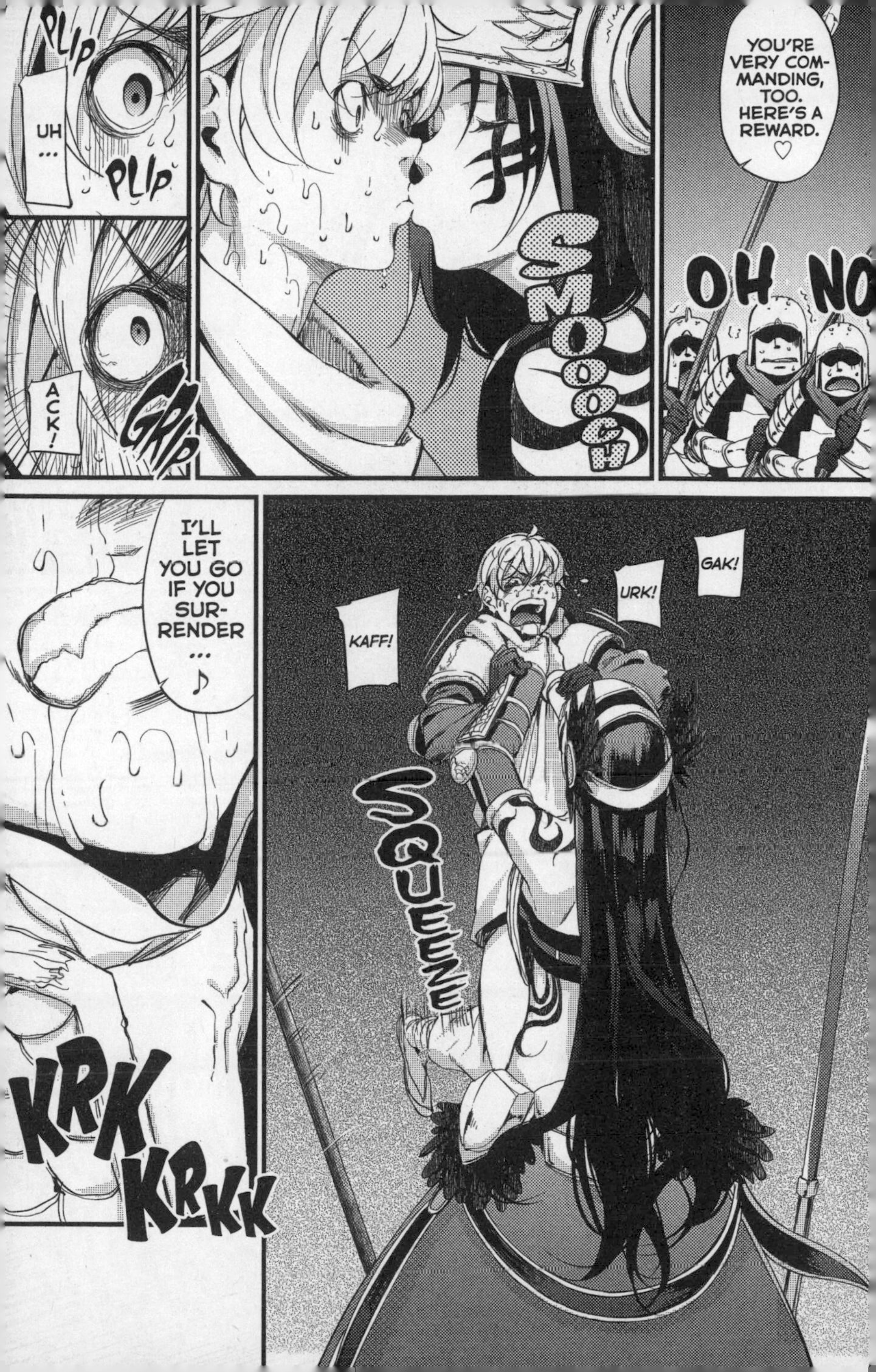
YOU'RE VERY COMMANDING, TOO. HERE'S A REWARD. ♡
OH NO
SMOOCH
PLIP
UH ...
PLIP
ACK!
GRIP
GAK!
URK!
KAFF!
SQUEEZE
I'LL LET YOU GO IF YOU SURRENDER ... ♪
KRK KRKK

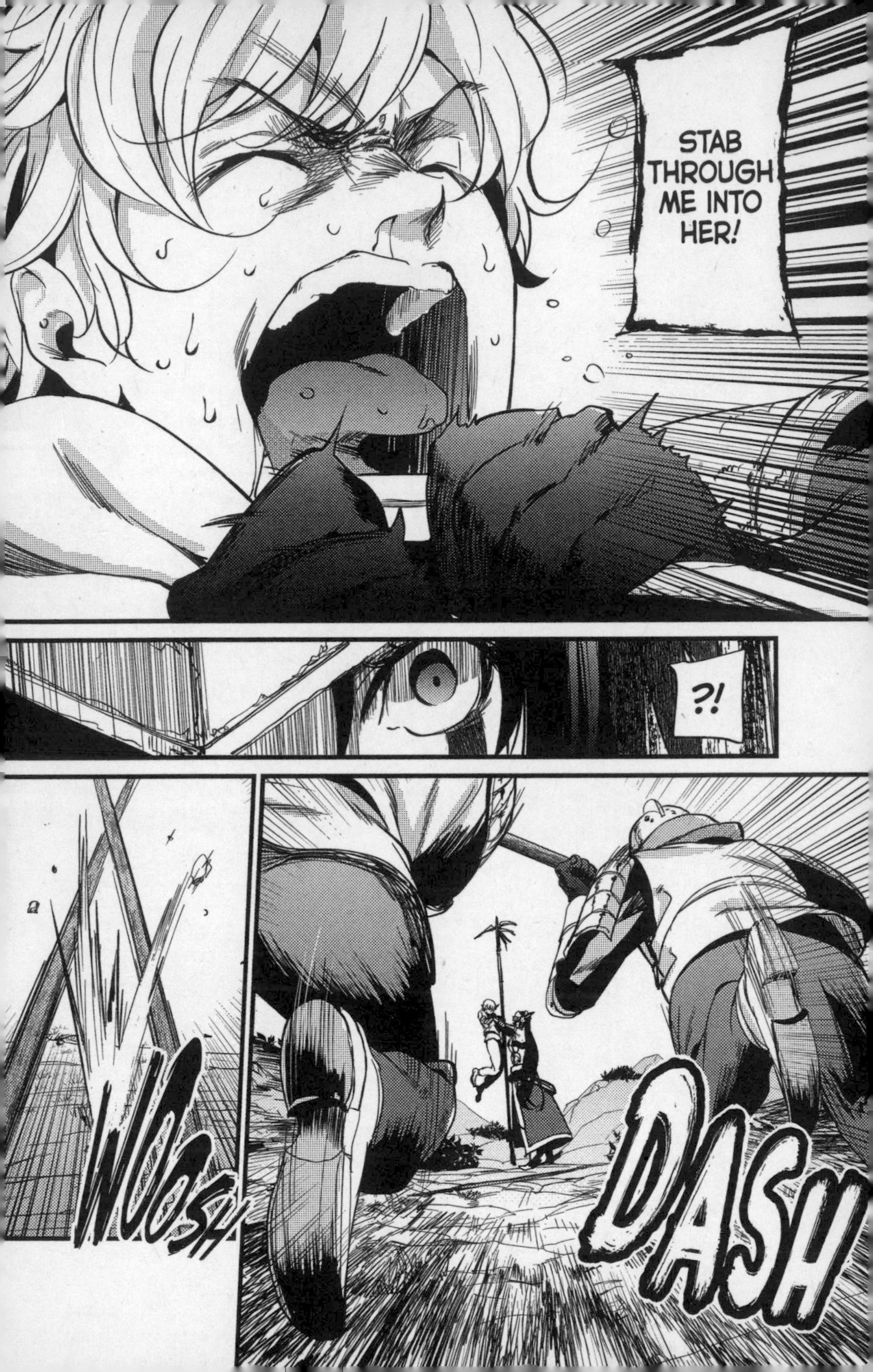
STAB THROUGH ME INTO HER!
?!
DASH
WHOOSH

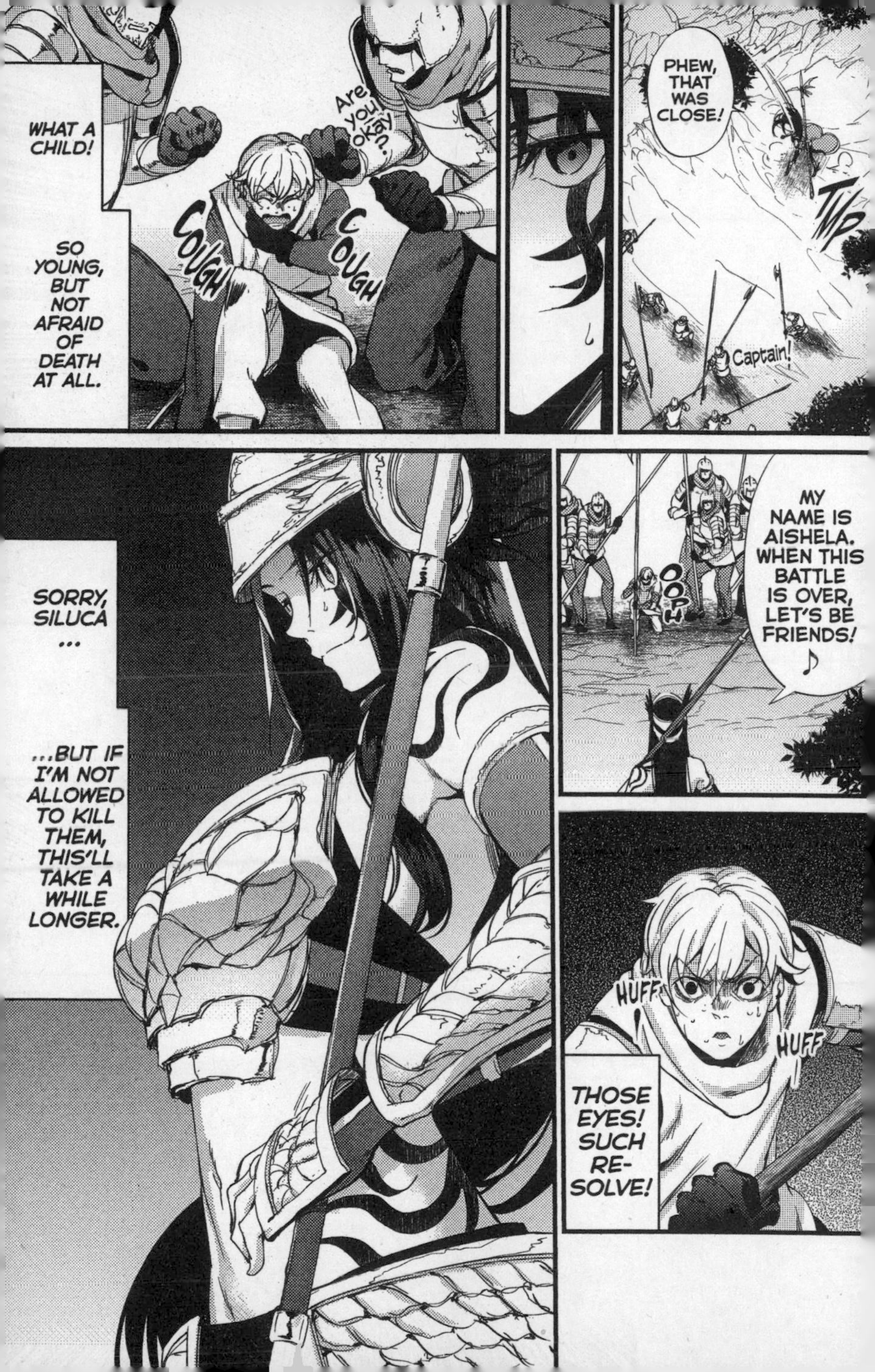
PHEW, THAT WAS CLOSE!
TNP
Captain!
Are you okay?
COUGH
COUGH
WHAT A CHILD!
SO YOUNG, BUT NOT AFRAID OF DEATH AT ALL.
MY NAME IS AISHELA. WHEN THIS BATTLE IS OVER, LET'S BE FRIENDS! ♪
OOPH
HUFF
HUFF
THOSE EYES! SUCH RE-SOLVE!
SORRY, SILUCA ...
...BUT IF I'M NOT ALLOWED TO KILL THEM, THIS'LL TAKE A WHILE LONGER.

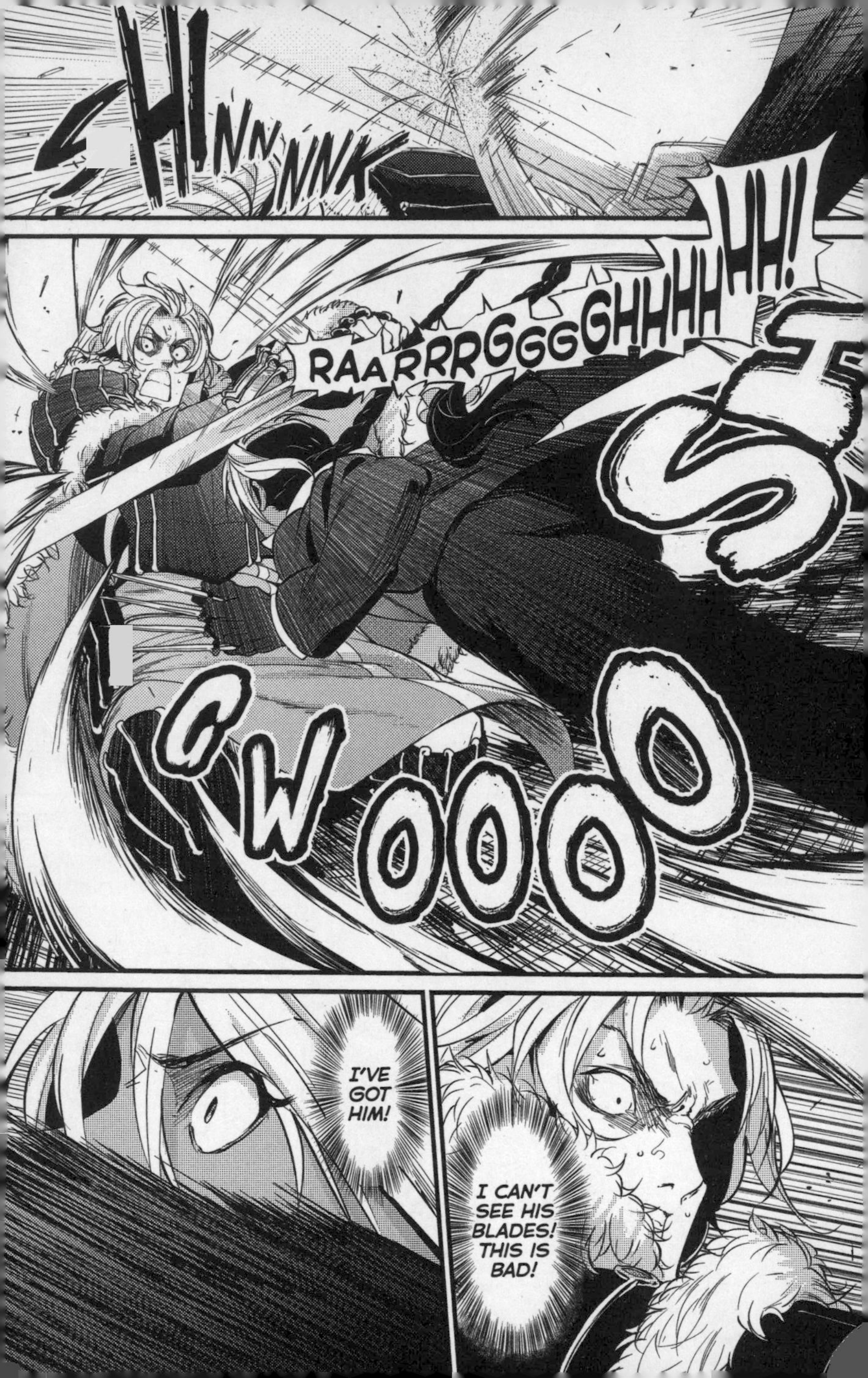
CHINNNNNK
RAARRRGGGGHHHHHHH!
I CAN'T SEE HIS BLADES! THIS IS BAD!
I'VE GOT HIM!

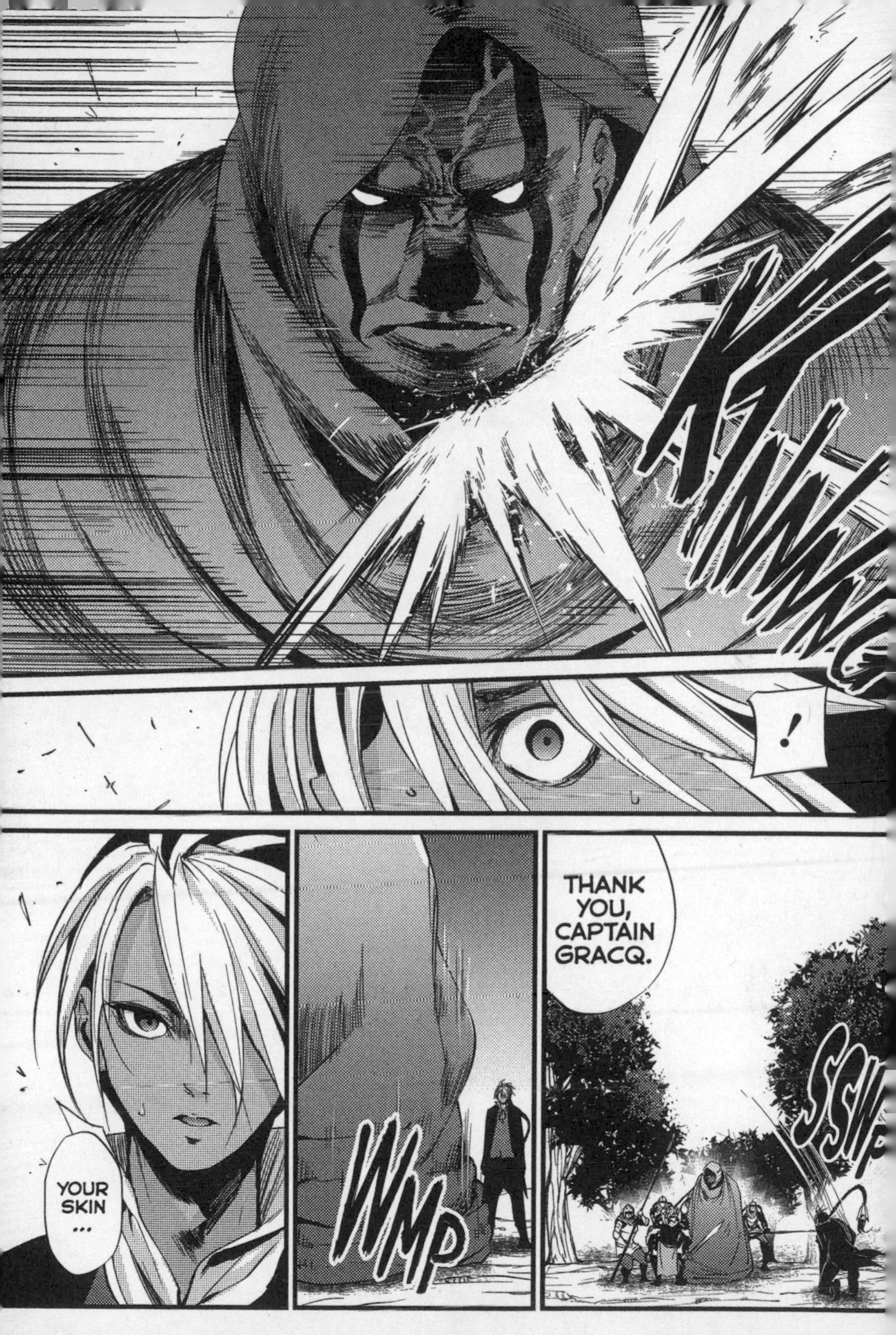
!
THANK YOU, CAPTAIN GRACQ.
WMP
YOUR SKIN ...

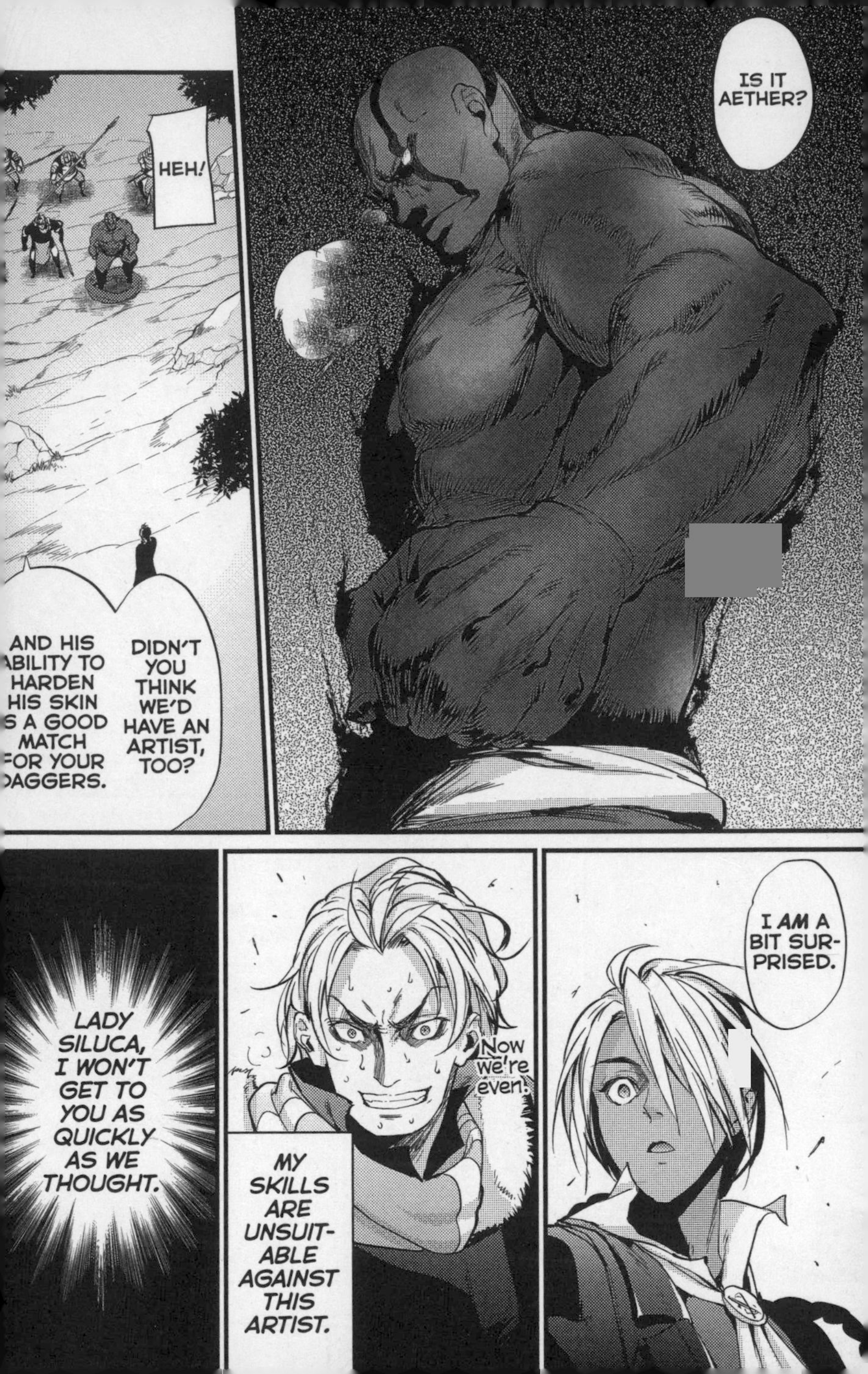
IS IT AETHER?
HEH!
DIDN'T YOU THINK WE'D HAVE AN ARTIST, TOO?
AND HIS ABILITY TO HARDEN HIS SKIN IS A GOOD MATCH FOR YOUR DAGGERS.
I *AM* A BIT SUR-PRISED.
Now we're even!
MY SKILLS ARE UNSUIT-ABLE AGAINST THIS ARTIST.
LADY SILUCA, I WON'T GET TO YOU AS QUICKLY AS WE THOUGHT.

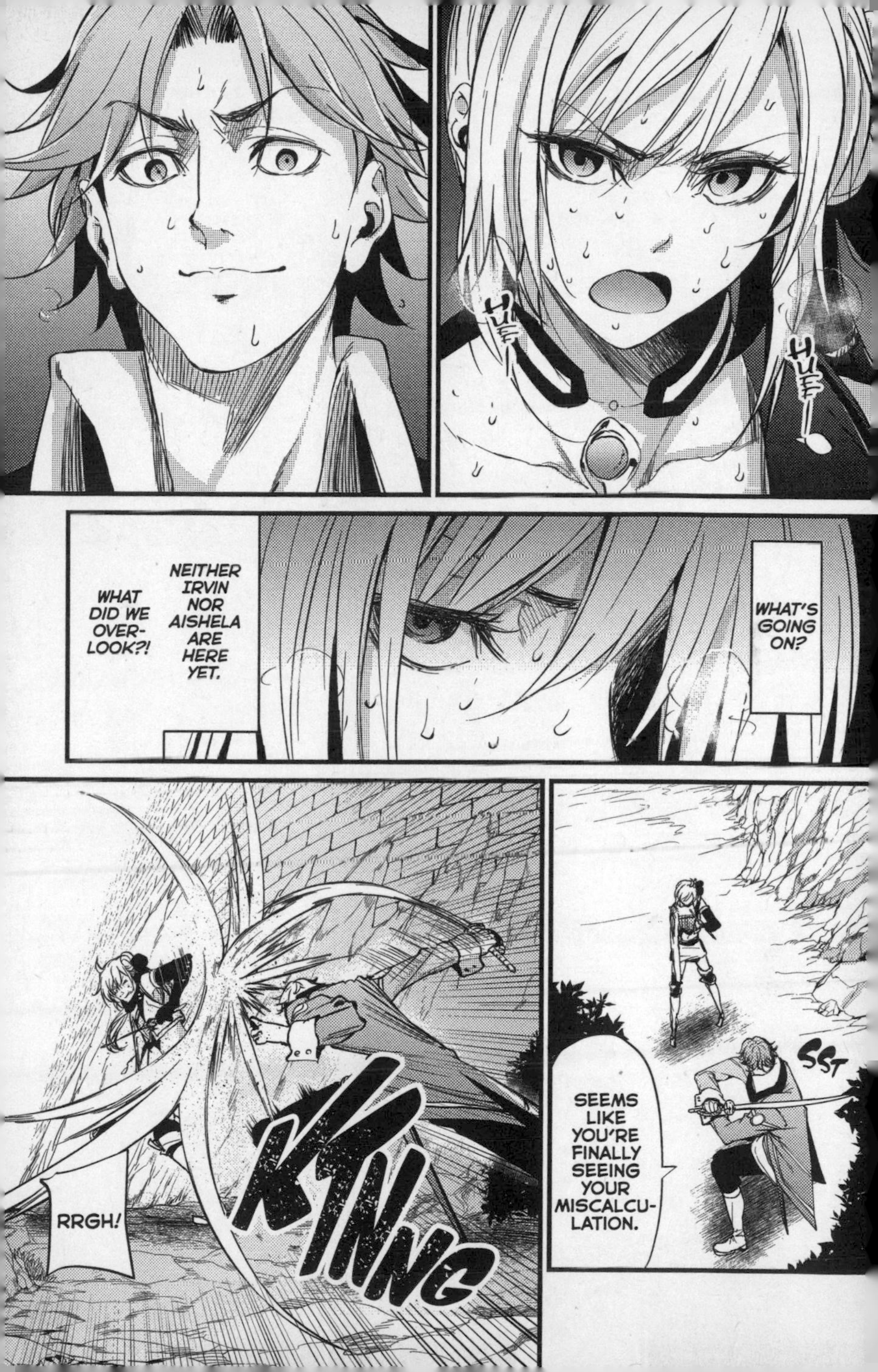
HUF
HUF
WHAT'S GOING ON?
NEITHER IRVIN NOR AISHELA ARE HERE YET.
WHAT DID WE OVER-LOOK?!
SST
SEEMS LIKE YOU'RE FINALLY SEEING YOUR MISCALCU-LATION.
KINNG
RRGH!

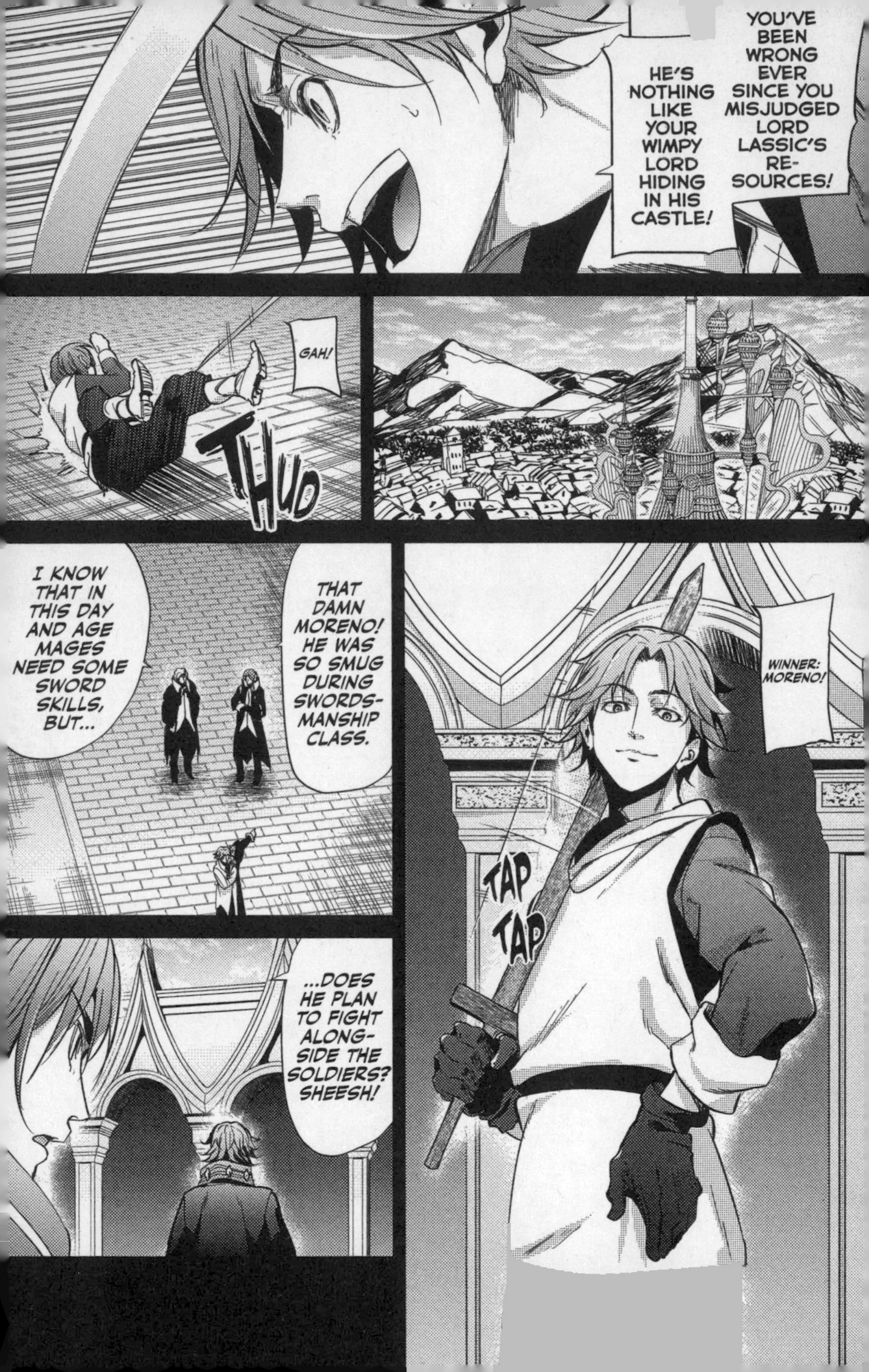
YOU'VE BEEN WRONG EVER SINCE YOU MISJUDGED LORD LASSIC'S RE-SOURCES!
HE'S NOTHING LIKE YOUR WIMPY LORD HIDING IN HIS CASTLE!
GAH!
THUD
WINNER: MORENO!
TAP TAP
THAT DAMN MORENO! HE WAS SO SMUG DURING SWORDS-MANSHIP CLASS.
I KNOW THAT IN THIS DAY AND AGE MAGES NEED SOME SWORD SKILLS, BUT...
...DOES HE PLAN TO FIGHT ALONG-SIDE THE SOLDIERS? SHEESH!

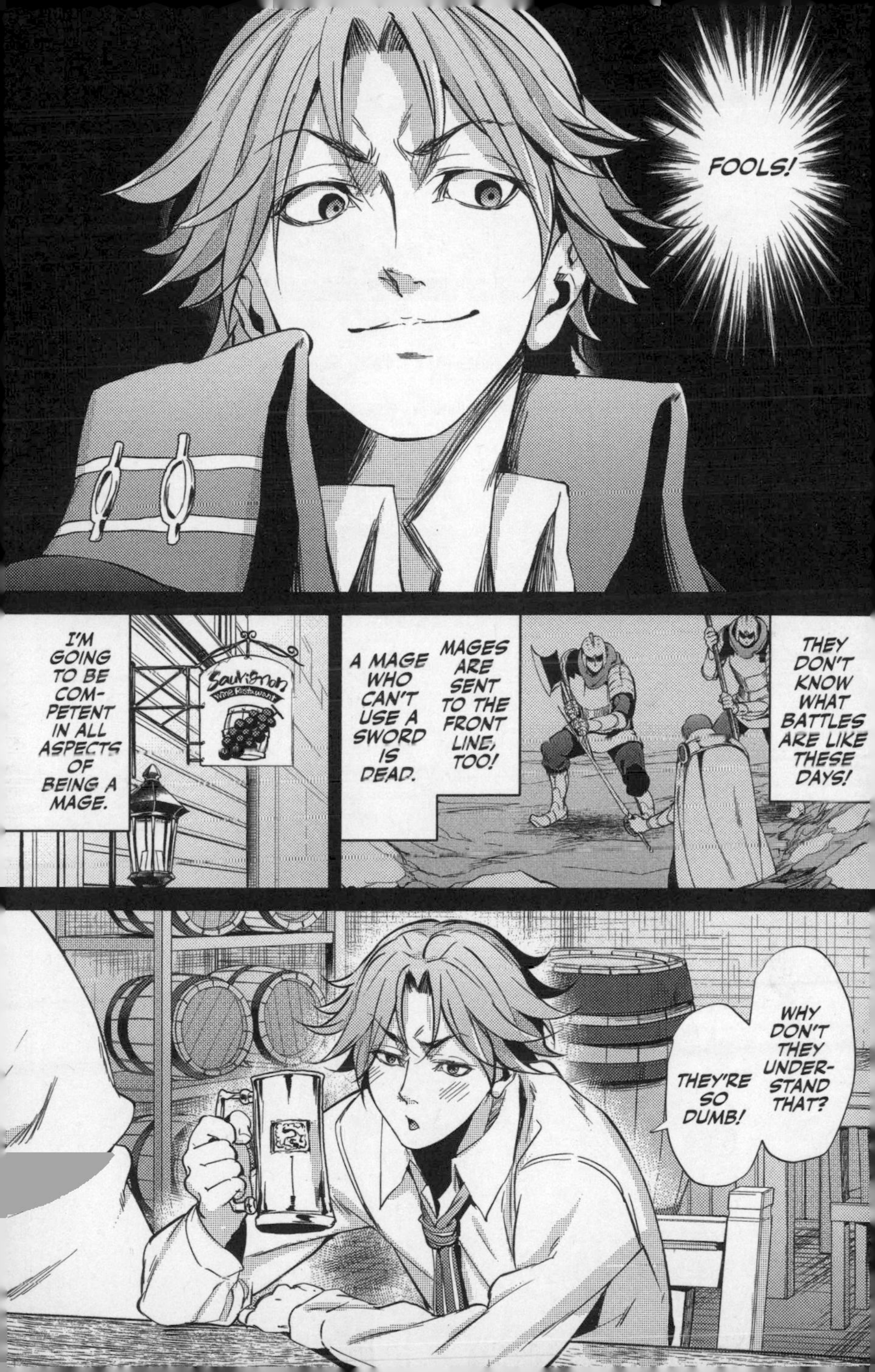
FOOLS!
THEY DON'T KNOW WHAT BATTLES ARE LIKE THESE DAYS!
MAGES ARE SENT TO THE FRONT LINE, TOO!
A MAGE WHO CAN'T USE A SWORD IS DEAD.
I'M GOING TO BE COMPETENT IN ALL ASPECTS OF BEING A MAGE.
Sauvignon
Wine Restaurant
WHY DON'T THEY UNDERSTAND THAT?
THEY'RE SO DUMB!

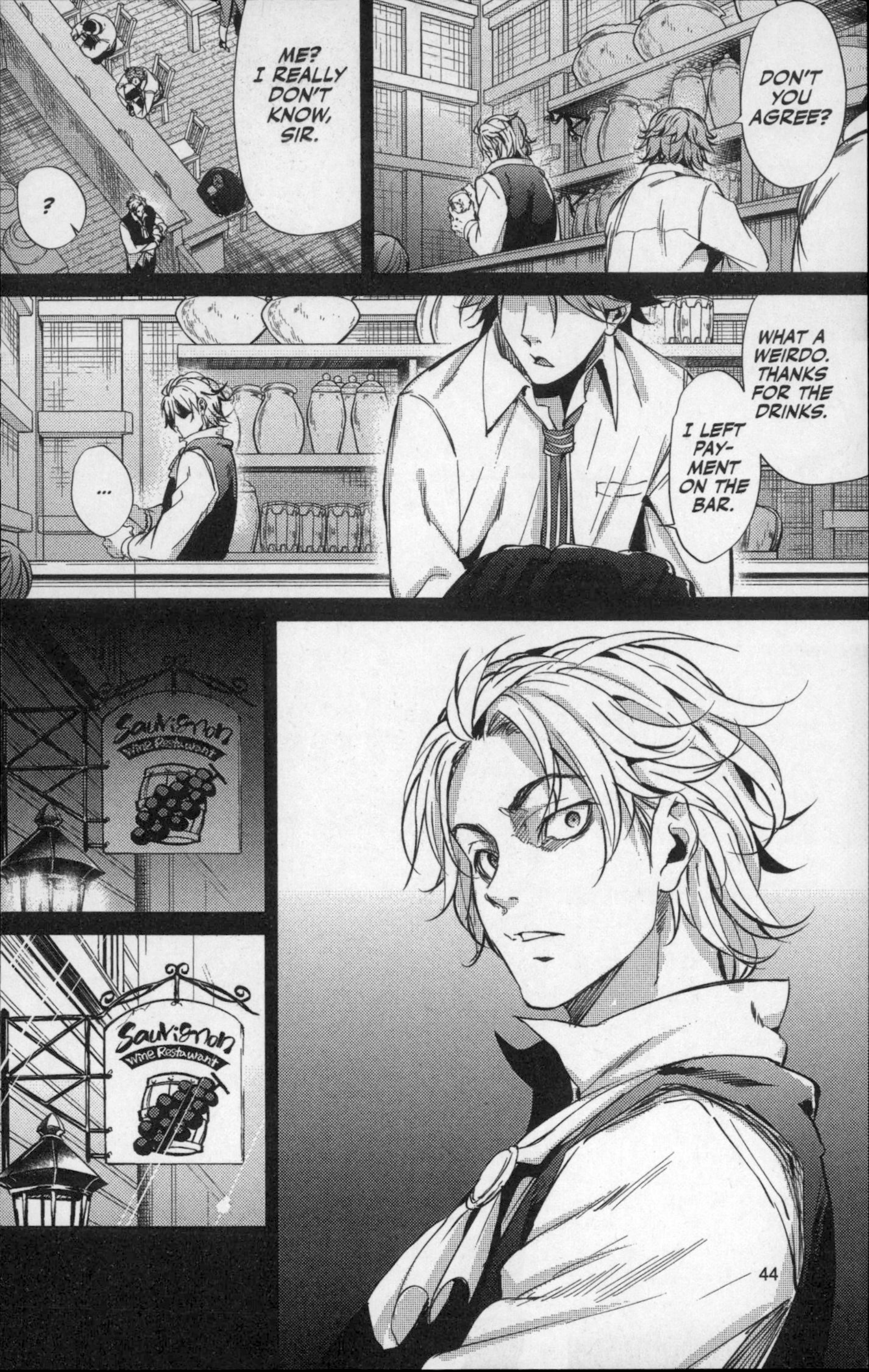
DON'T YOU AGREE?
ME? I REALLY DON'T KNOW, SIR.
?
WHAT A WEIRDO. THANKS FOR THE DRINKS.
I LEFT PAY-MENT ON THE BAR.
...
Sauvignon
Wine Restaurant
Sauvignon
Wine Restaurant

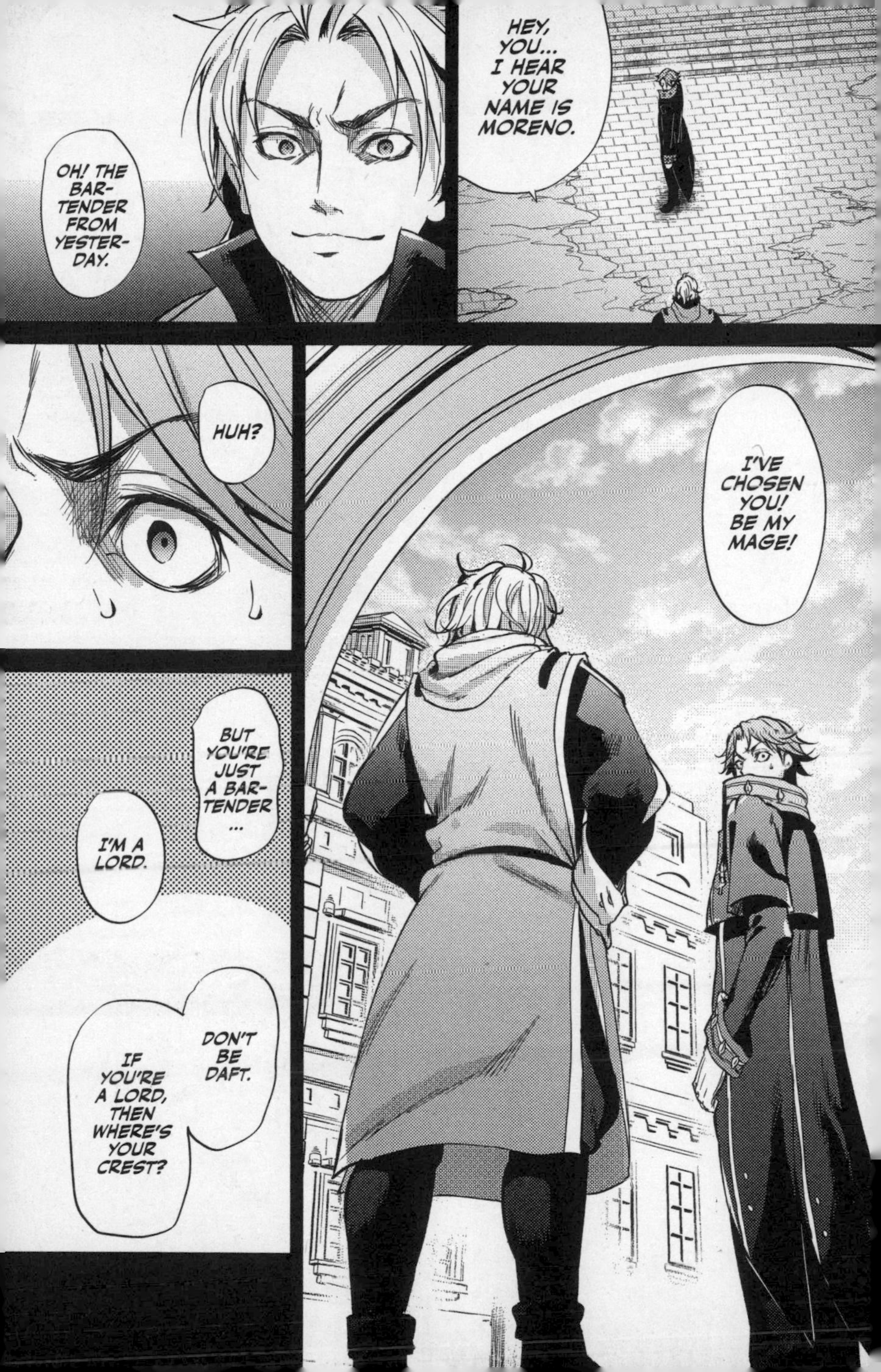

HEY, YOU... I HEAR YOUR NAME IS MORENO.
OH! THE BARTENDER FROM YESTERDAY.
I'VE CHOSEN YOU! BE MY MAGE!
HUH?
BUT YOU'RE JUST A BARTENDER...
I'M A LORD.
DON'T BE DAFT.
IF YOU'RE A LORD, THEN WHERE'S YOUR CREST?

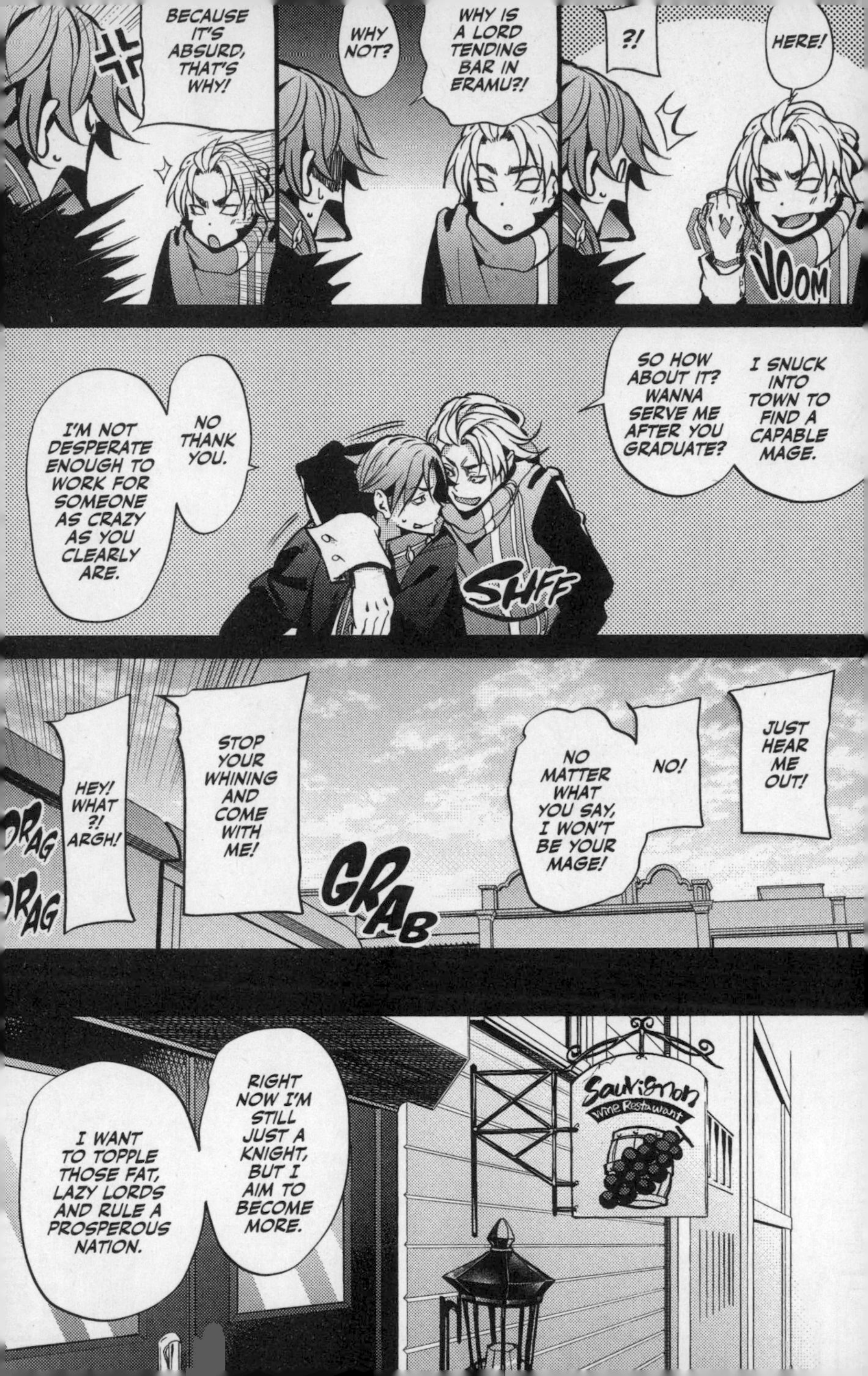
HERE!
?!
VOOM
WHY IS A LORD TENDING BAR IN ERAMU?!
WHY NOT?
BECAUSE IT'S ABSURD, THAT'S WHY!
I SNUCK INTO TOWN TO FIND A CAPABLE MAGE.
SO HOW ABOUT IT? WANNA SERVE ME AFTER YOU GRADUATE?
SHFF
NO THANK YOU.
I'M NOT DESPERATE ENOUGH TO WORK FOR SOMEONE AS CRAZY AS YOU CLEARLY ARE.
JUST HEAR ME OUT!
NO!
NO MATTER WHAT YOU SAY, I WON'T BE YOUR MAGE!
GRAB
STOP YOUR WHINING AND COME WITH ME!
HEY! WHAT ?! ARGH!
Sauvignon
Wine Restaurant
RIGHT NOW I'M STILL JUST A KNIGHT, BUT I AIM TO BECOME MORE.
I WANT TO TOPPLE THOSE FAT, LAZY LORDS AND RULE A PROSPEROUS NATION.

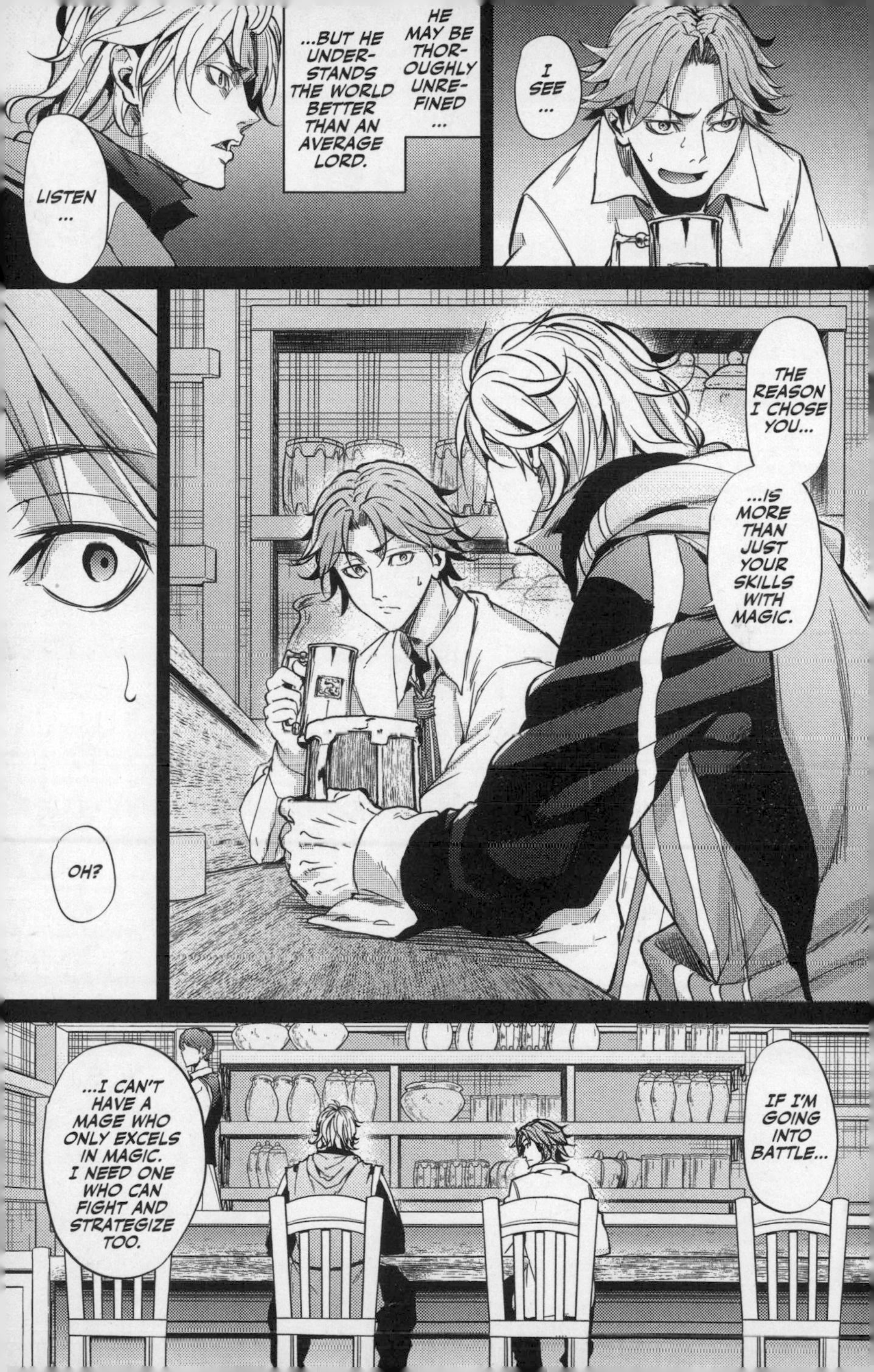
I SEE...
HE MAY BE THOROUGHLY UNREFINED...
...BUT HE UNDERSTANDS THE WORLD BETTER THAN AN AVERAGE LORD.
LISTEN...
THE REASON I CHOSE YOU...
...IS MORE THAN JUST YOUR SKILLS WITH MAGIC.
OH?
IF I'M GOING INTO BATTLE...
...I CAN'T HAVE A MAGE WHO ONLY EXCELS IN MAGIC. I NEED ONE WHO CAN FIGHT AND STRATEGIZE TOO.

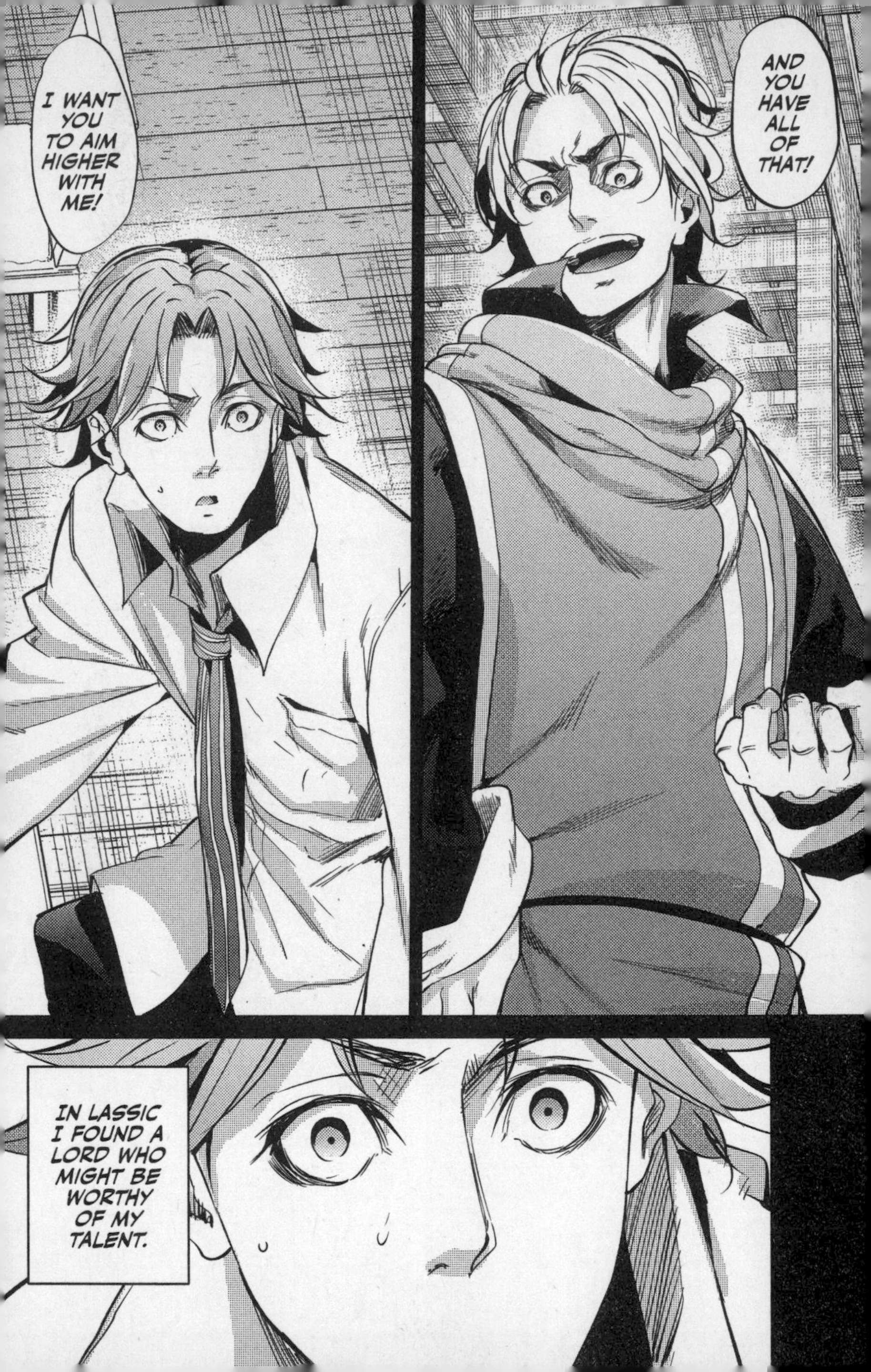
AND YOU HAVE ALL OF THAT!
I WANT YOU TO AIM HIGHER WITH ME!
IN LASSIC I FOUND A LORD WHO MIGHT BE WORTHY OF MY TALENT.

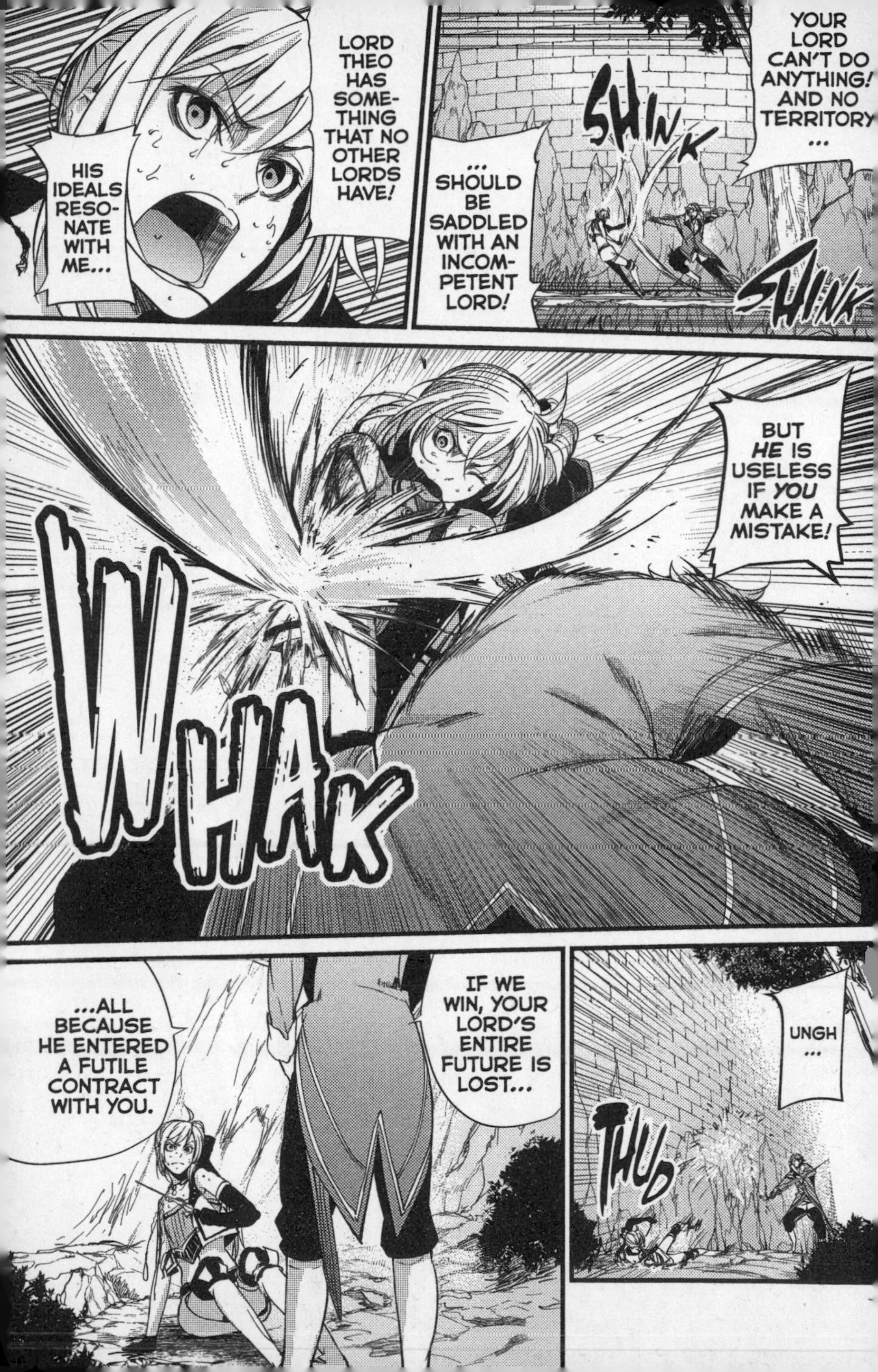
YOUR LORD CAN'T DO ANYTHING! AND NO TERRITORY ...
SHINK
... SHOULD BE SADDLED WITH AN INCOMPETENT LORD!
SHINK
LORD THEO HAS SOMETHING THAT NO OTHER LORDS HAVE!
HIS IDEALS RESONATE WITH ME...
BUT *HE* IS USELESS IF *YOU* MAKE A MISTAKE!
WHAK
UNGH ...
THUD
IF WE WIN, YOUR LORD'S ENTIRE FUTURE IS LOST...
...ALL BECAUSE HE ENTERED A FUTILE CONTRACT WITH YOU.

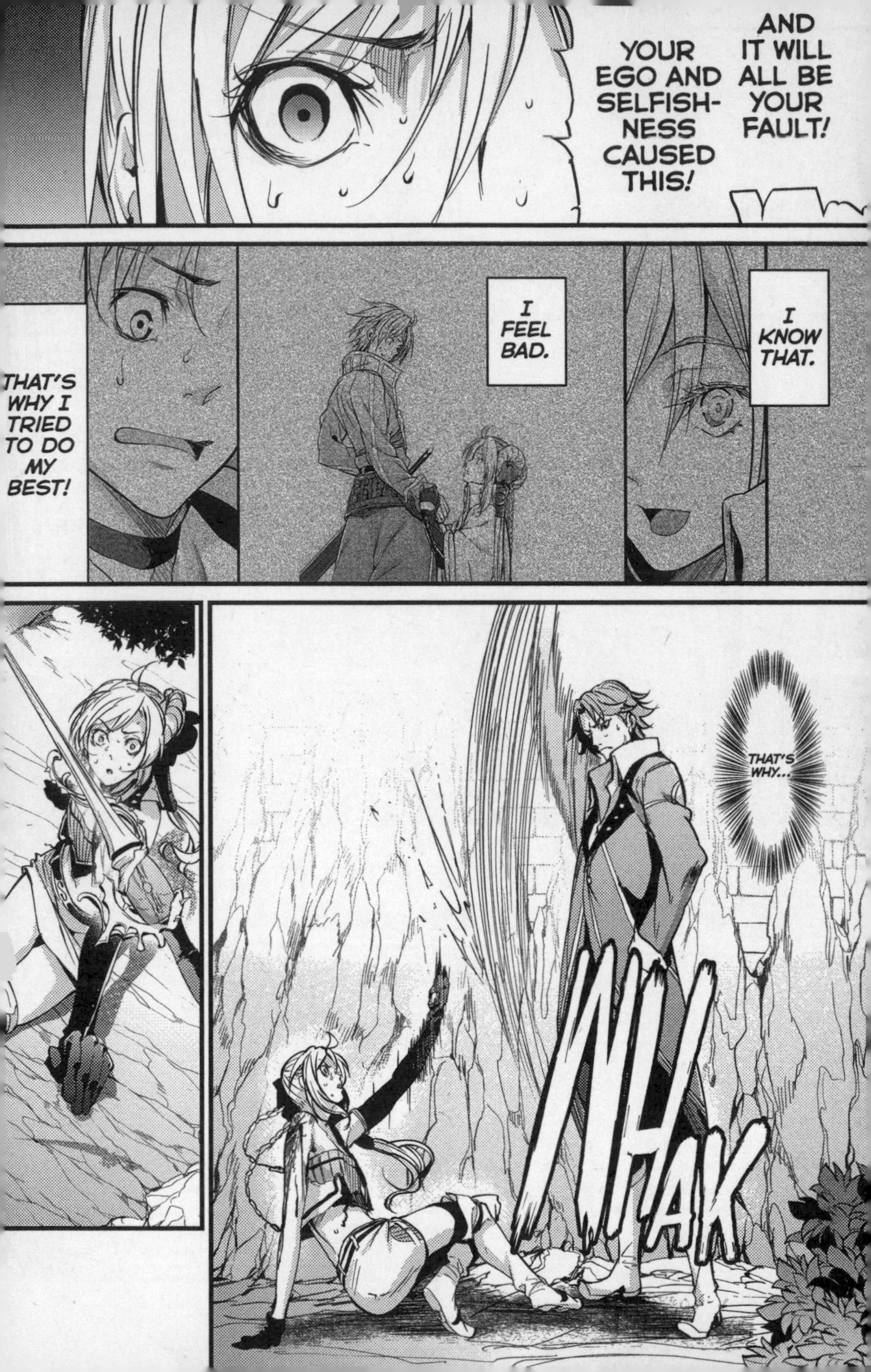
YOUR EGO AND SELFISHNESS CAUSED THIS!
AND IT WILL ALL BE YOUR FAULT!
I KNOW THAT.
I FEEL BAD.
THAT'S WHY I TRIED TO DO MY BEST!
THAT'S WHY...
WHAK

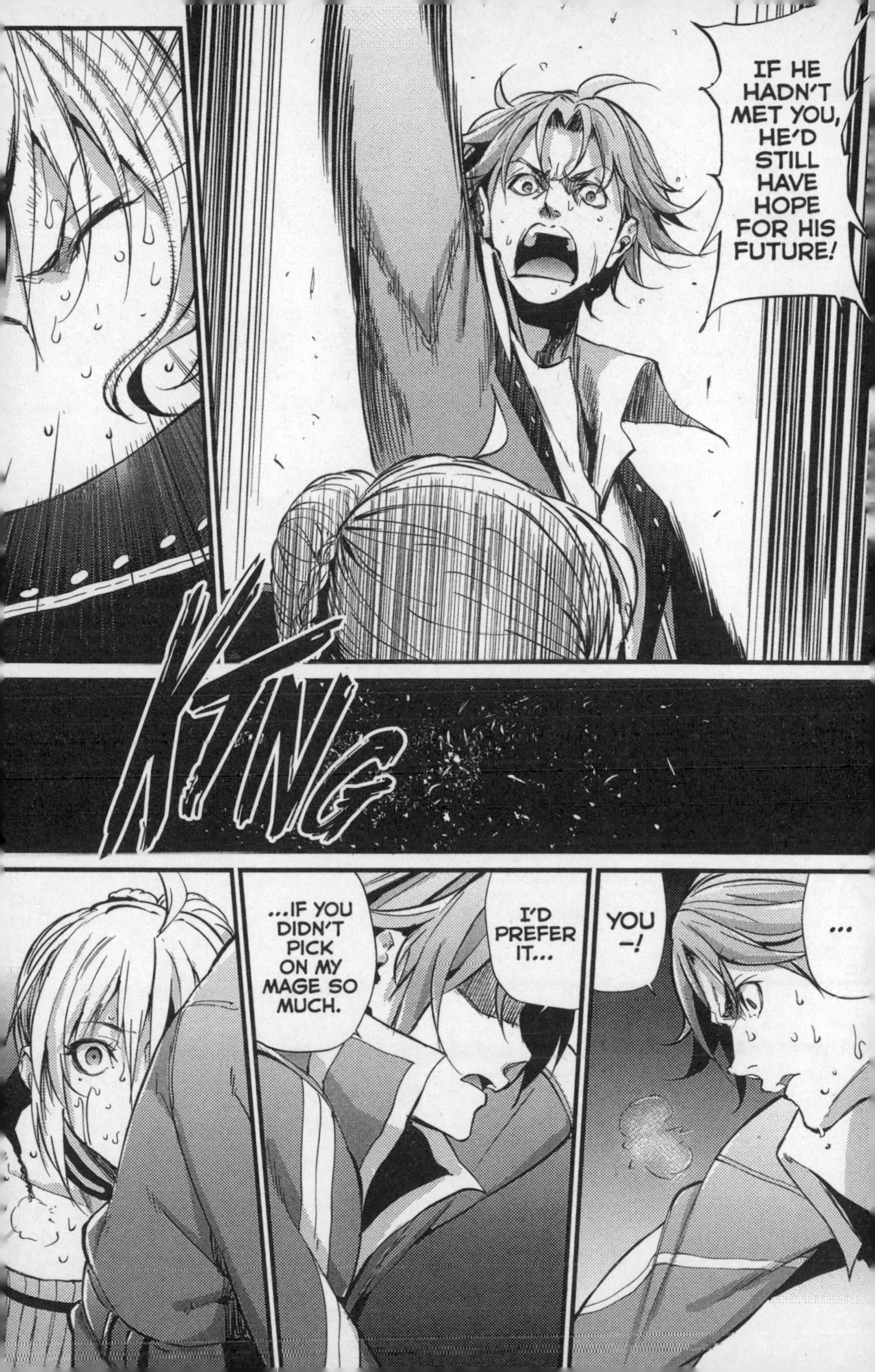
IF HE HADN'T MET YOU, HE'D STILL HAVE HOPE FOR HIS FUTURE!
KING
...
YOU —!
I'D PREFER IT...
...IF YOU DIDN'T PICK ON MY MAGE SO MUCH.

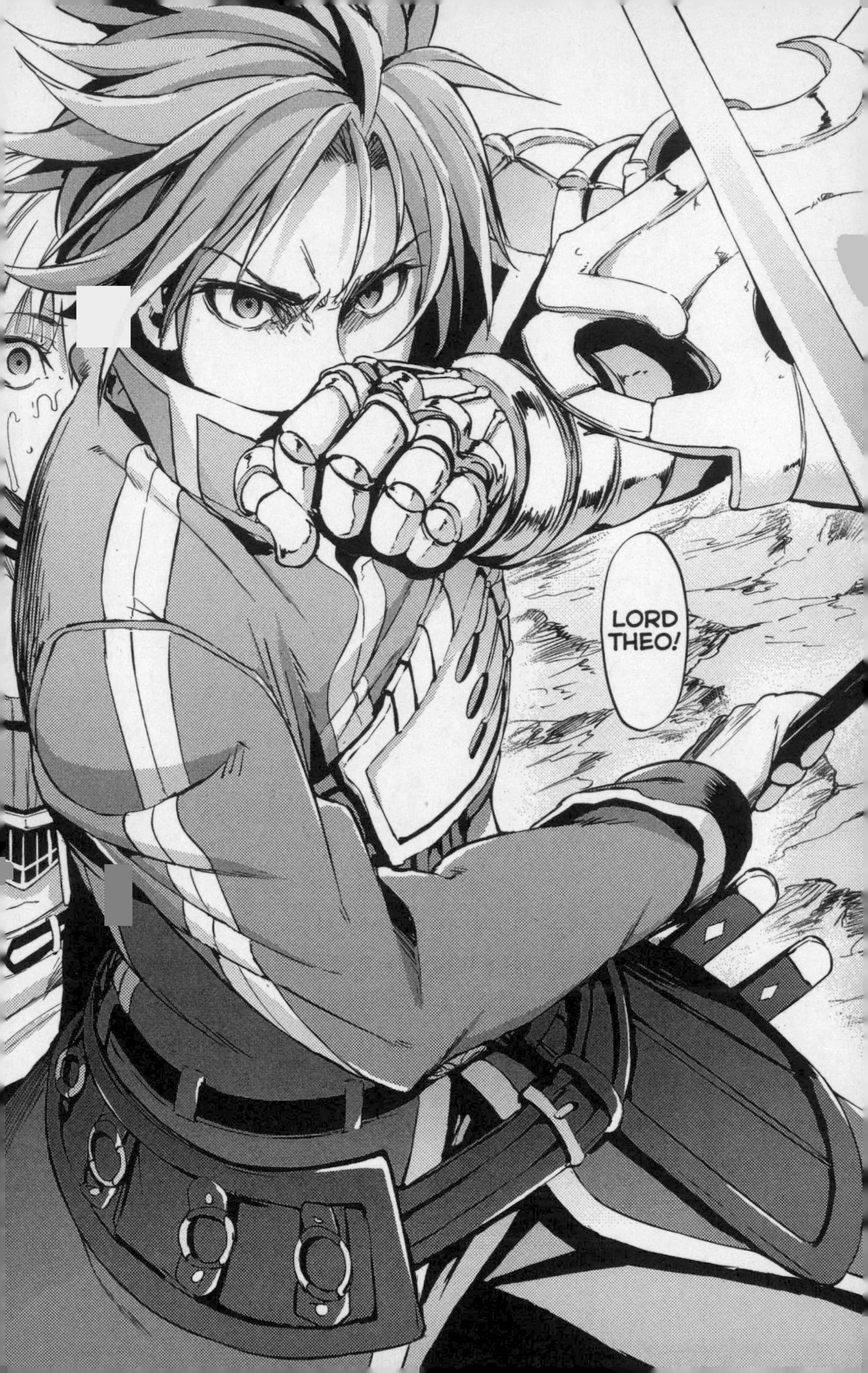
LORD THEO!

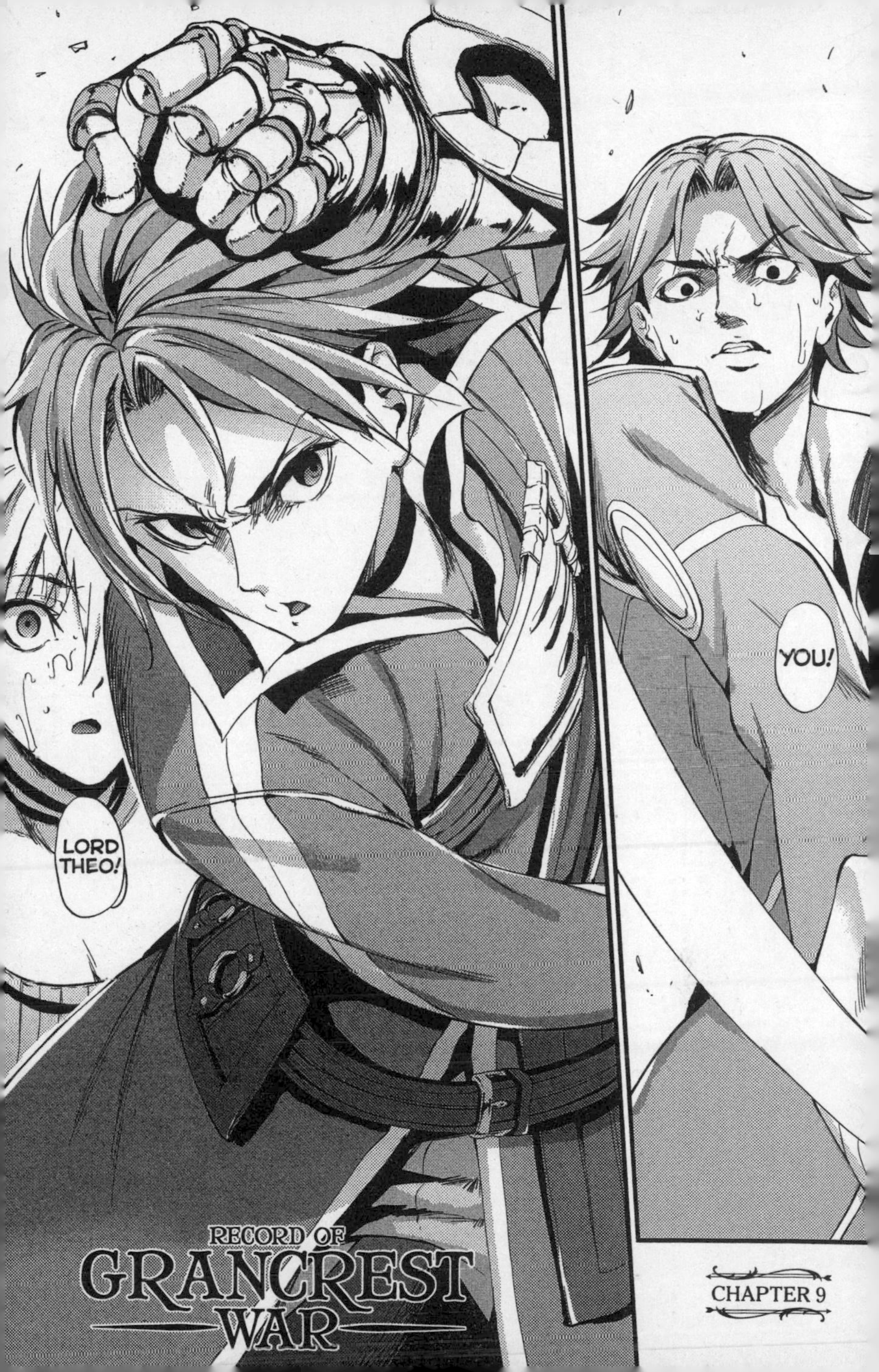
YOU!
LORD THEO!
RECORD OF GRANCREST WAR
CHAPTER 9

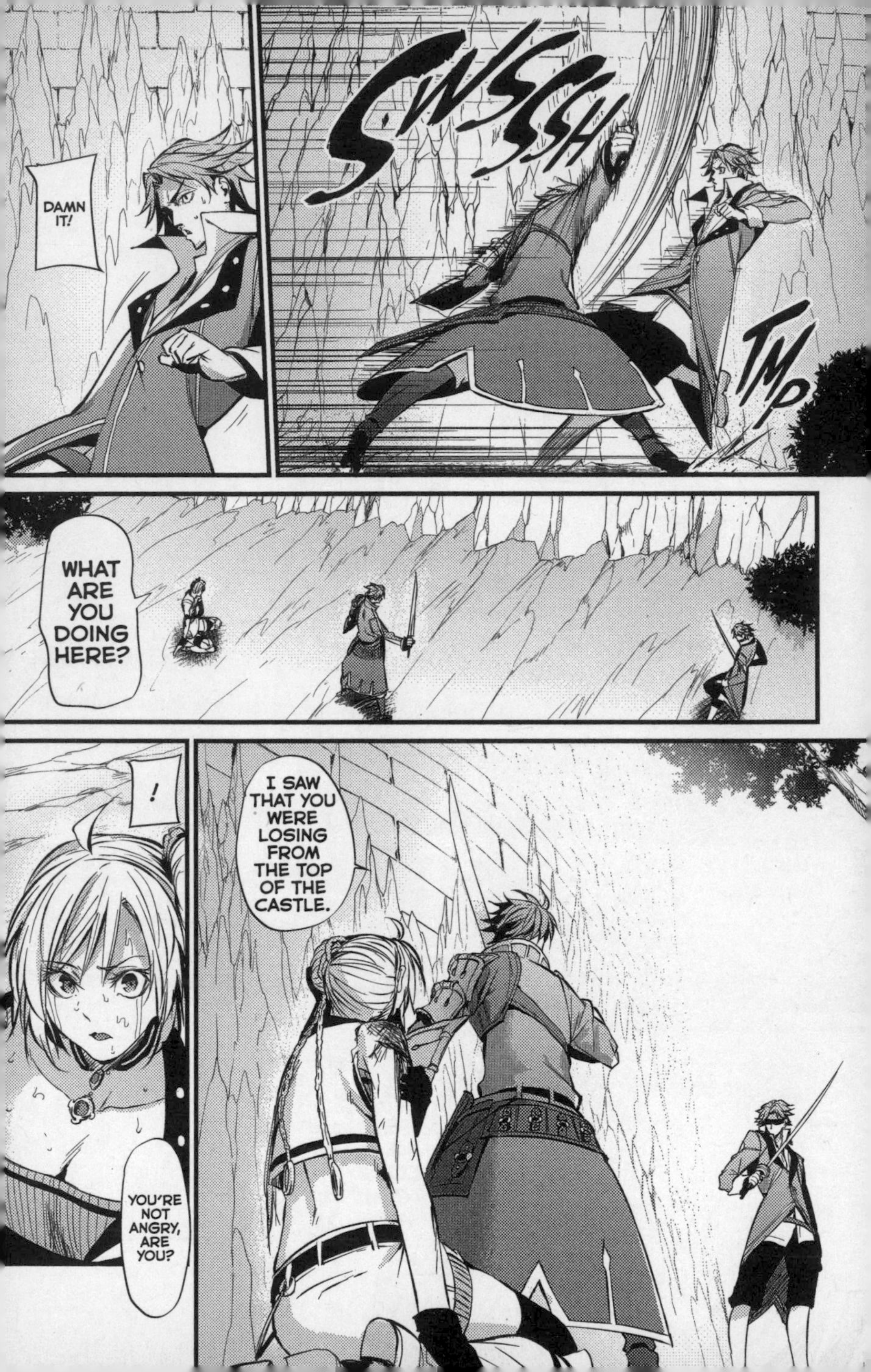
SWSSH
TMP
DAMN IT!
WHAT ARE YOU DOING HERE?
I SAW THAT YOU WERE LOSING FROM THE TOP OF THE CASTLE.
!
YOU'RE NOT ANGRY, ARE YOU?

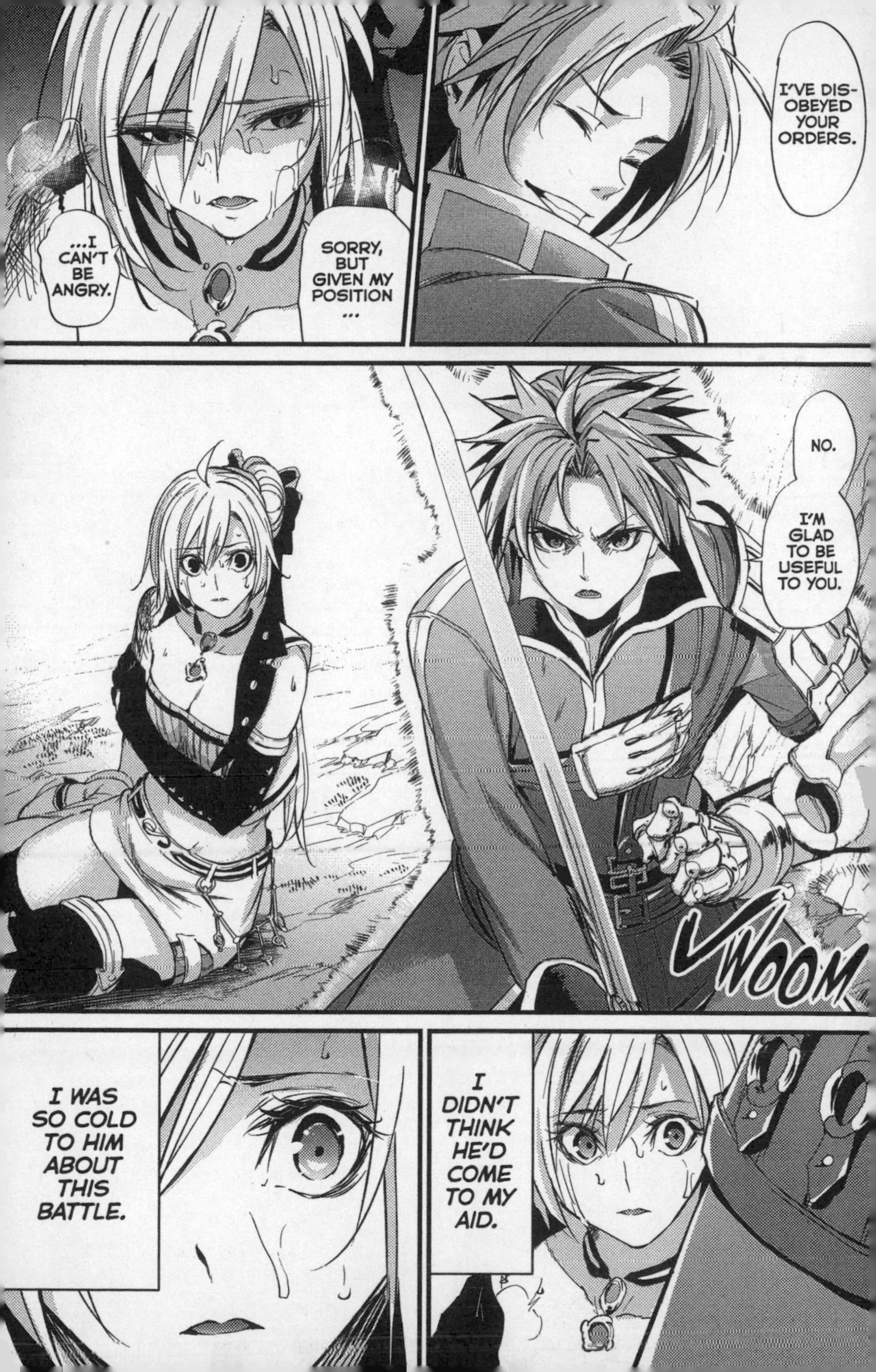
I'VE DIS-OBEYED YOUR ORDERS.
SORRY, BUT GIVEN MY POSITION ...
...I CAN'T BE ANGRY.
NO.
I'M GLAD TO BE USEFUL TO YOU.
VWOOM
I DIDN'T THINK HE'D COME TO MY AID.
I WAS SO COLD TO HIM ABOUT THIS BATTLE.

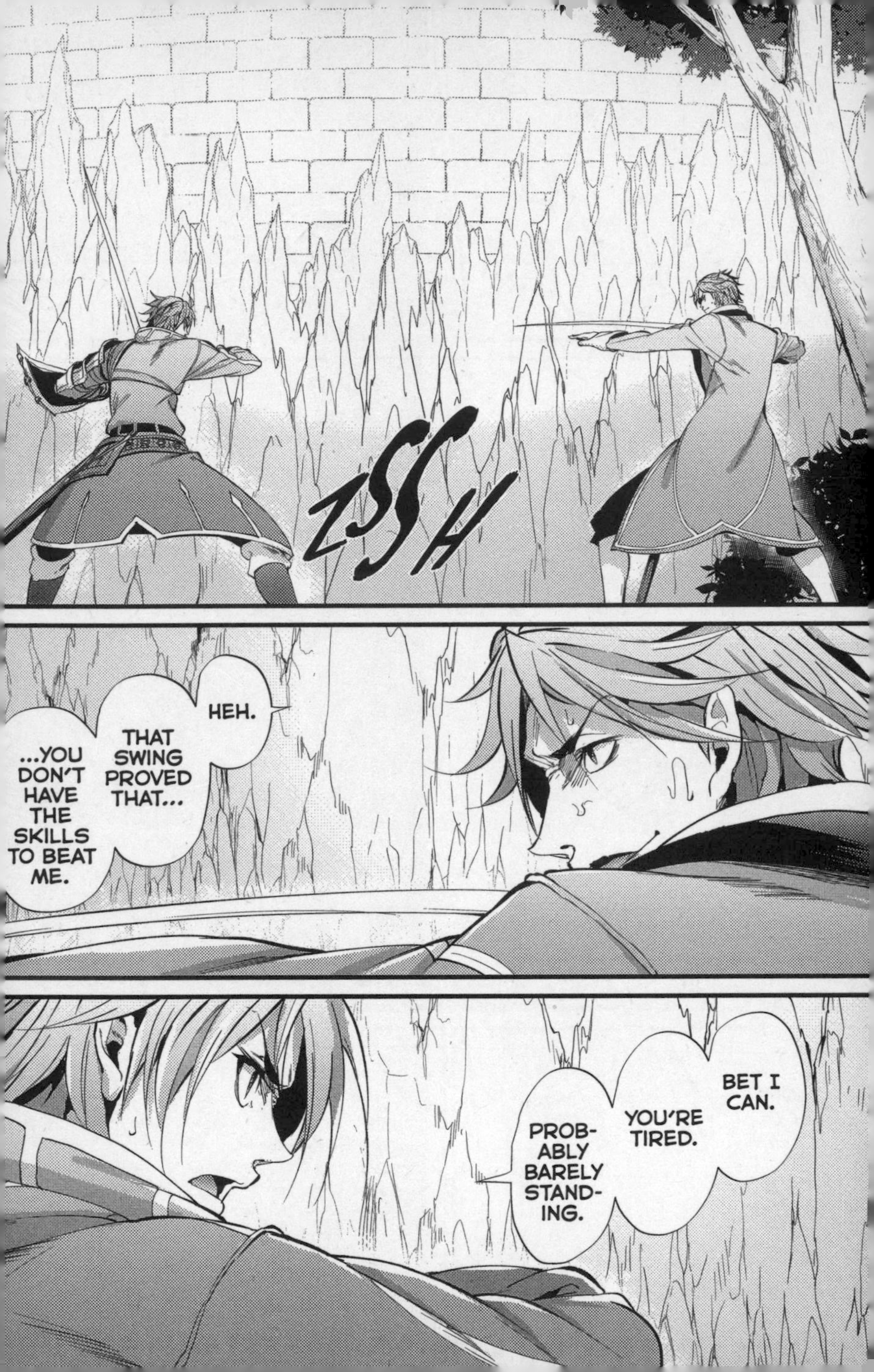
ZSH
HEH.
THAT SWING PROVED THAT...
...YOU DON'T HAVE THE SKILLS TO BEAT ME.
BET I CAN.
YOU'RE TIRED.
PROB-ABLY BARELY STAND-ING.

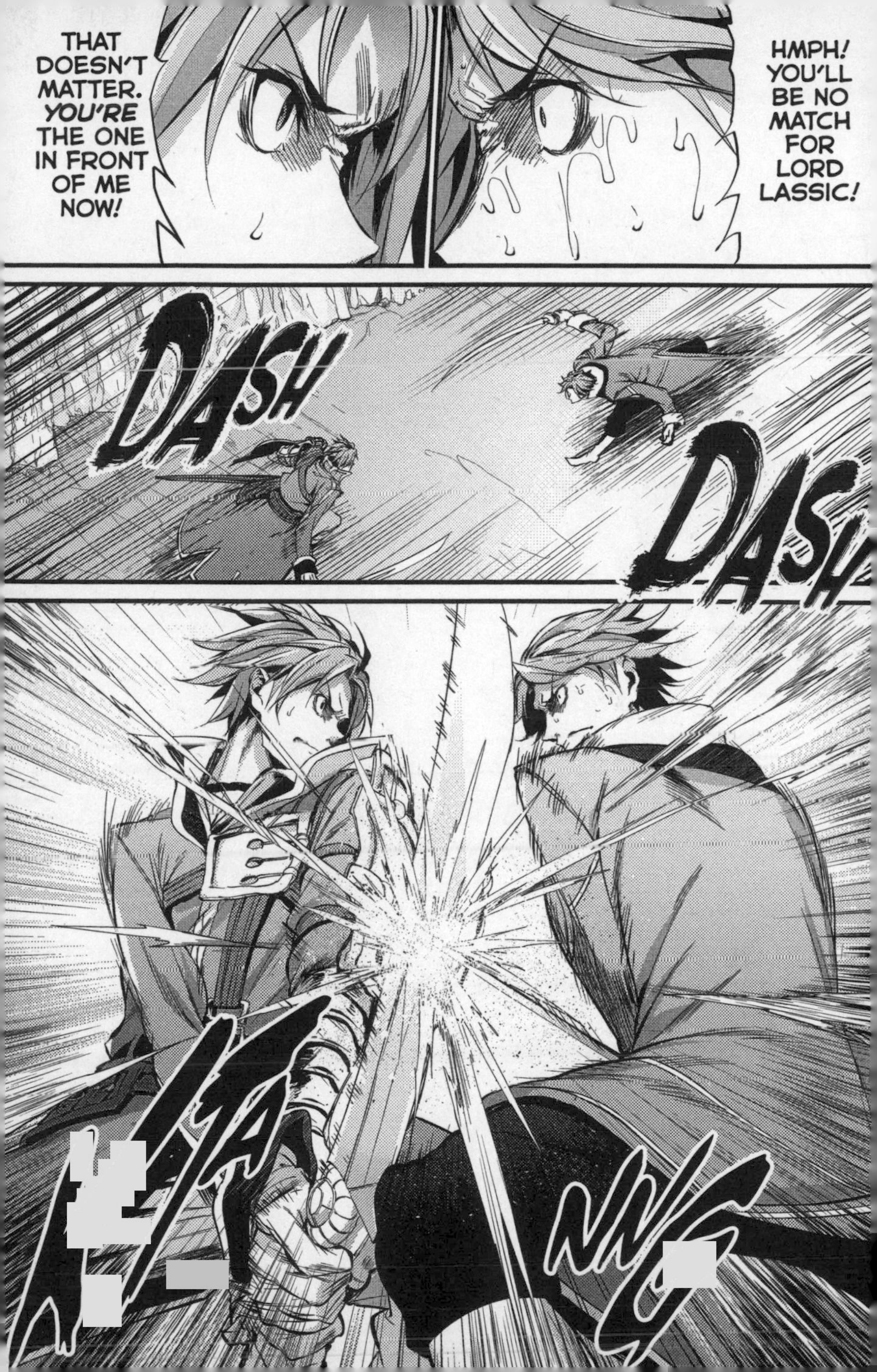
HMPH! YOU'LL BE NO MATCH FOR LORD LASSIC!
THAT DOESN'T MATTER. *YOU'RE* THE ONE IN FRONT OF ME NOW!
DASH
DASH
NNG

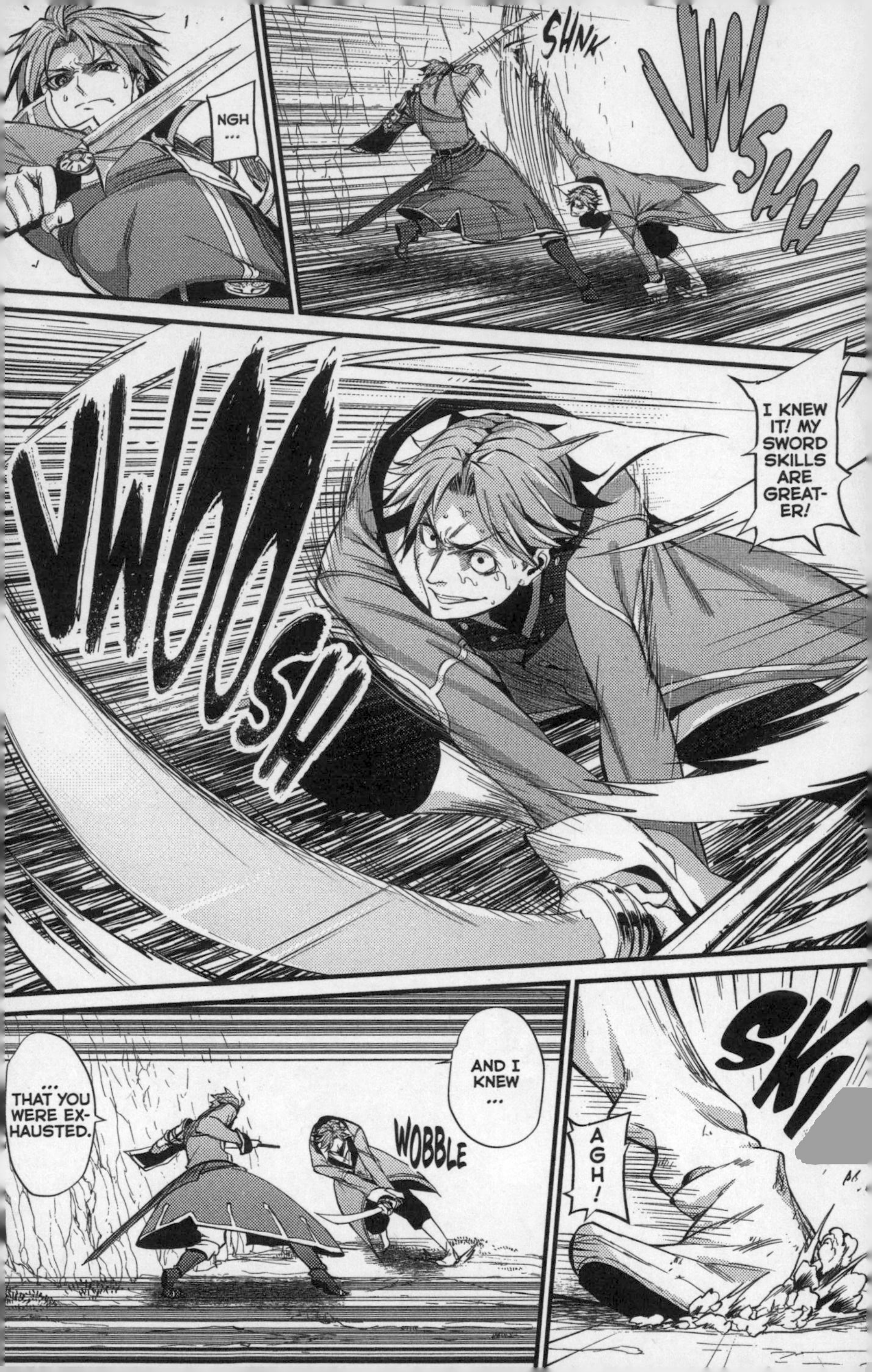
SHNK
VWSHW
NGH ...
VWUUSH!
I KNEW IT! MY SWORD SKILLS ARE GREATER!
SKI
AGH!
AND I KNEW ...
WOBBLE
... THAT YOU WERE EXHAUSTED.

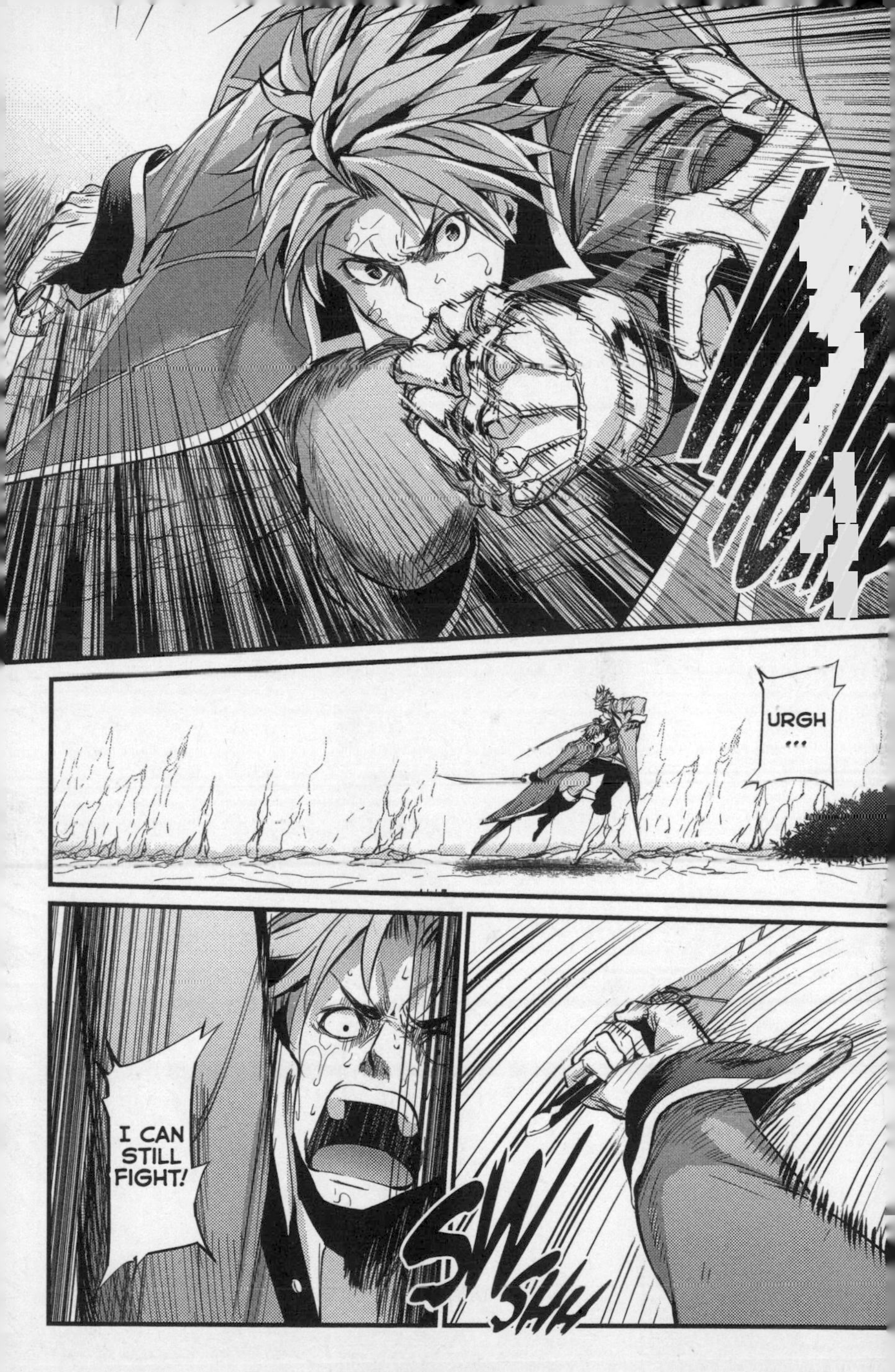
URGH ...
SWSHH
I CAN STILL FIGHT!

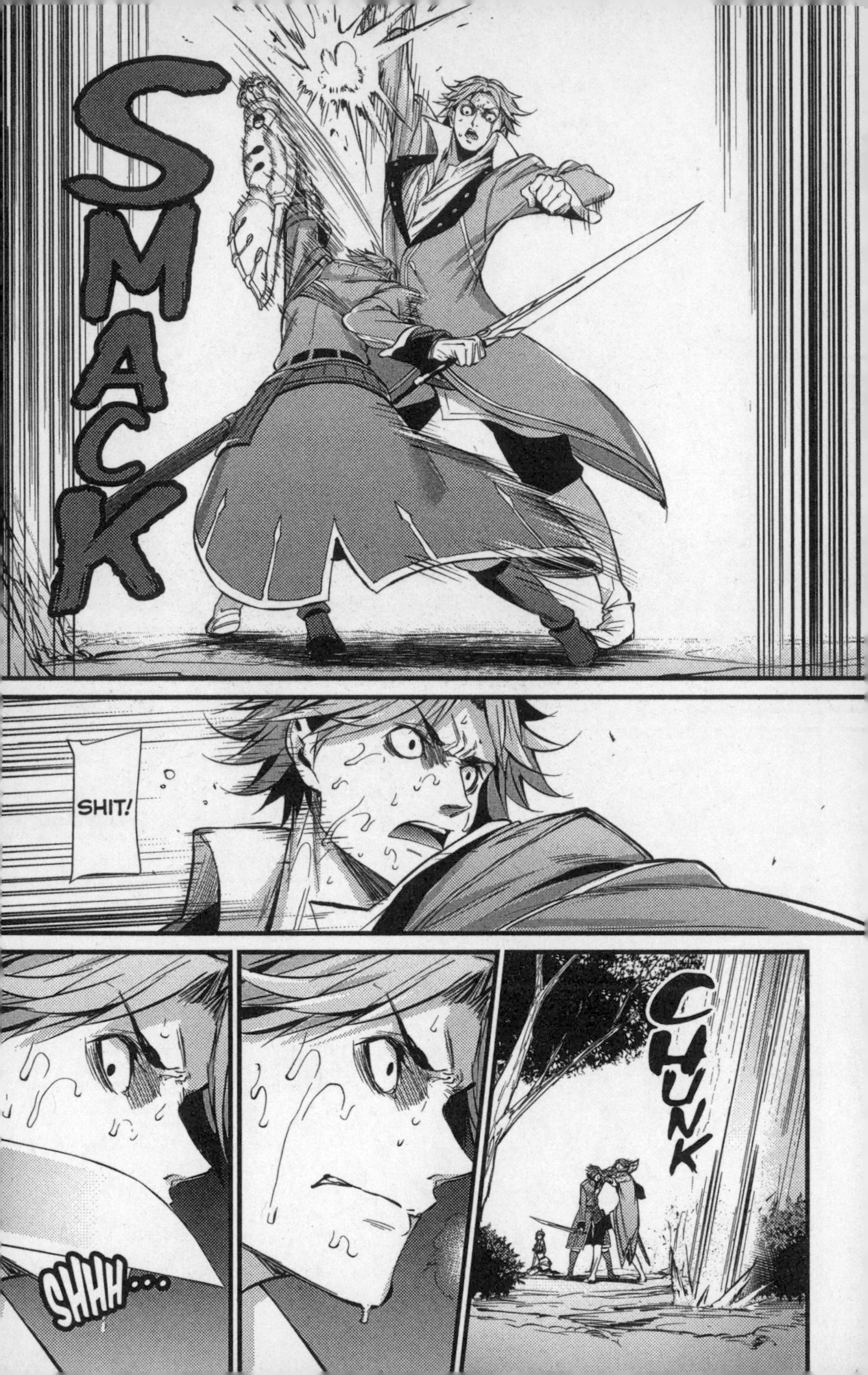
SMACK
SHIT!
CHUNK
SHHH...

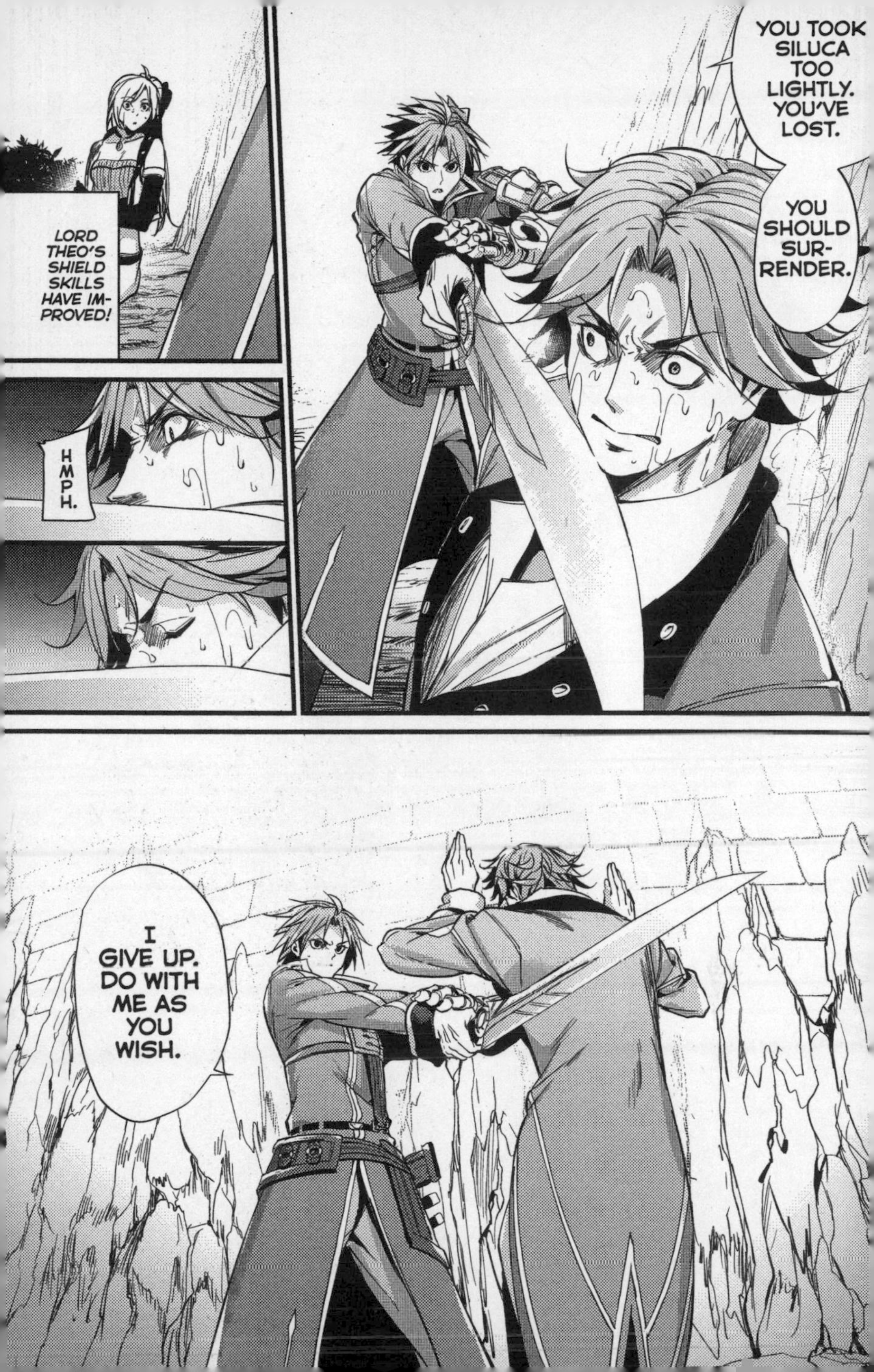
YOU TOOK SILUCA TOO LIGHTLY. YOU'VE LOST.
YOU SHOULD SUR-RENDER.
LORD THEO'S SHIELD SKILLS HAVE IM-PROVED!
HMPH.
I GIVE UP. DO WITH ME AS YOU WISH.

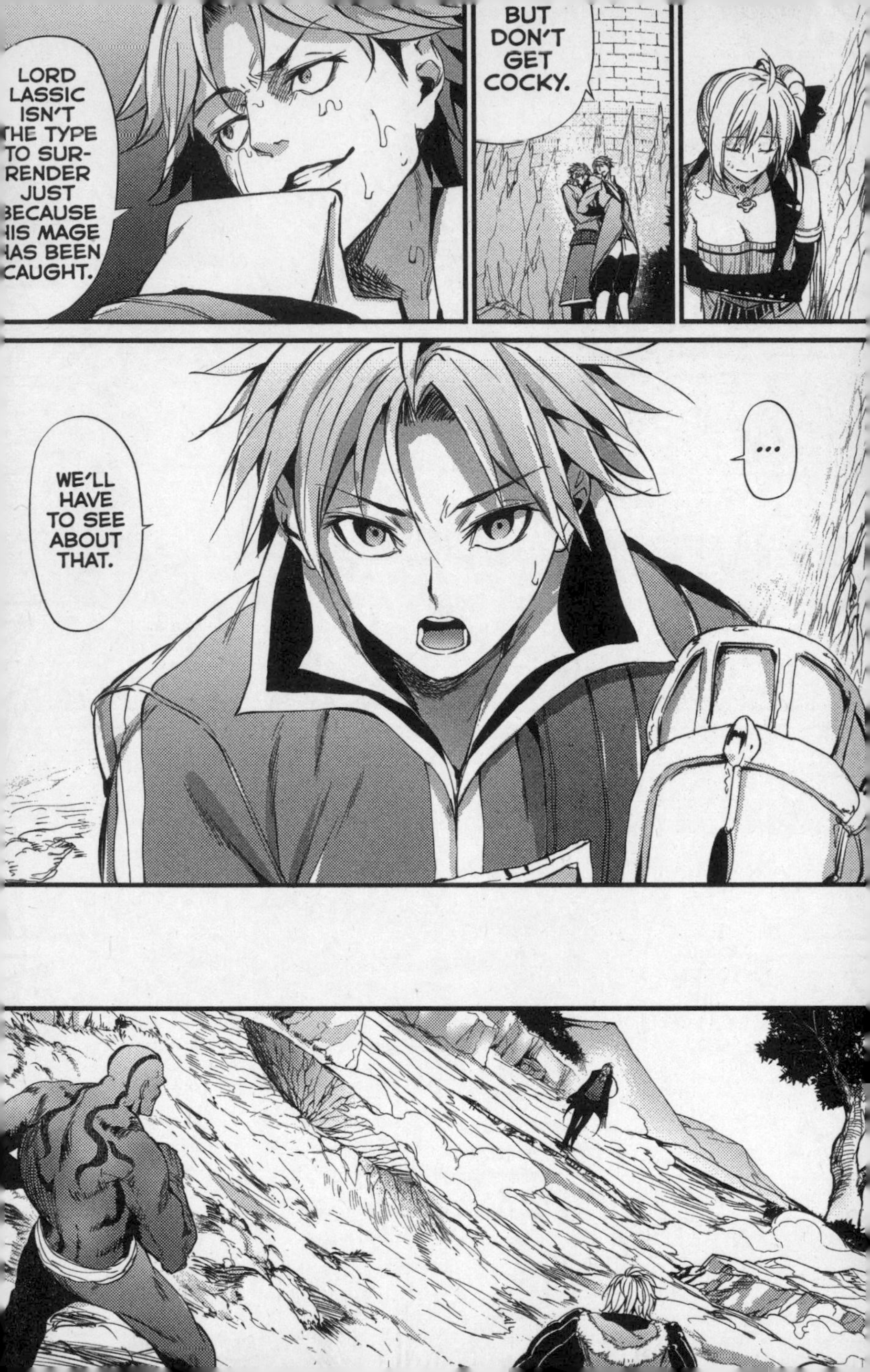
BUT DON'T GET COCKY.
LORD LASSIC ISN'T THE TYPE TO SUR-RENDER JUST BECAUSE HIS MAGE HAS BEEN CAUGHT.
...
WE'LL HAVE TO SEE ABOUT THAT.

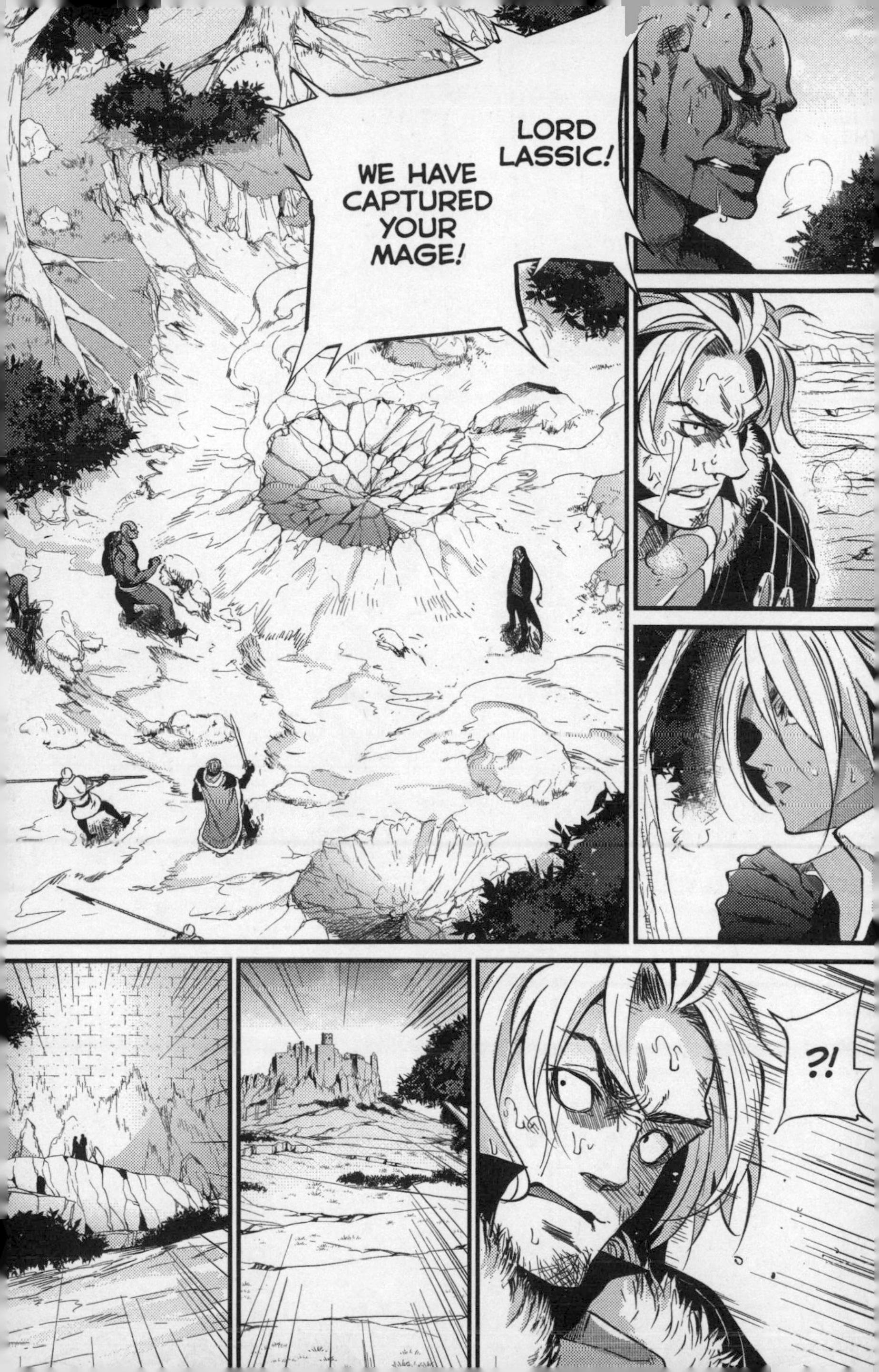
LORD LASSIC!
WE HAVE CAPTURED YOUR MAGE!
?!

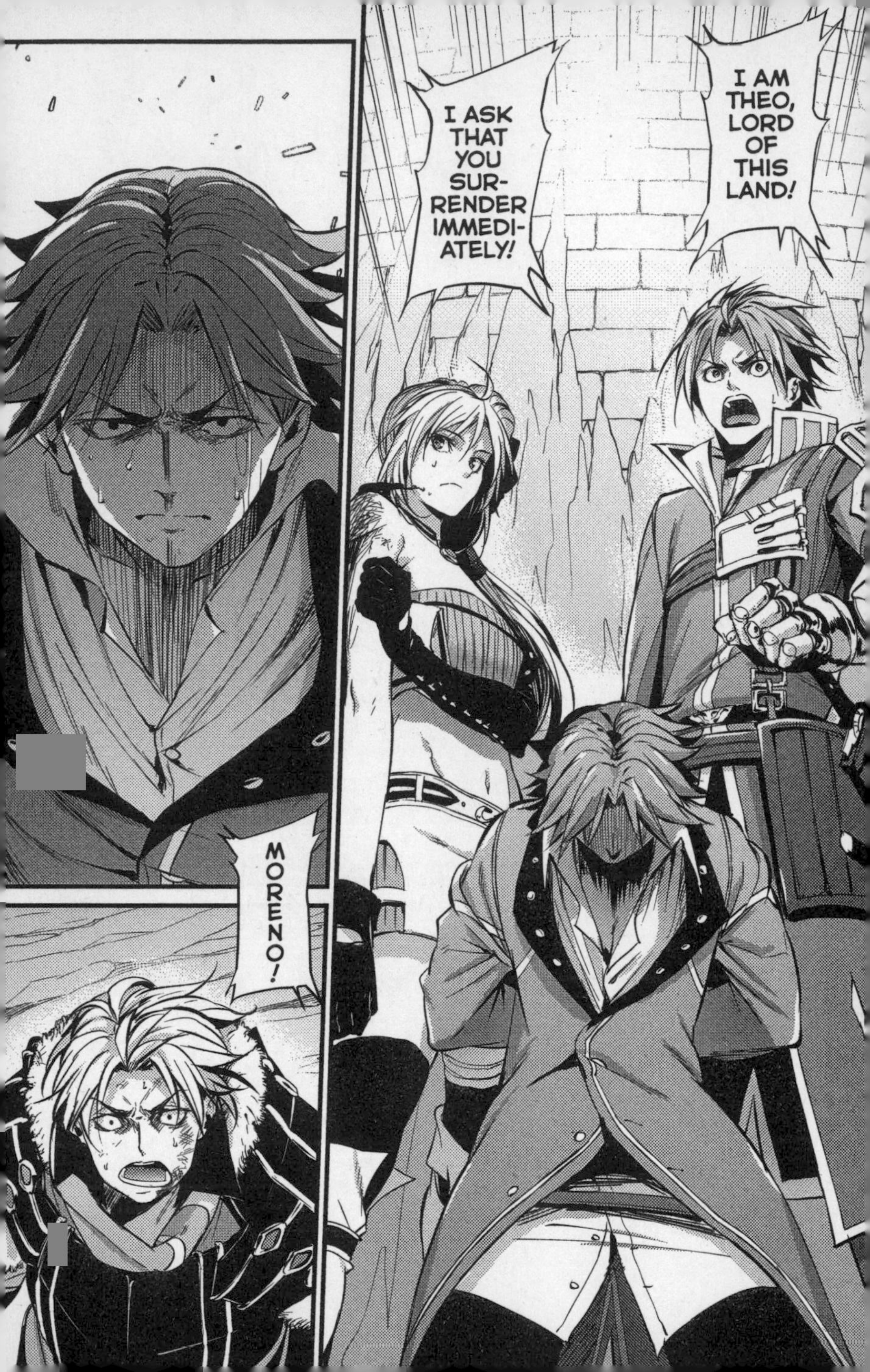
I AM THEO, LORD OF THIS LAND!
I ASK THAT YOU SUR-RENDER IMMEDI-ATELY!
MORENO!

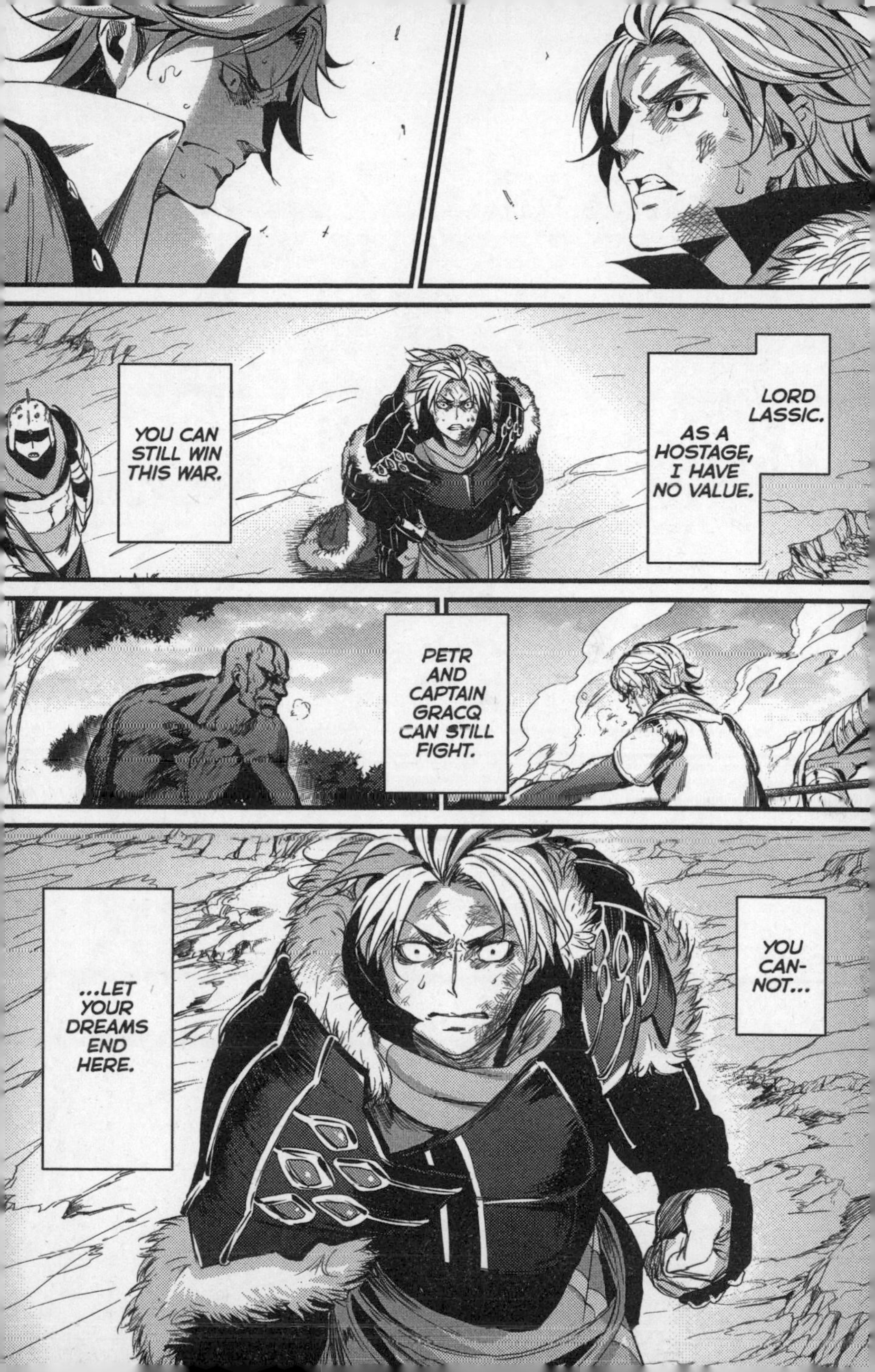
LORD LASSIC.
AS A HOSTAGE, I HAVE NO VALUE.
YOU CAN STILL WIN THIS WAR.
PETR AND CAPTAIN GRACQ CAN STILL FIGHT.
YOU CAN-NOT...
...LET YOUR DREAMS END HERE.

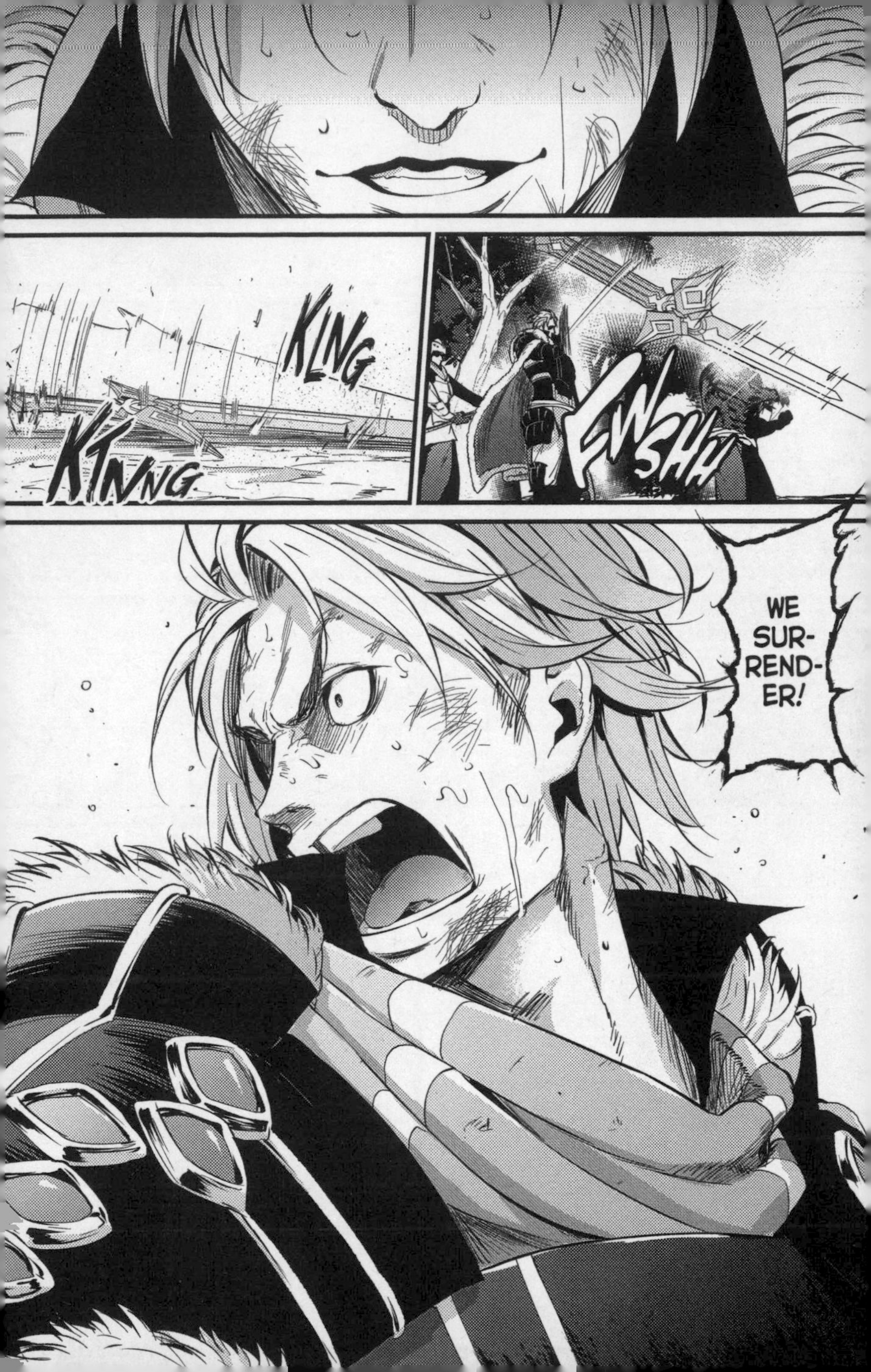
FWSHH
KLING
KTNNG
WE SURRENDER!

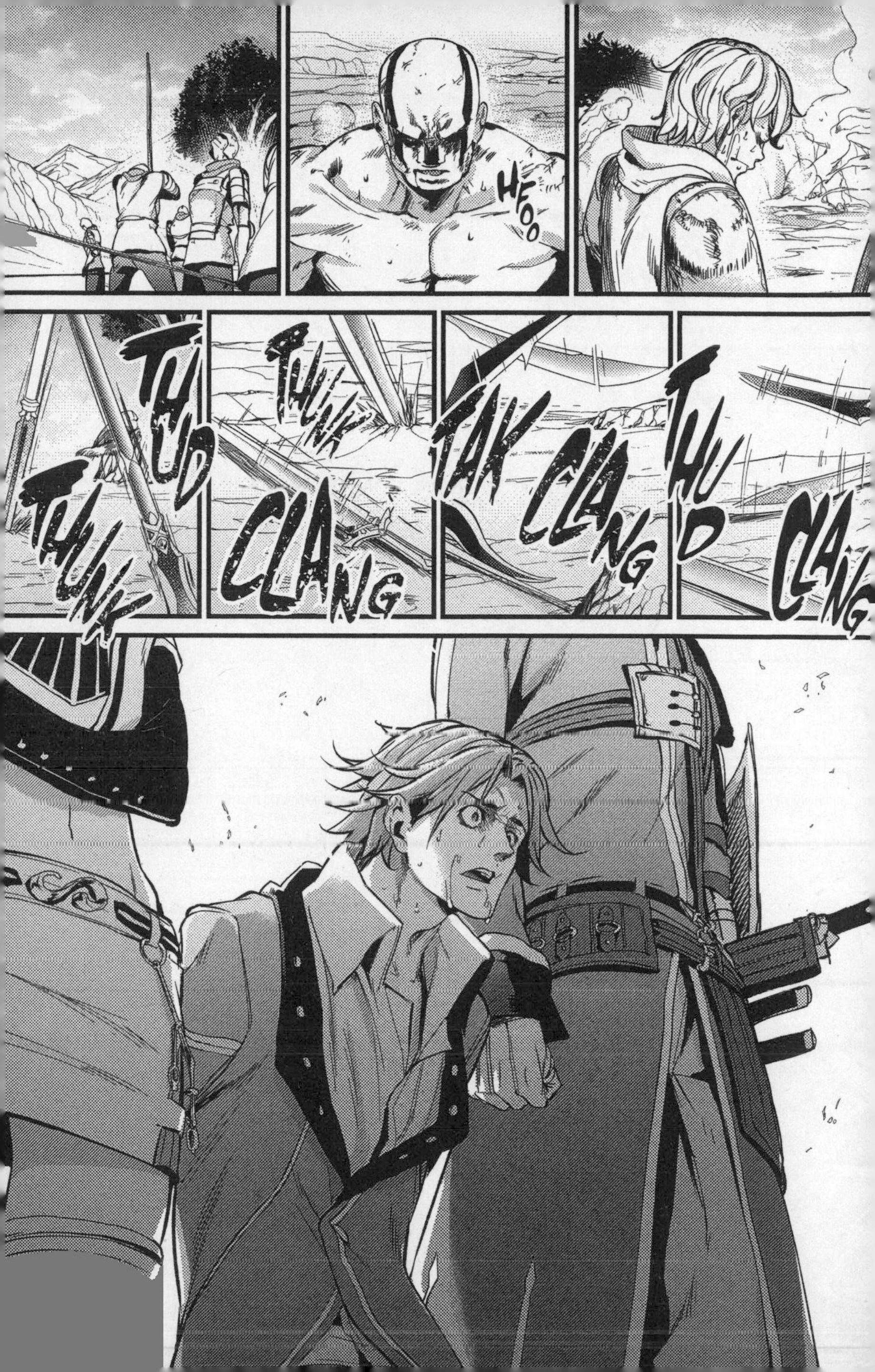
HFOO
THUD
CLANG
TAK
CLANG
THUNK
CLANG
THUD
THUNK

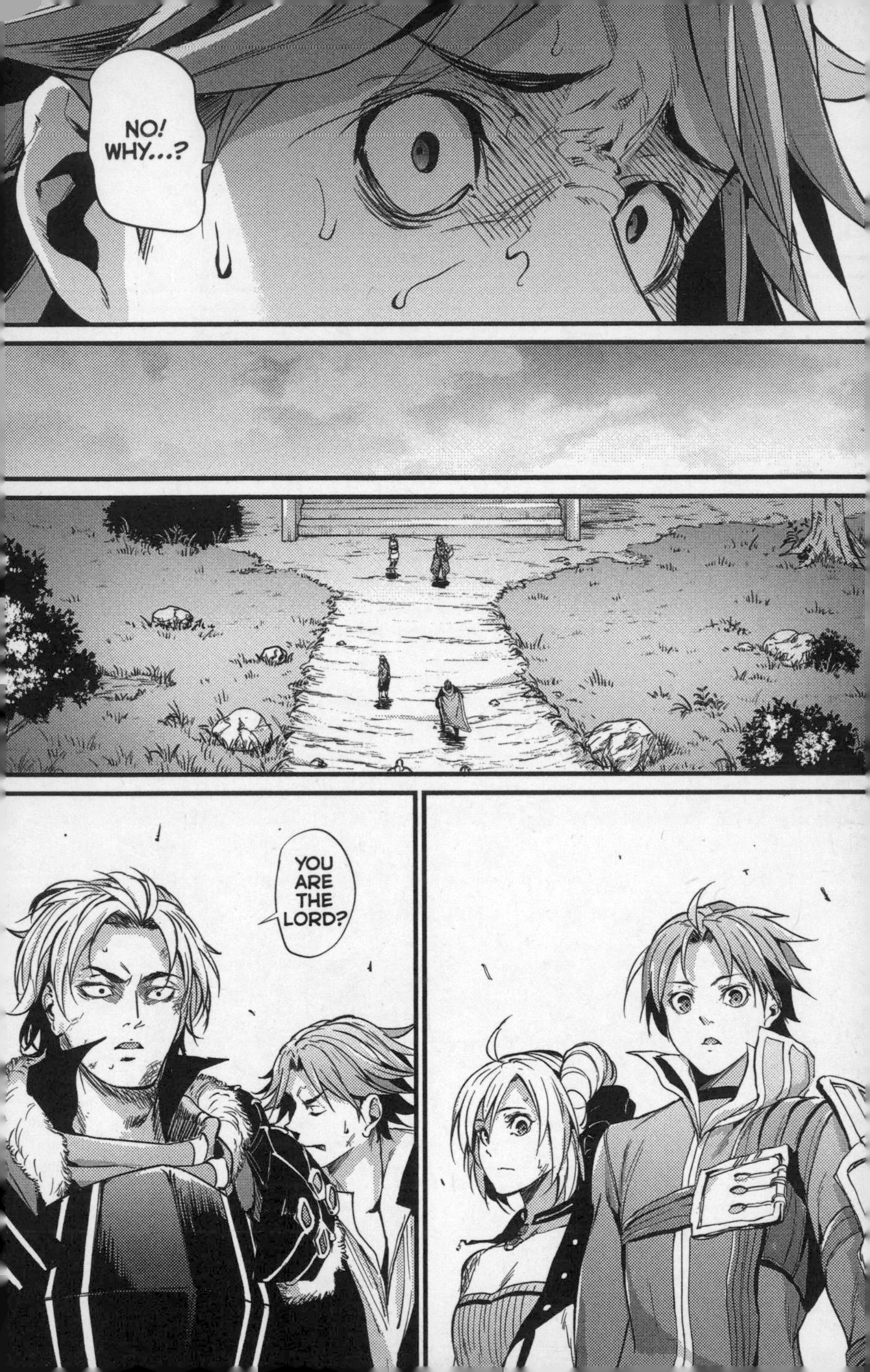
NO! WHY...?
YOU ARE THE LORD?

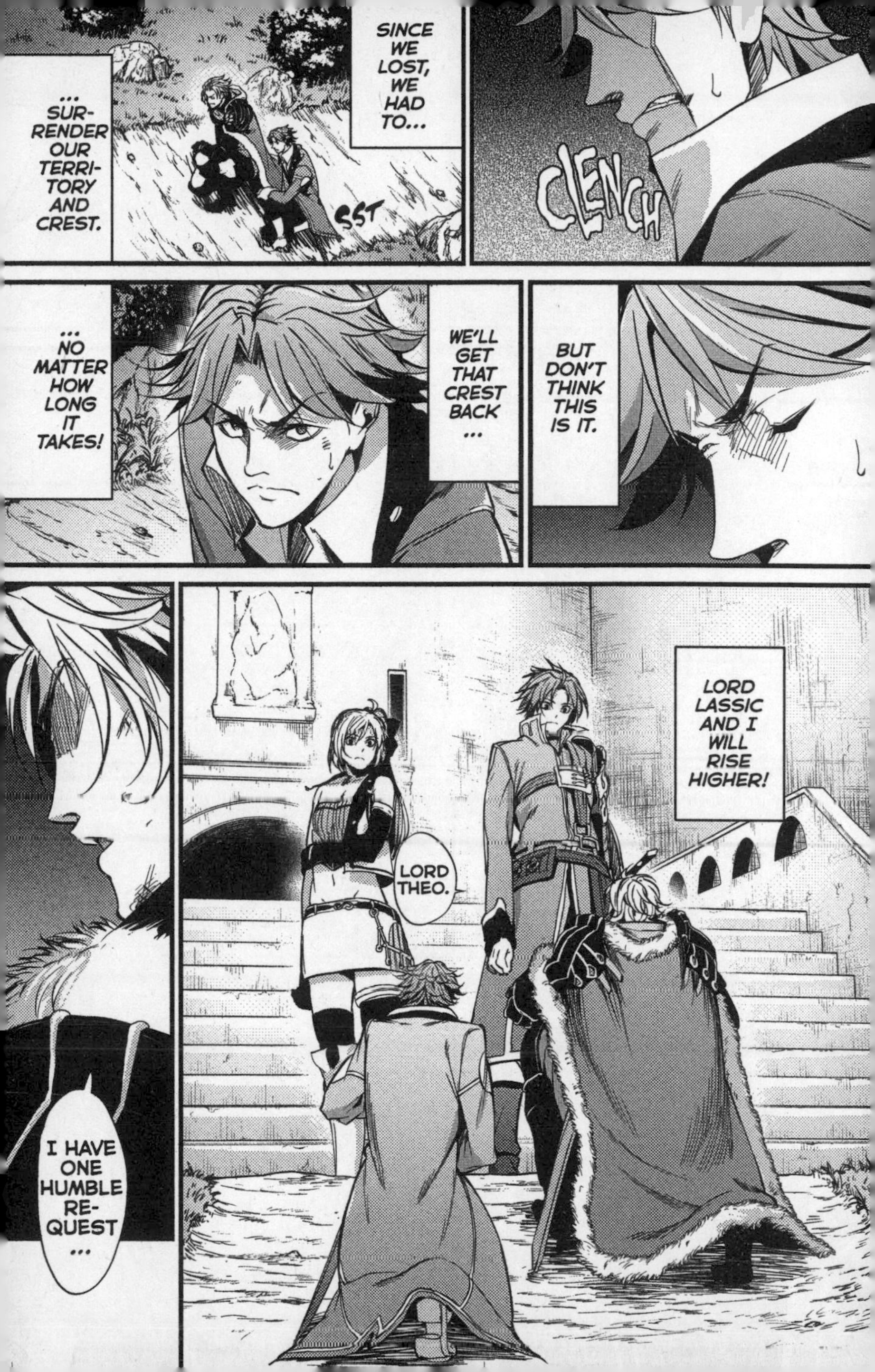
CLENCH
SINCE WE LOST, WE HAD TO...
...SURRENDER OUR TERRITORY AND CREST.
SST
BUT DON'T THINK THIS IS IT.
WE'LL GET THAT CREST BACK...
...NO MATTER HOW LONG IT TAKES!
LORD LASSIC AND I WILL RISE HIGHER!
LORD THEO.
I HAVE ONE HUMBLE REQUEST...

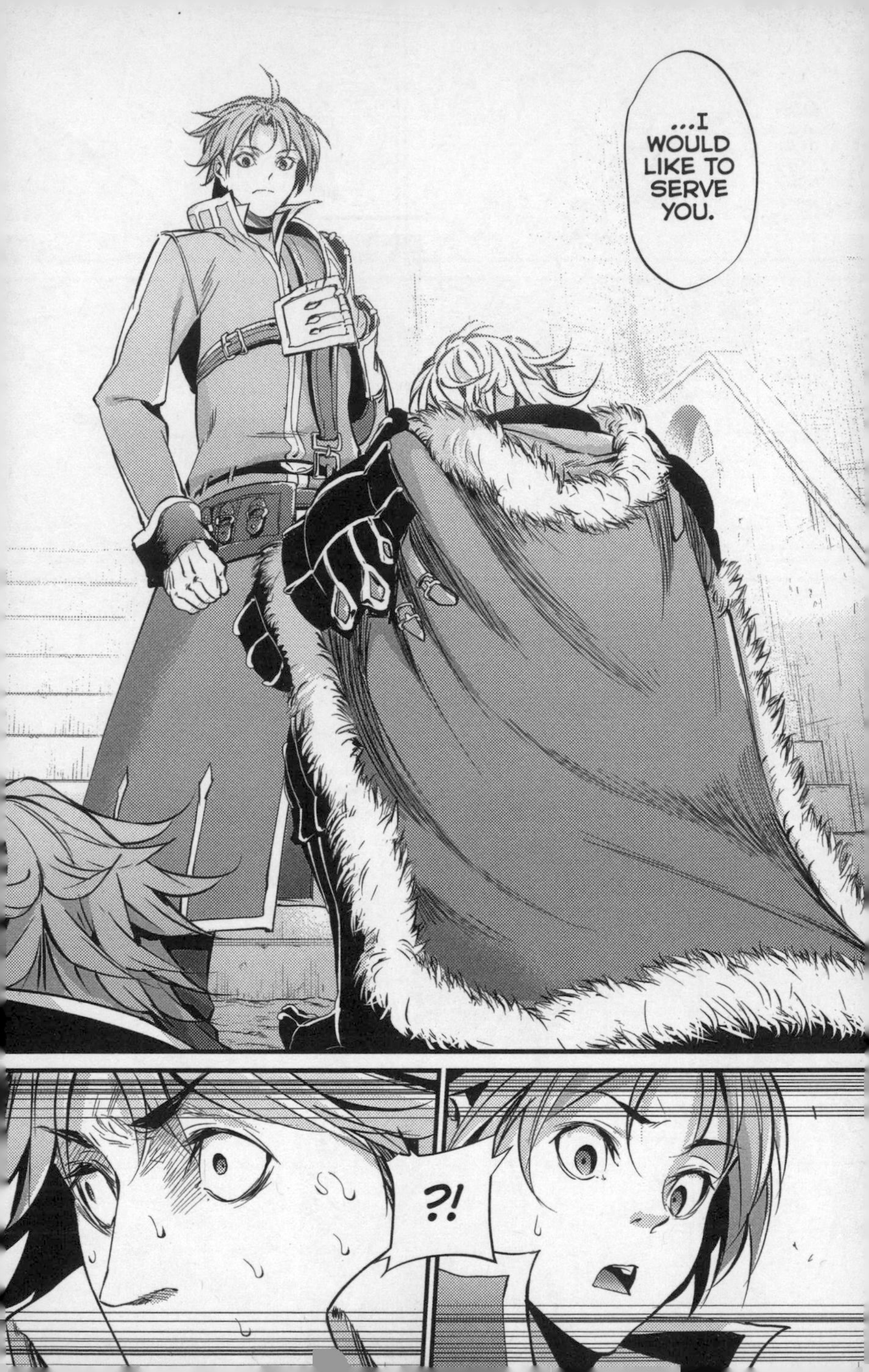
...I WOULD LIKE TO SERVE YOU.
?!

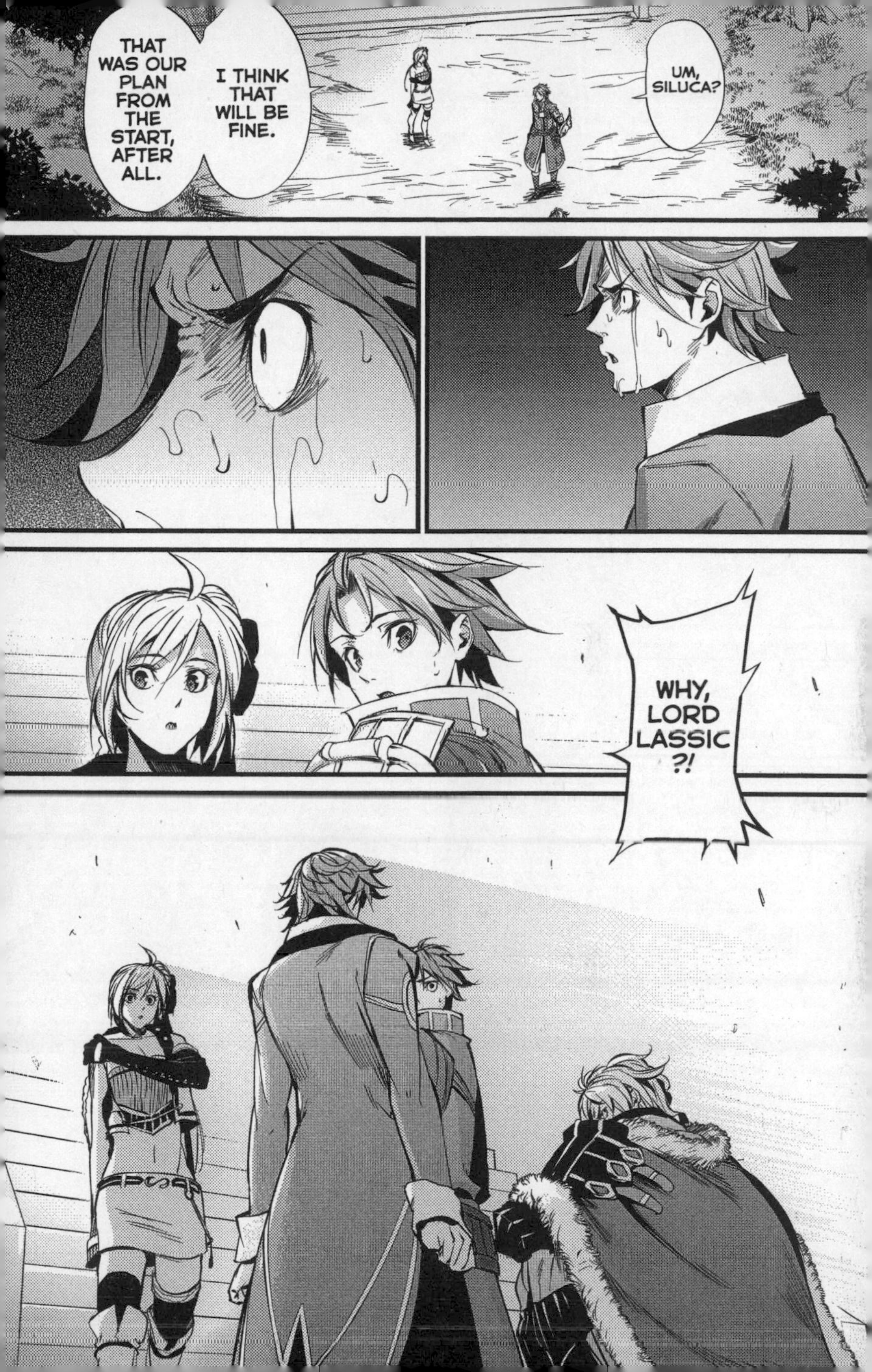
UM, SILUCA?
I THINK THAT WILL BE FINE.
THAT WAS OUR PLAN FROM THE START, AFTER ALL.
WHY, LORD LASSIC?!

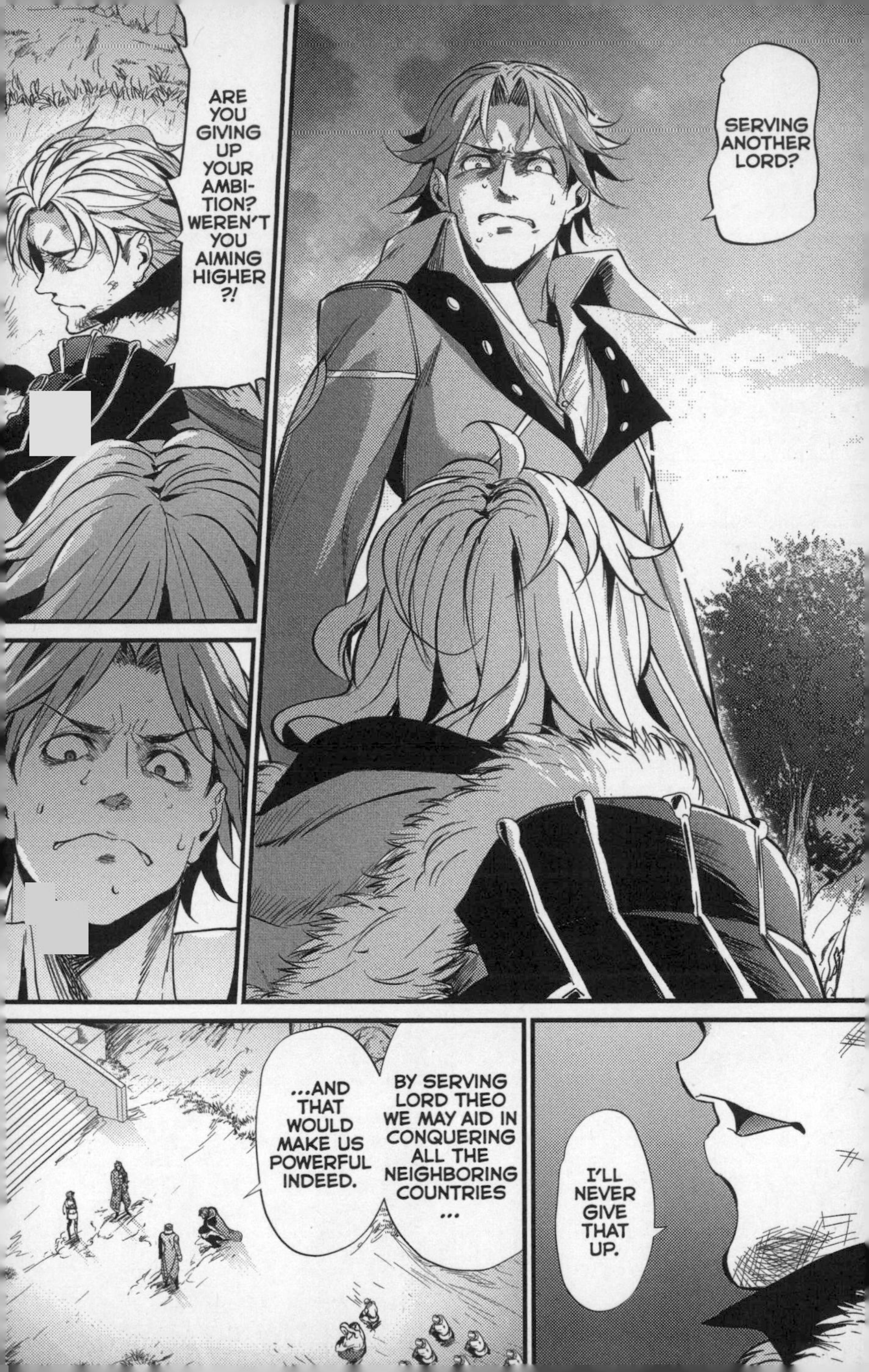
SERVING ANOTHER LORD?
ARE YOU GIVING UP YOUR AMBITION? WEREN'T YOU AIMING HIGHER?!
I'LL NEVER GIVE THAT UP.
BY SERVING LORD THEO WE MAY AID IN CONQUERING ALL THE NEIGHBORING COUNTRIES...
...AND THAT WOULD MAKE US POWERFUL INDEED.

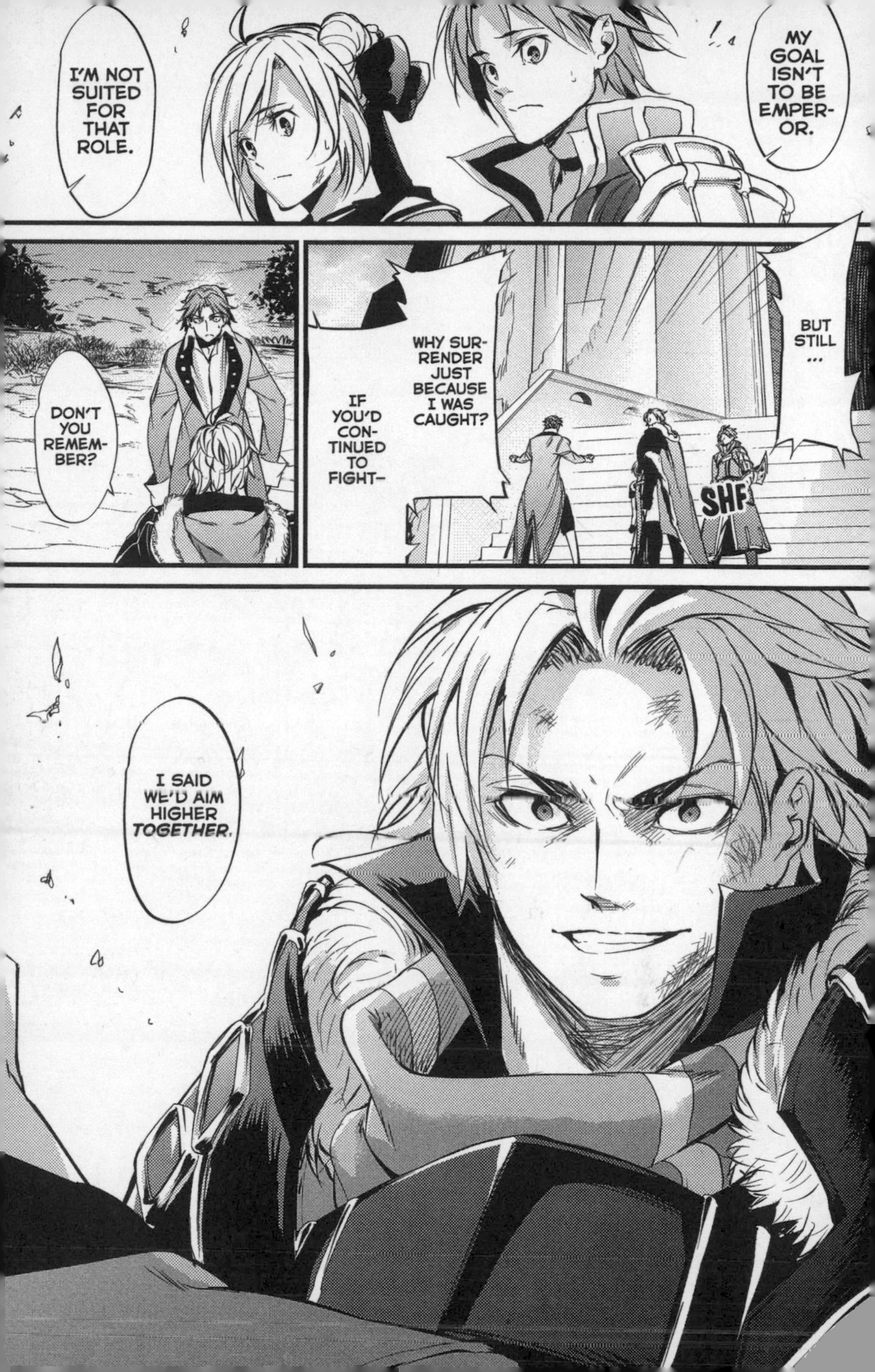
MY GOAL ISN'T TO BE EMPEROR.
I'M NOT SUITED FOR THAT ROLE.
BUT STILL ...
WHY SURRENDER JUST BECAUSE I WAS CAUGHT?
IF YOU'D CONTINUED TO FIGHT—
SHF
DON'T YOU REMEMBER?
I SAID WE'D AIM HIGHER *TOGETHER*.

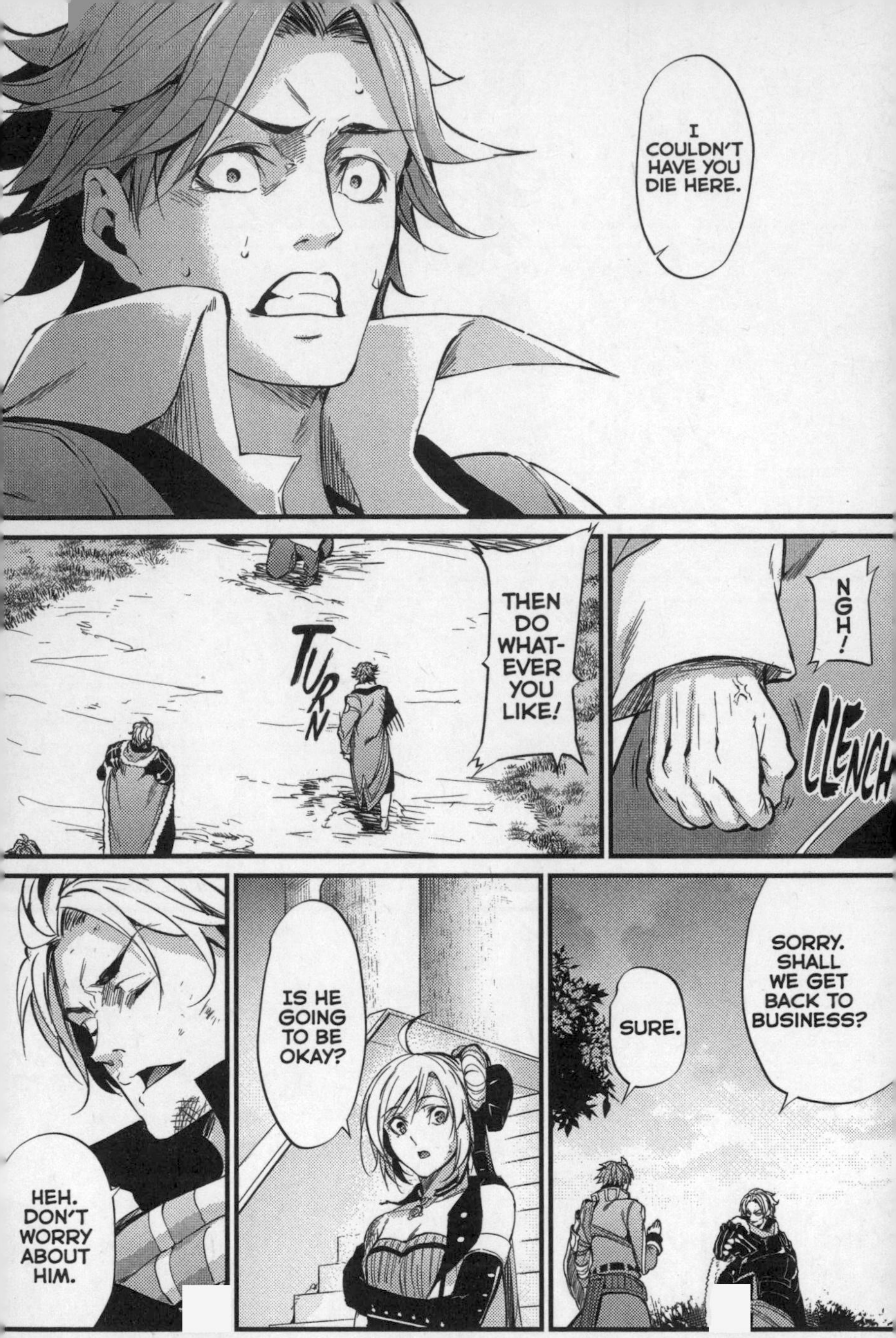
I COULDN'T HAVE YOU DIE HERE.
NGH!
CLENCH
THEN DO WHATEVER YOU LIKE!
TURN
SORRY. SHALL WE GET BACK TO BUSINESS?
SURE.
IS HE GOING TO BE OKAY?
HEH. DON'T WORRY ABOUT HIM.

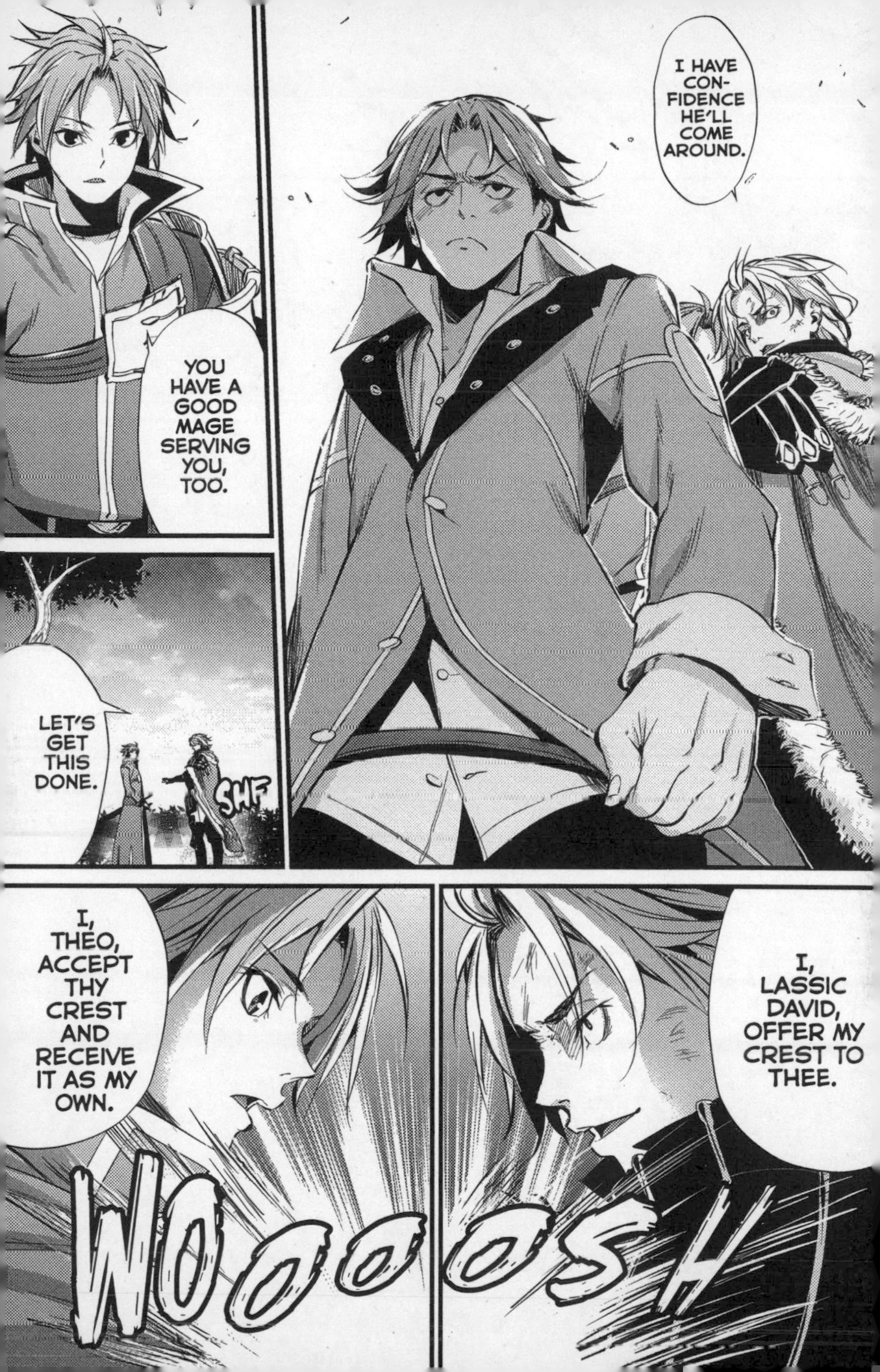
I HAVE CONFIDENCE HE'LL COME AROUND.
YOU HAVE A GOOD MAGE SERVING YOU, TOO.
LET'S GET THIS DONE.
SHF
I, LASSIC DAVID, OFFER MY CREST TO THEE.
I, THEO, ACCEPT THY CREST AND RECEIVE IT AS MY OWN.
WOOOOSH

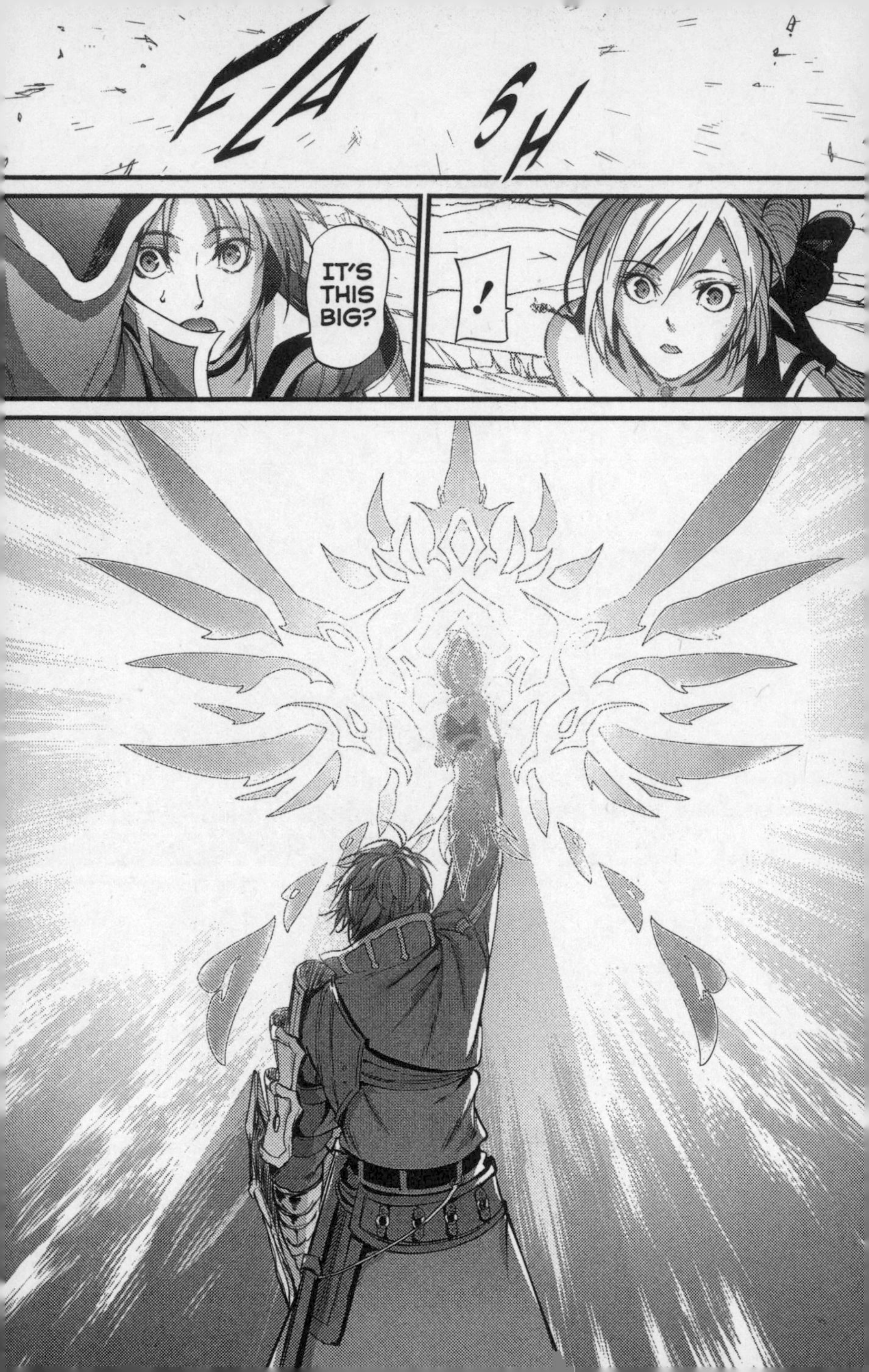
FLASH
!
IT'S THIS BIG?

RECORD OF
GRANCREST
WAR

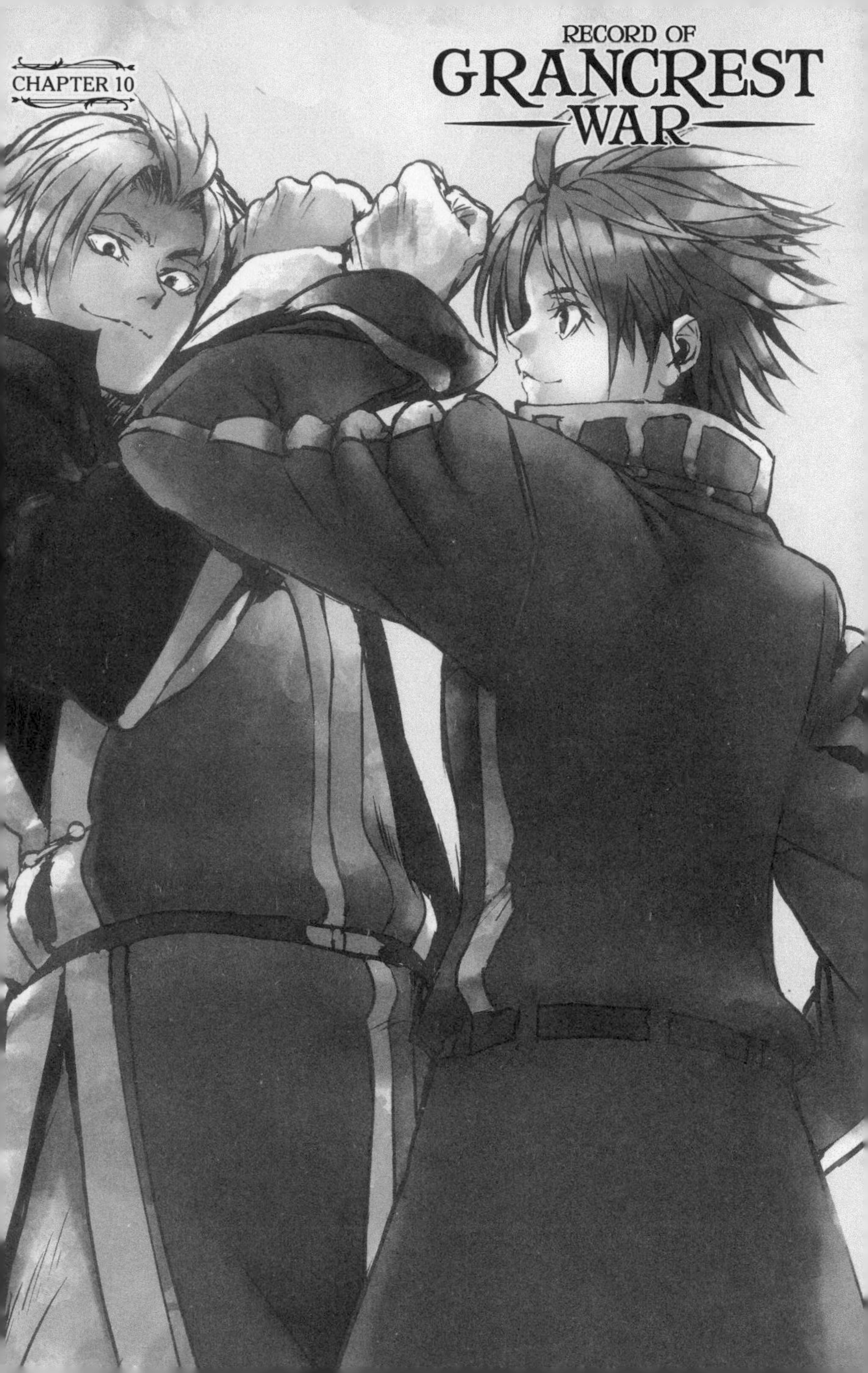
CHAPTER 10
RECORD OF
GRANCREST
WAR

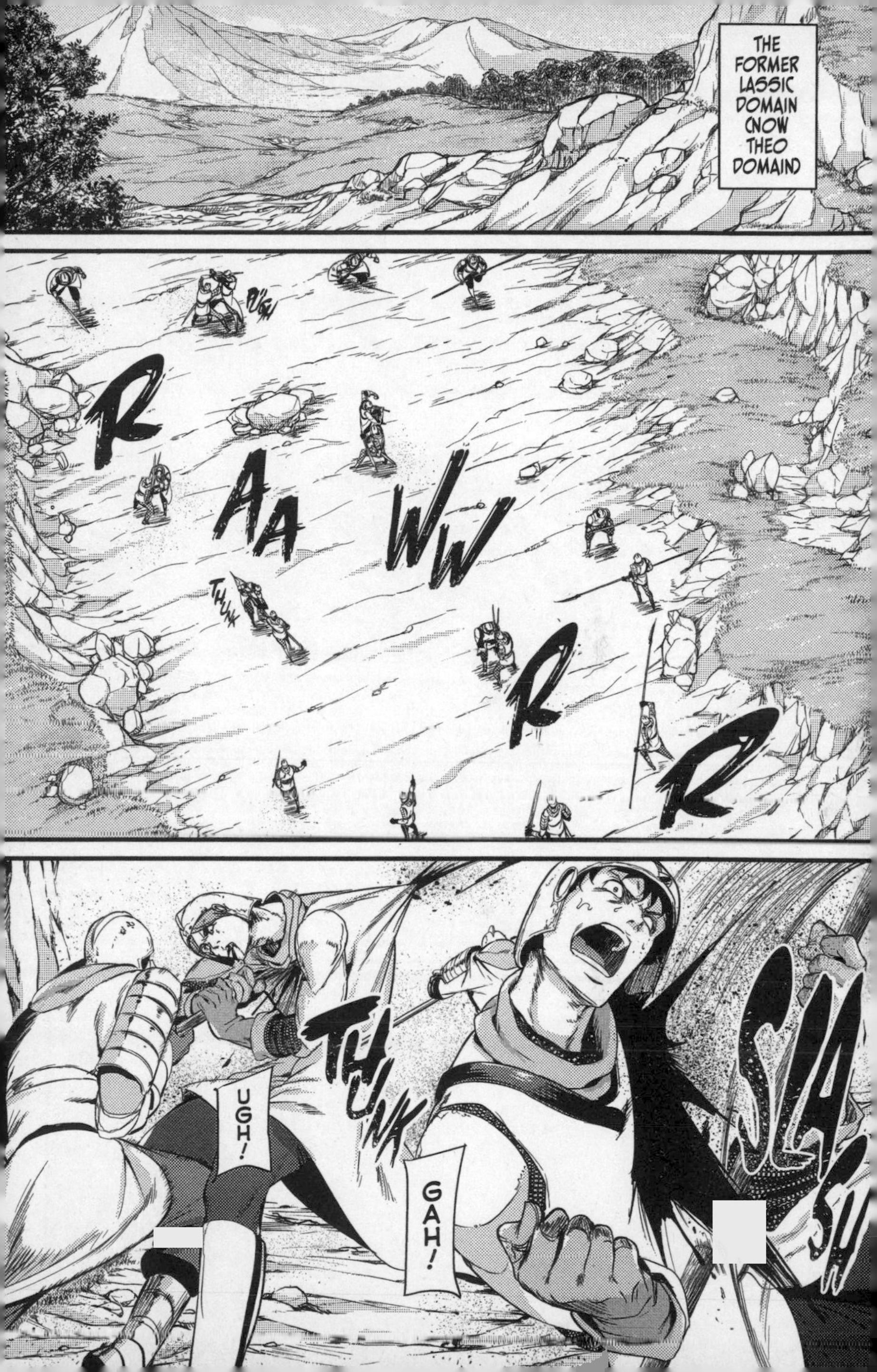
THE FORMER LASSIC DOMAIN (NOW THEO DOMAIN)
RAAWRRR
THUNK
SLASH
GAH!
THUNK
UGH!

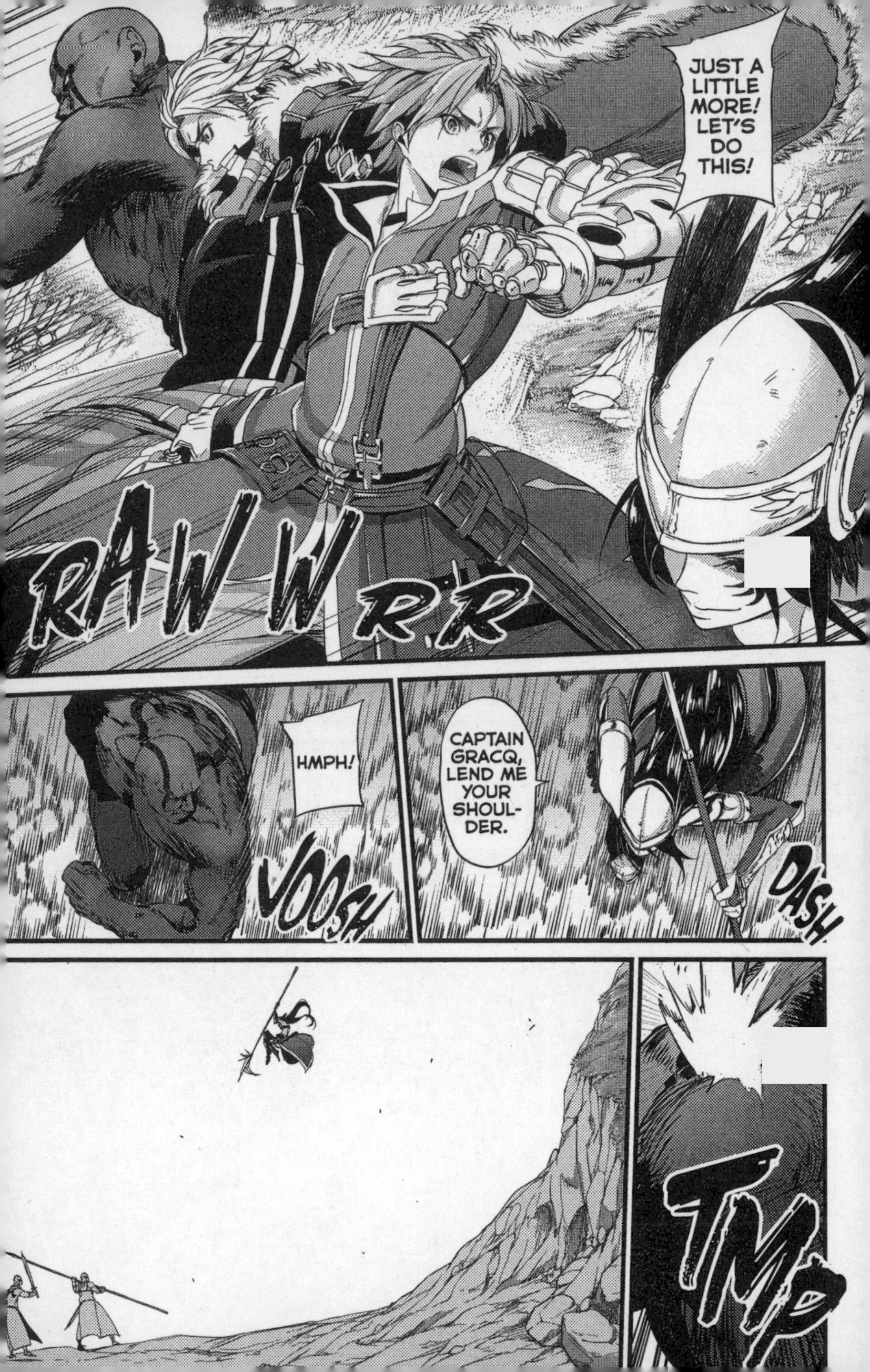
JUST A LITTLE MORE! LET'S DO THIS!
RAWWRR
CAPTAIN GRACQ, LEND ME YOUR SHOUL-DER.
DASH
HMPH!
VOOSH
TMP

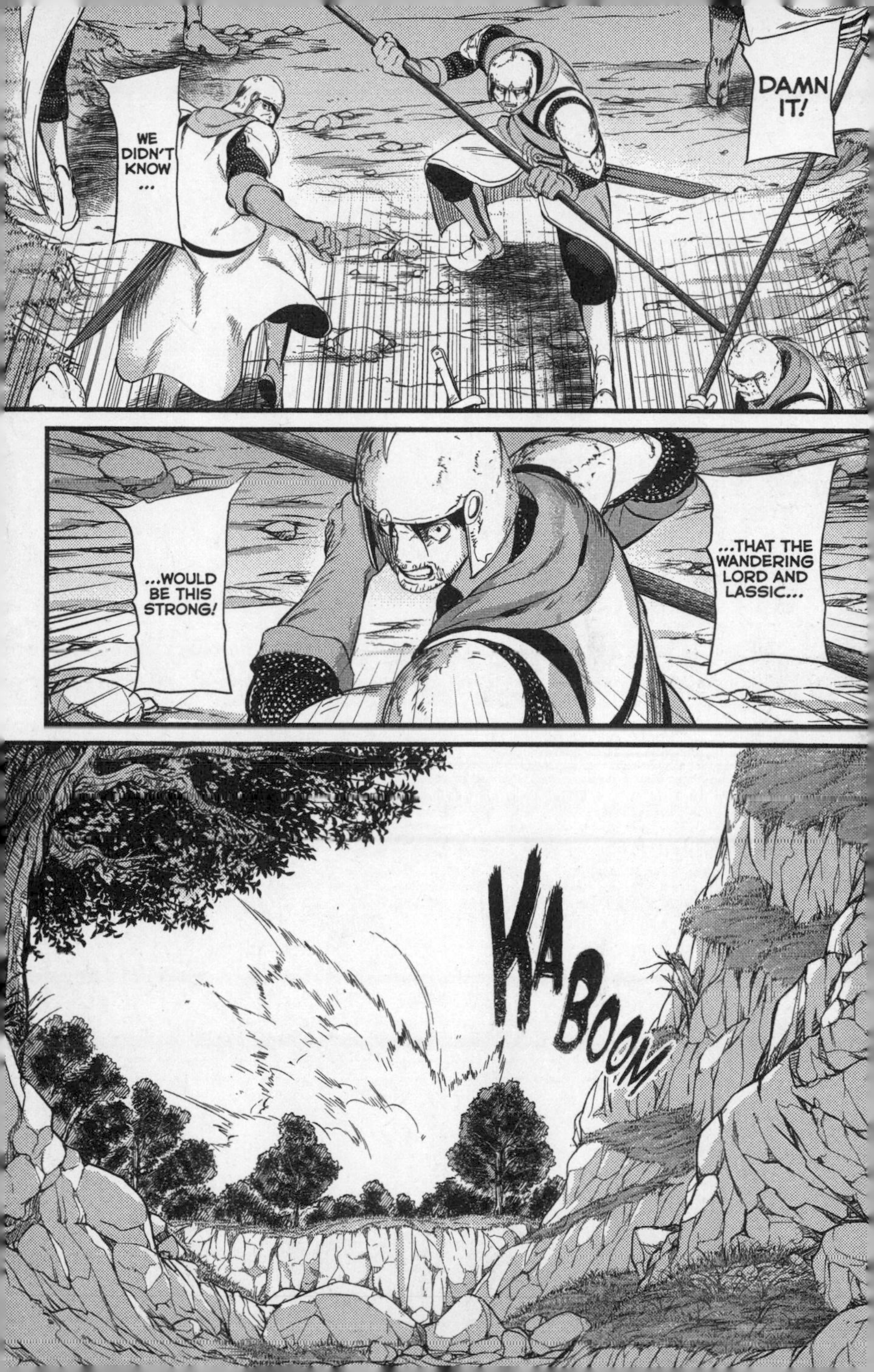
DAMN IT!
WE DIDN'T KNOW...
...THAT THE WANDERING LORD AND LASSIC...
...WOULD BE THIS STRONG!
KA BOOM

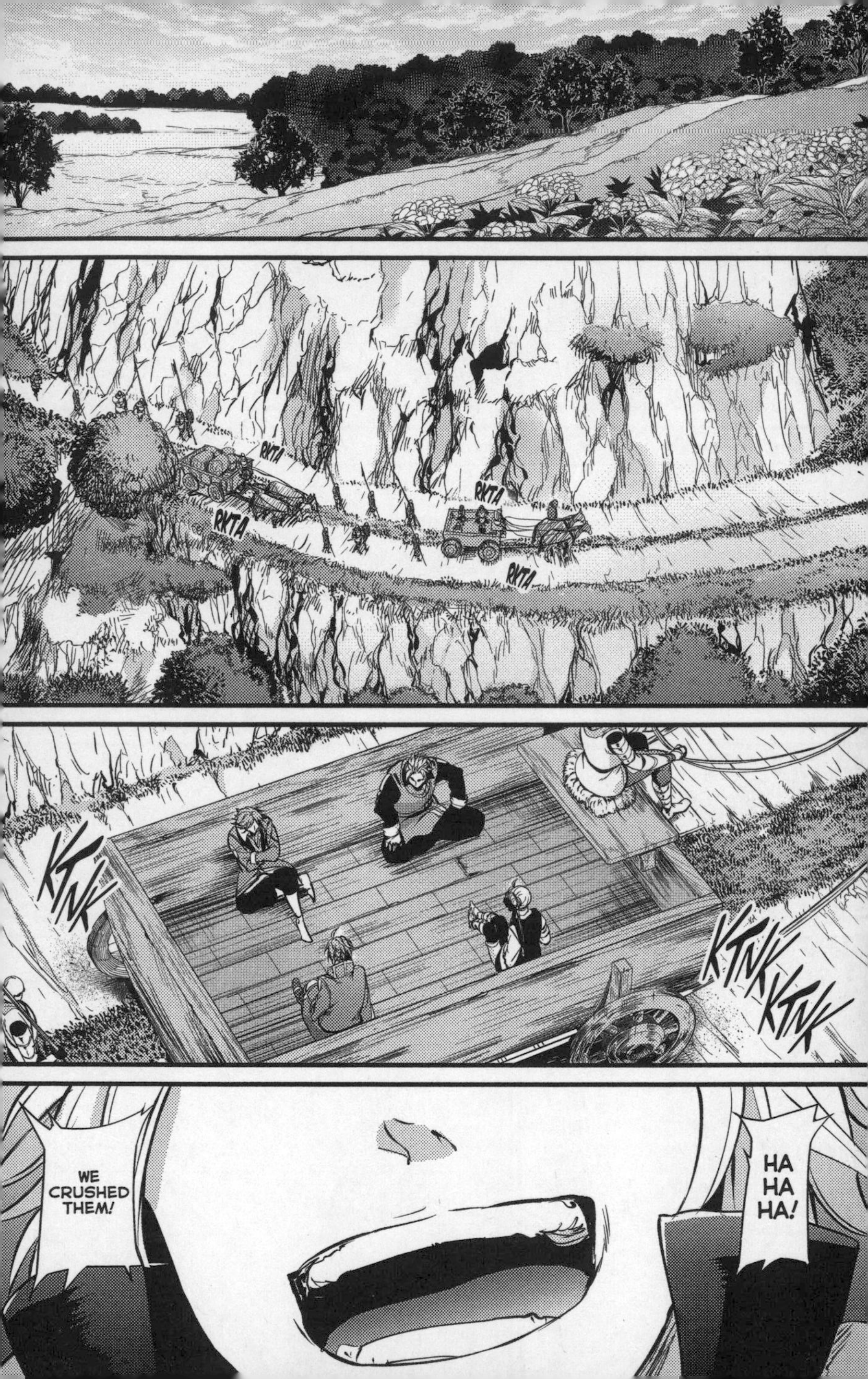
RKTA
RKTA
RKTA
RKTA
KTNK KTNK
KTNK
HA HA HA!
WE CRUSHED THEM!

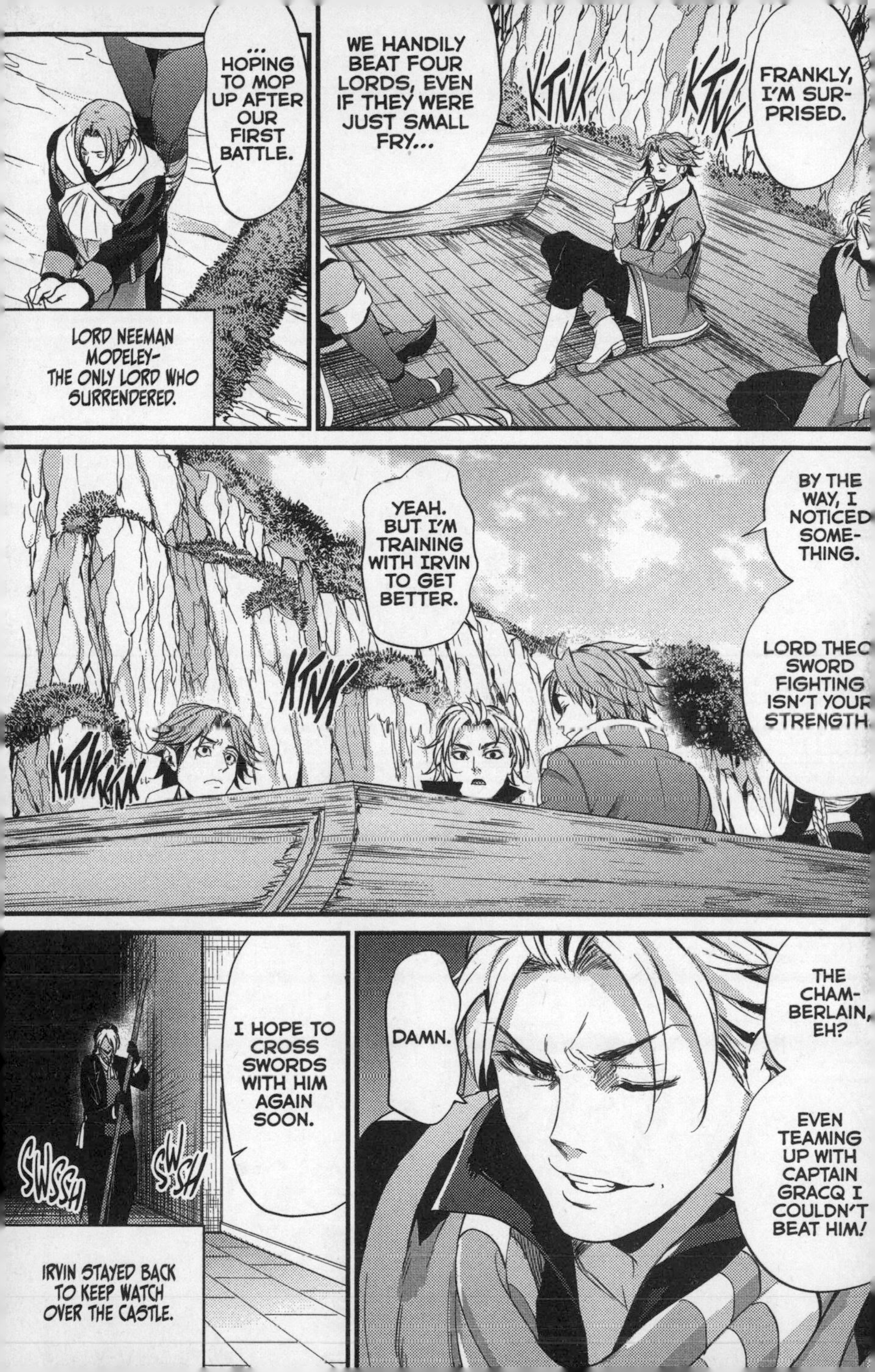
FRANKLY, I'M SUR-PRISED.
KTNK KTNK
WE HANDILY BEAT FOUR LORDS, EVEN IF THEY WERE JUST SMALL FRY...
...HOPING TO MOP UP AFTER OUR FIRST BATTLE.
LORD NEEMAN MODELEY- THE ONLY LORD WHO SURRENDERED.
BY THE WAY, I NOTICED SOME-THING.
LORD THEO SWORD FIGHTING ISN'T YOUR STRENGTH
YEAH. BUT I'M TRAINING WITH IRVIN TO GET BETTER.
KTNK
KTNKKINK
THE CHAM-BERLAIN, EH?
EVEN TEAMING UP WITH CAPTAIN GRACQ I COULDN'T BEAT HIM!
DAMN.
I HOPE TO CROSS SWORDS WITH HIM AGAIN SOON.
SWSH
SWSSH
IRVIN STAYED BACK TO KEEP WATCH OVER THE CASTLE.

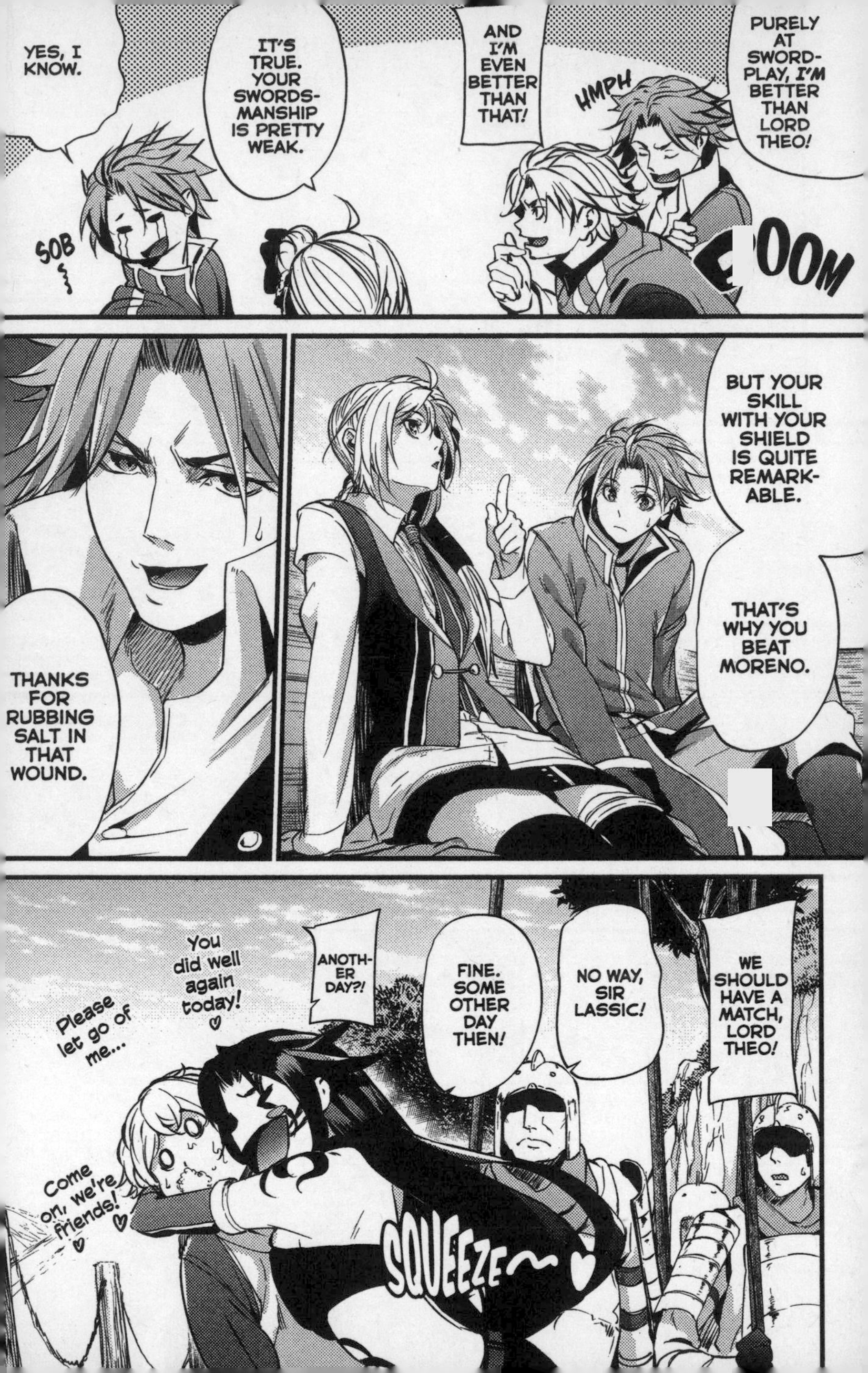
PURELY AT SWORD-PLAY, I'M BETTER THAN LORD THEO!
HMPH
AND I'M EVEN BETTER THAN THAT!
OOM
IT'S TRUE. YOUR SWORDS-MANSHIP IS PRETTY WEAK.
YES, I KNOW.
SOB
BUT YOUR SKILL WITH YOUR SHIELD IS QUITE REMARK-ABLE.
THAT'S WHY YOU BEAT MORENO.
THANKS FOR RUBBING SALT IN THAT WOUND.
WE SHOULD HAVE A MATCH, LORD THEO!
NO WAY, SIR LASSIC!
FINE. SOME OTHER DAY THEN!
ANOTH-ER DAY?!
You did well again today! ♡
Please let go of me...
Come on, we're friends! ♡
SQUEEZE~ ♡

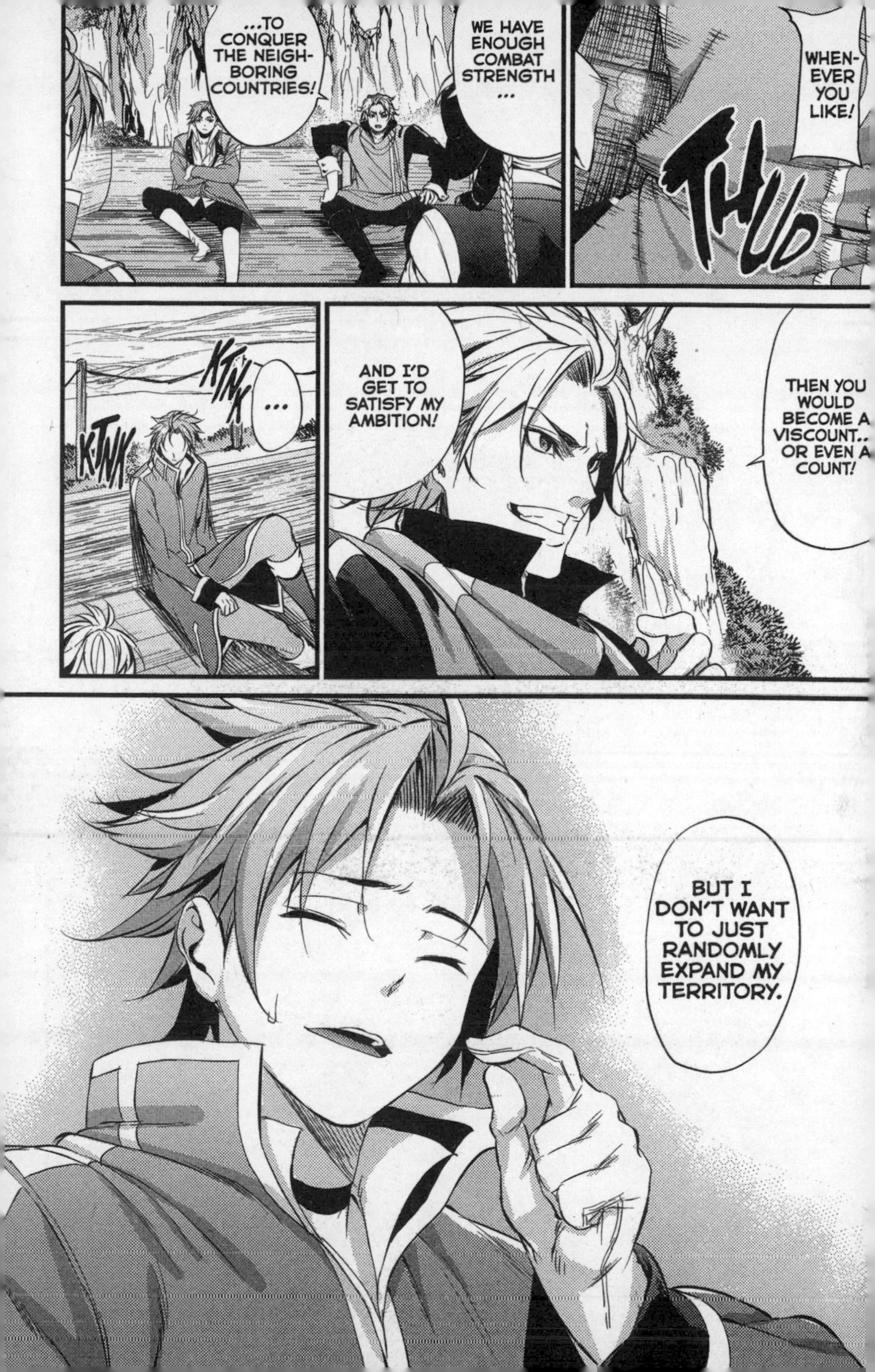
WHEN-EVER YOU LIKE!
THUD
WE HAVE ENOUGH COMBAT STRENGTH ...
...TO CONQUER THE NEIGH-BORING COUNTRIES!
THEN YOU WOULD BECOME A VISCOUNT.. OR EVEN A COUNT!
AND I'D GET TO SATISFY MY AMBITION!
K-TNK
...
K-TNK
BUT I DON'T WANT TO JUST RANDOMLY EXPAND MY TERRITORY.

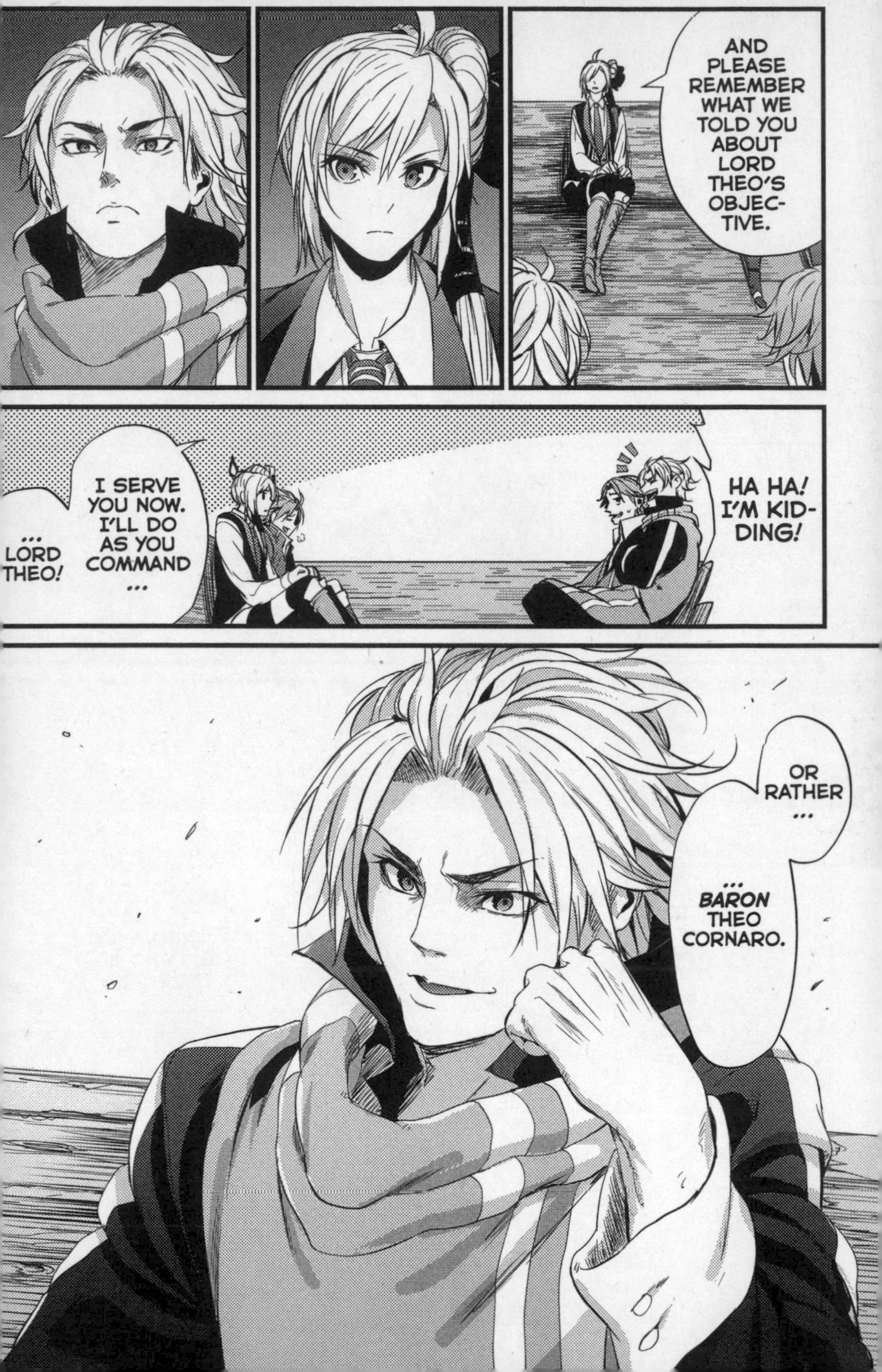
AND PLEASE REMEMBER WHAT WE TOLD YOU ABOUT LORD THEO'S OBJEC-TIVE.
HA HA! I'M KID-DING!
I SERVE YOU NOW. I'LL DO AS YOU COMMAND ...
... LORD THEO!
OR RATHER ...
... *BARON* THEO CORNARO.

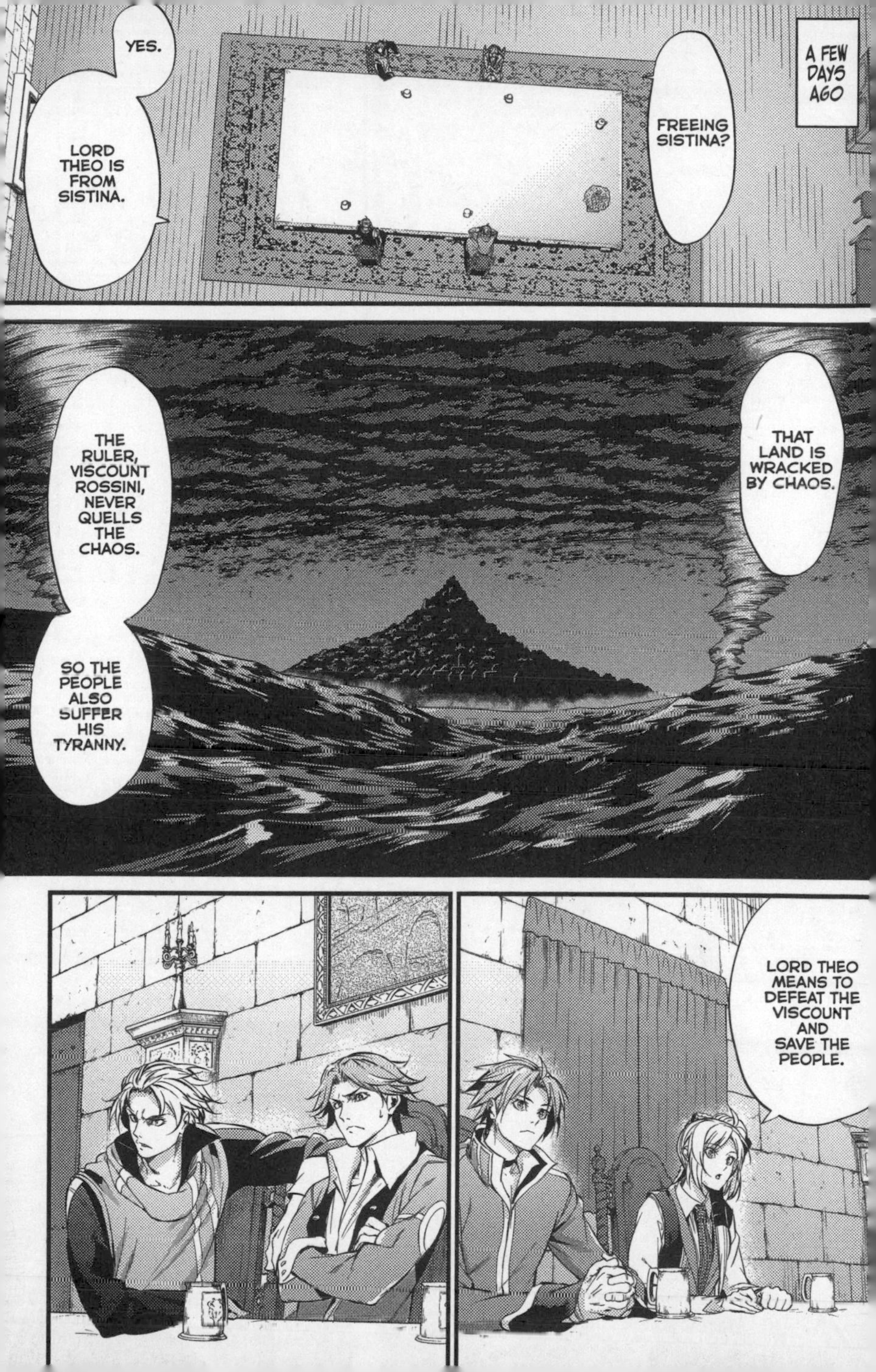
A FEW DAYS AGO
FREEING SISTINA?
YES.
LORD THEO IS FROM SISTINA.
THAT LAND IS WRACKED BY CHAOS.
THE RULER, VISCOUNT ROSSINI, NEVER QUELLS THE CHAOS.
SO THE PEOPLE ALSO SUFFER HIS TYRANNY.
LORD THEO MEANS TO DEFEAT THE VISCOUNT AND SAVE THE PEOPLE.

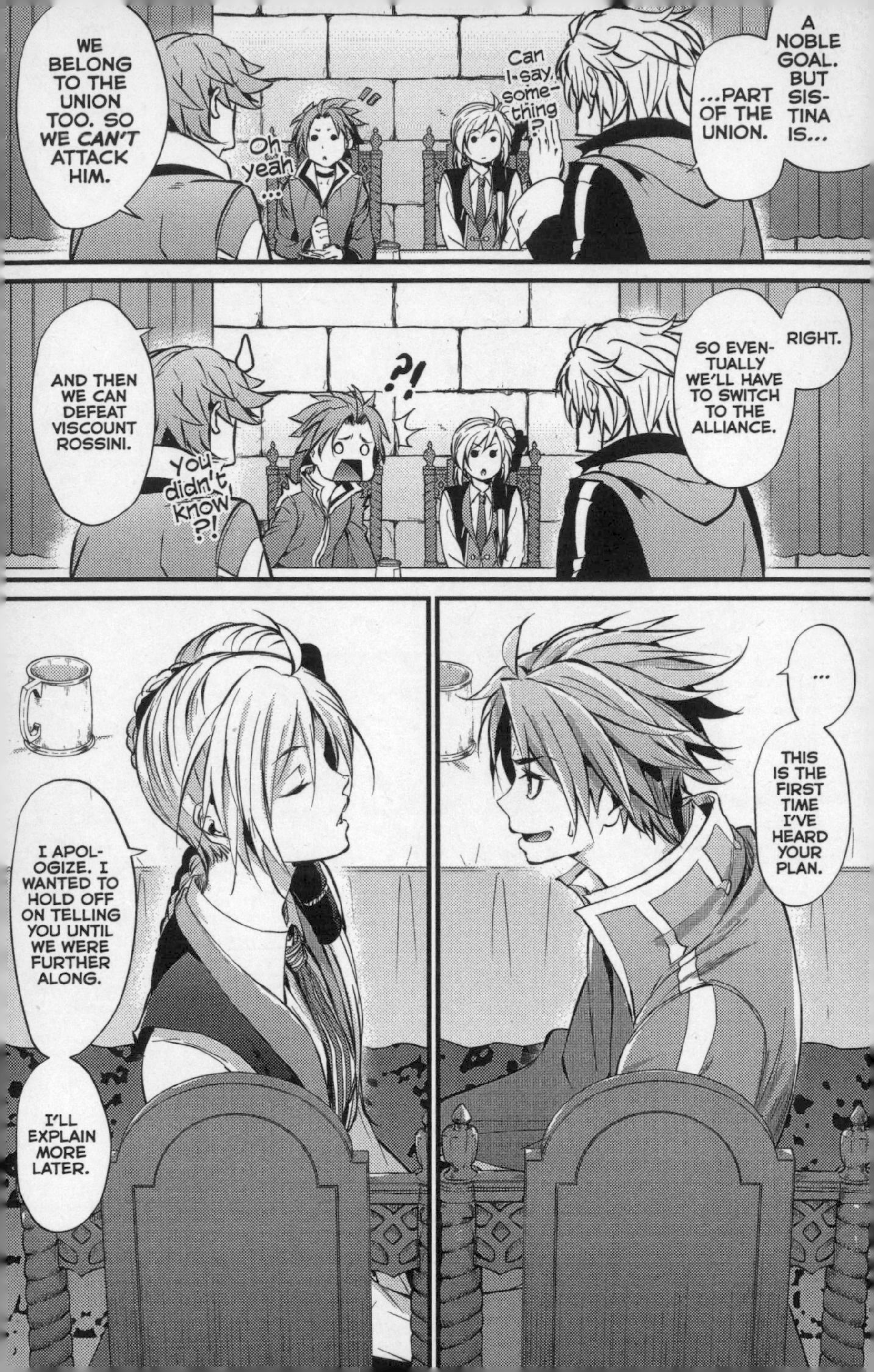
A NOBLE GOAL. BUT SISTINA IS...
...PART OF THE UNION.
Can I say something?
!!
Oh yeah...
WE BELONG TO THE UNION TOO. SO WE *CAN'T* ATTACK HIM.
RIGHT.
SO EVENTUALLY WE'LL HAVE TO SWITCH TO THE ALLIANCE.
?!
AND THEN WE CAN DEFEAT VISCOUNT ROSSINI.
You didn't know?!
...
THIS IS THE FIRST TIME I'VE HEARD YOUR PLAN.
I APOLOGIZE. I WANTED TO HOLD OFF ON TELLING YOU UNTIL WE WERE FURTHER ALONG.
I'LL EXPLAIN MORE LATER.

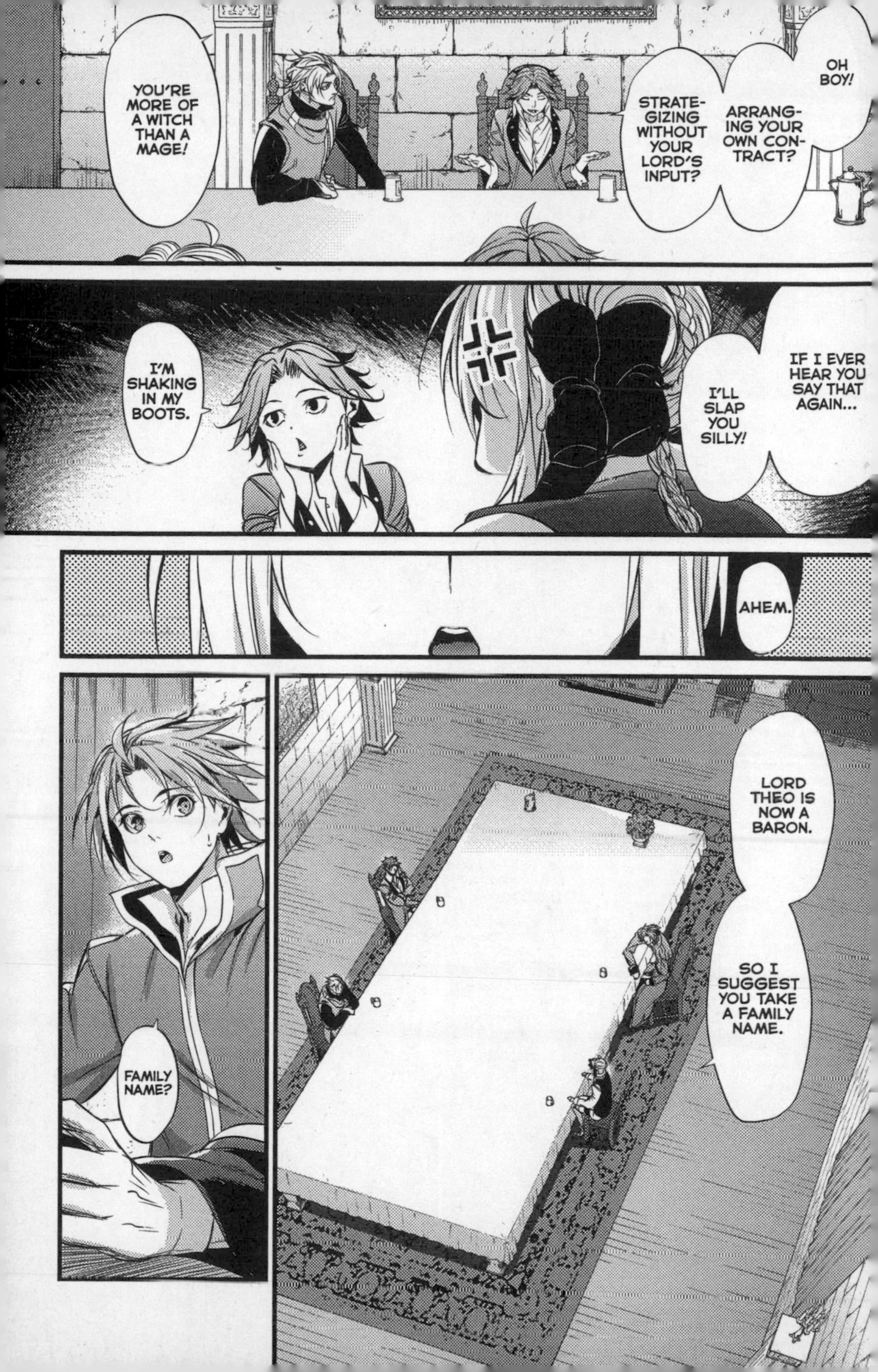
OH BOY!
ARRANGING YOUR OWN CONTRACT?
STRATEGIZING WITHOUT YOUR LORD'S INPUT?
YOU'RE MORE OF A WITCH THAN A MAGE!
IF I EVER HEAR YOU SAY THAT AGAIN...
I'LL SLAP YOU SILLY!
I'M SHAKING IN MY BOOTS.
AHEM.
LORD THEO IS NOW A BARON.
SO I SUGGEST YOU TAKE A FAMILY NAME.
FAMILY NAME?

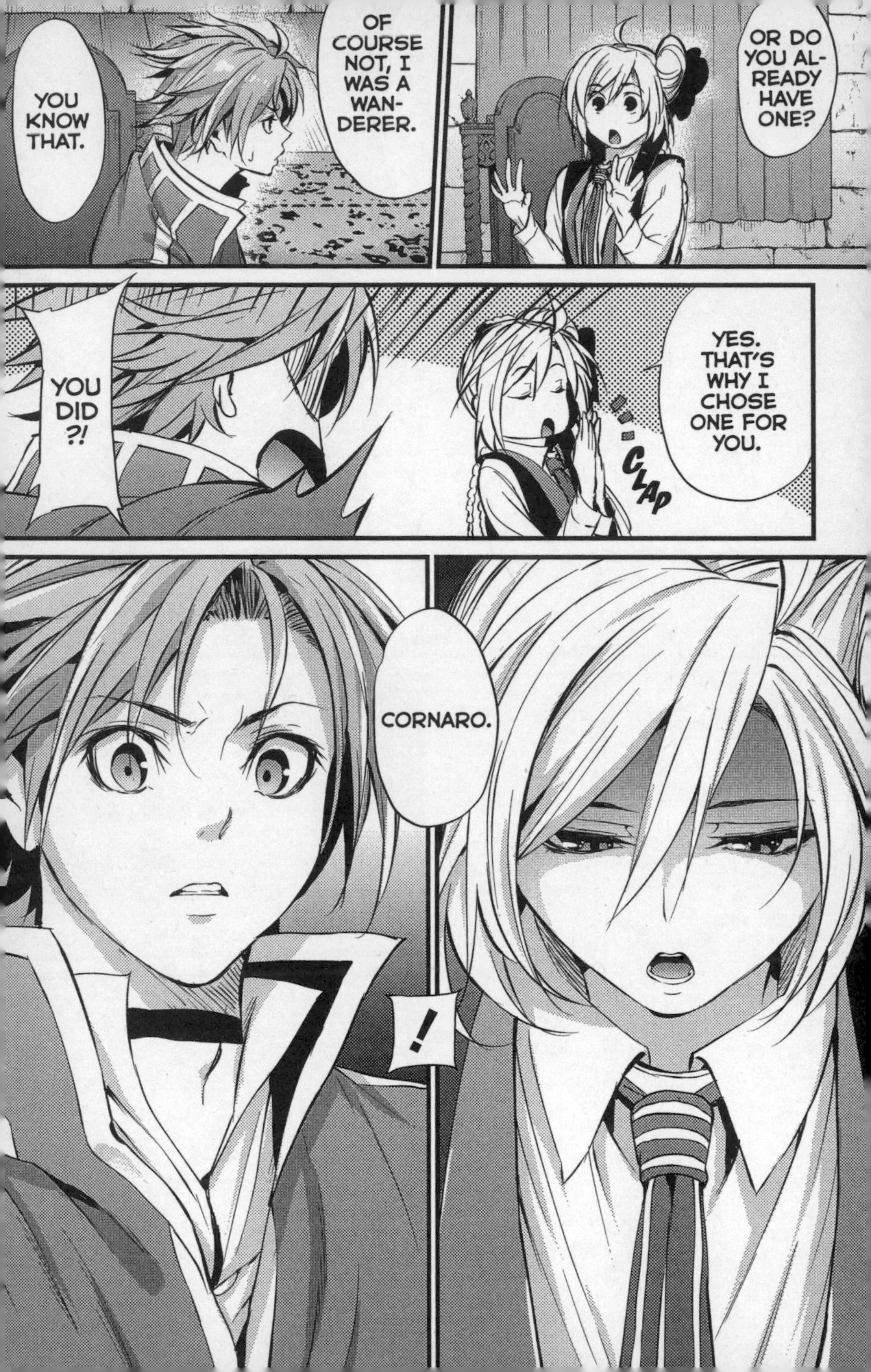
OR DO YOU AL-READY HAVE ONE?
OF COURSE NOT, I WAS A WAN-DERER.
YOU KNOW THAT.
YES. THAT'S WHY I CHOSE ONE FOR YOU.
CLAP
YOU DID ?!
CORNARO.
!

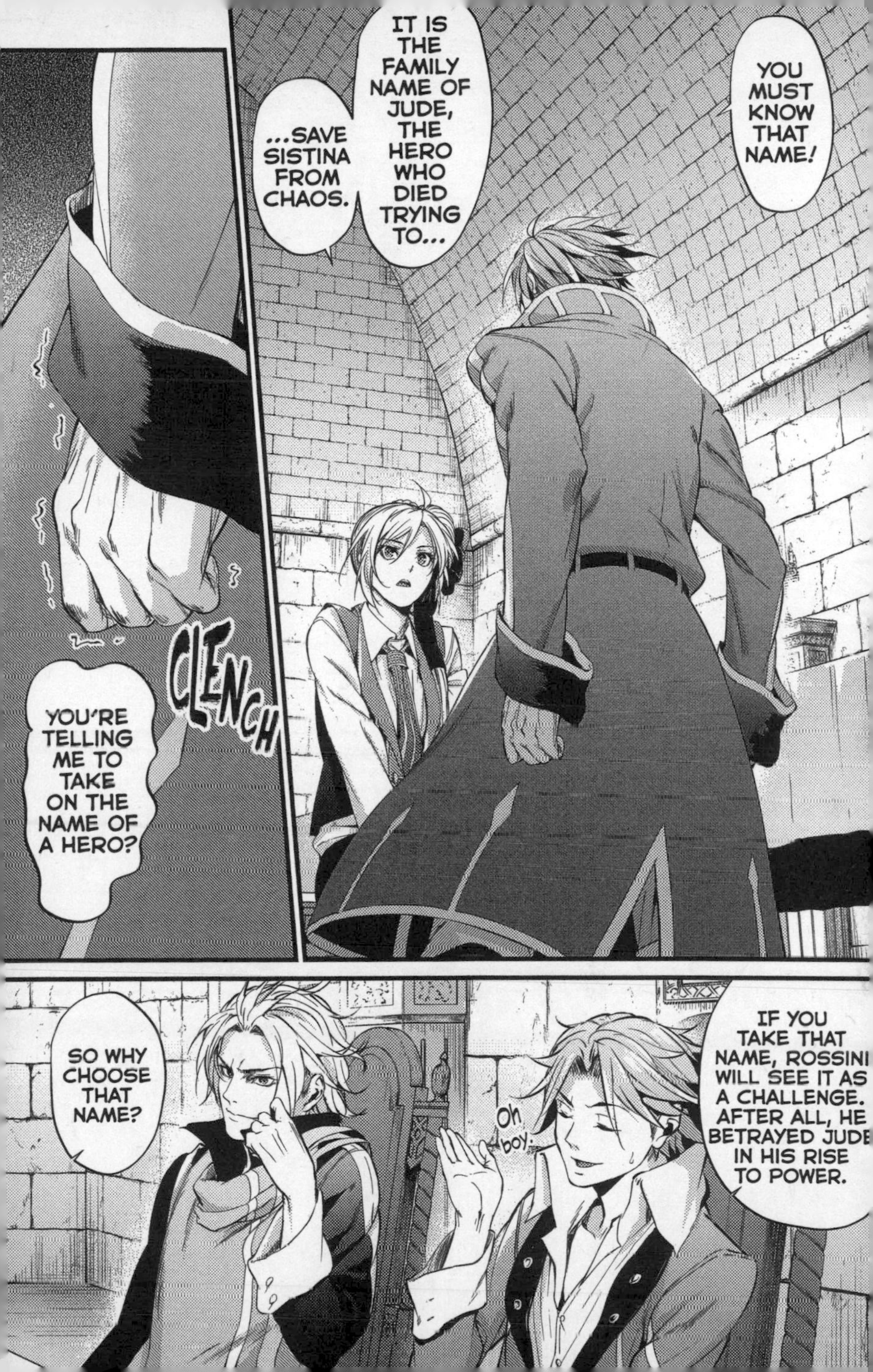
YOU MUST KNOW THAT NAME!
IT IS THE FAMILY NAME OF JUDE, THE HERO WHO DIED TRYING TO...
...SAVE SISTINA FROM CHAOS.
CLENCH
YOU'RE TELLING ME TO TAKE ON THE NAME OF A HERO?
IF YOU TAKE THAT NAME, ROSSINI WILL SEE IT AS A CHALLENGE. AFTER ALL, HE BETRAYED JUDE IN HIS RISE TO POWER.
Oh boy.
SO WHY CHOOSE THAT NAME?

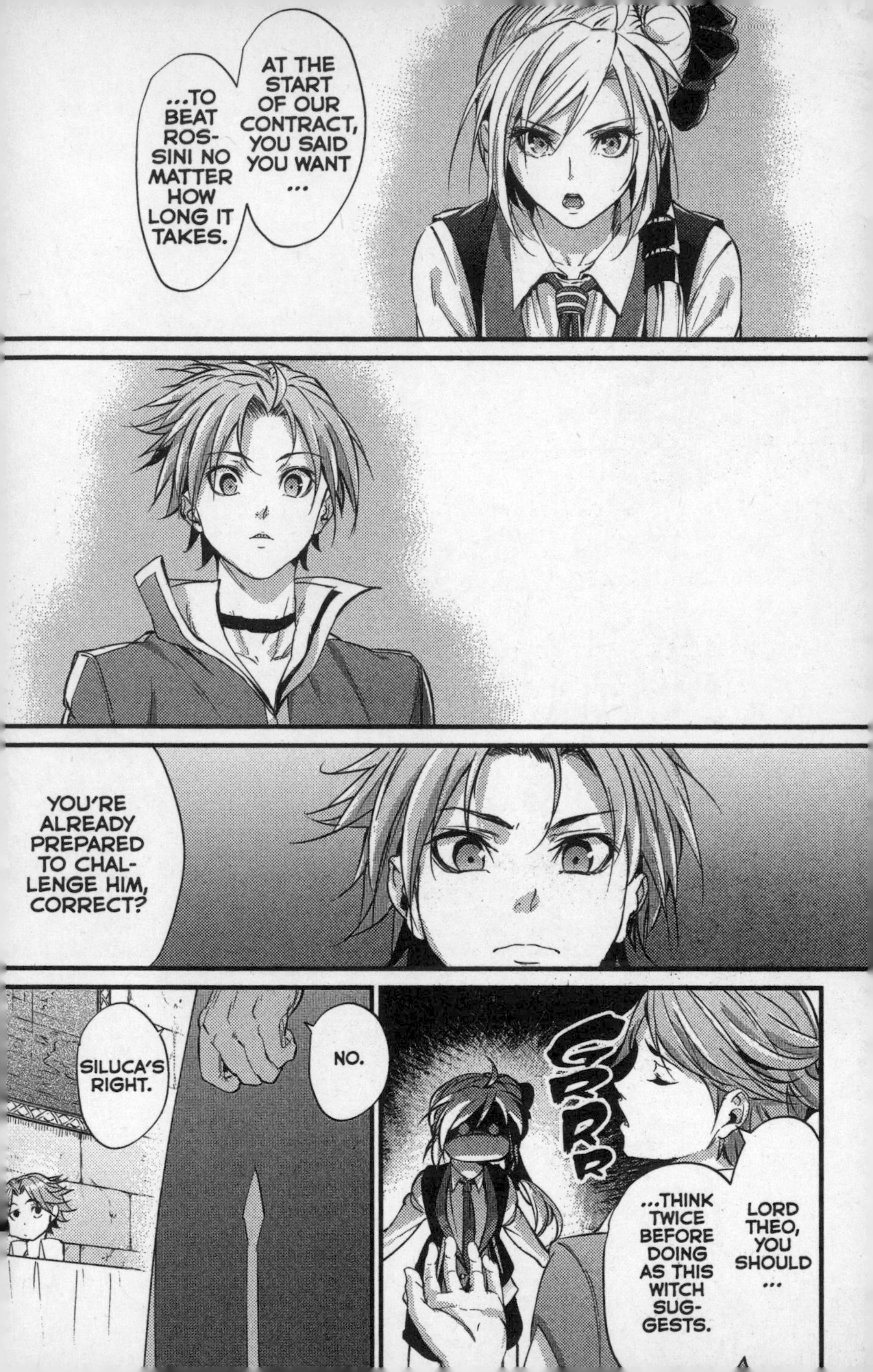
AT THE START OF OUR CONTRACT, YOU SAID YOU WANT...
...TO BEAT ROS-SINI NO MATTER HOW LONG IT TAKES.
YOU'RE ALREADY PREPARED TO CHAL-LENGE HIM, CORRECT?
GRRR
LORD THEO, YOU SHOULD...
...THINK TWICE BEFORE DOING AS THIS WITCH SUG-GESTS.
NO.
SILUCA'S RIGHT.

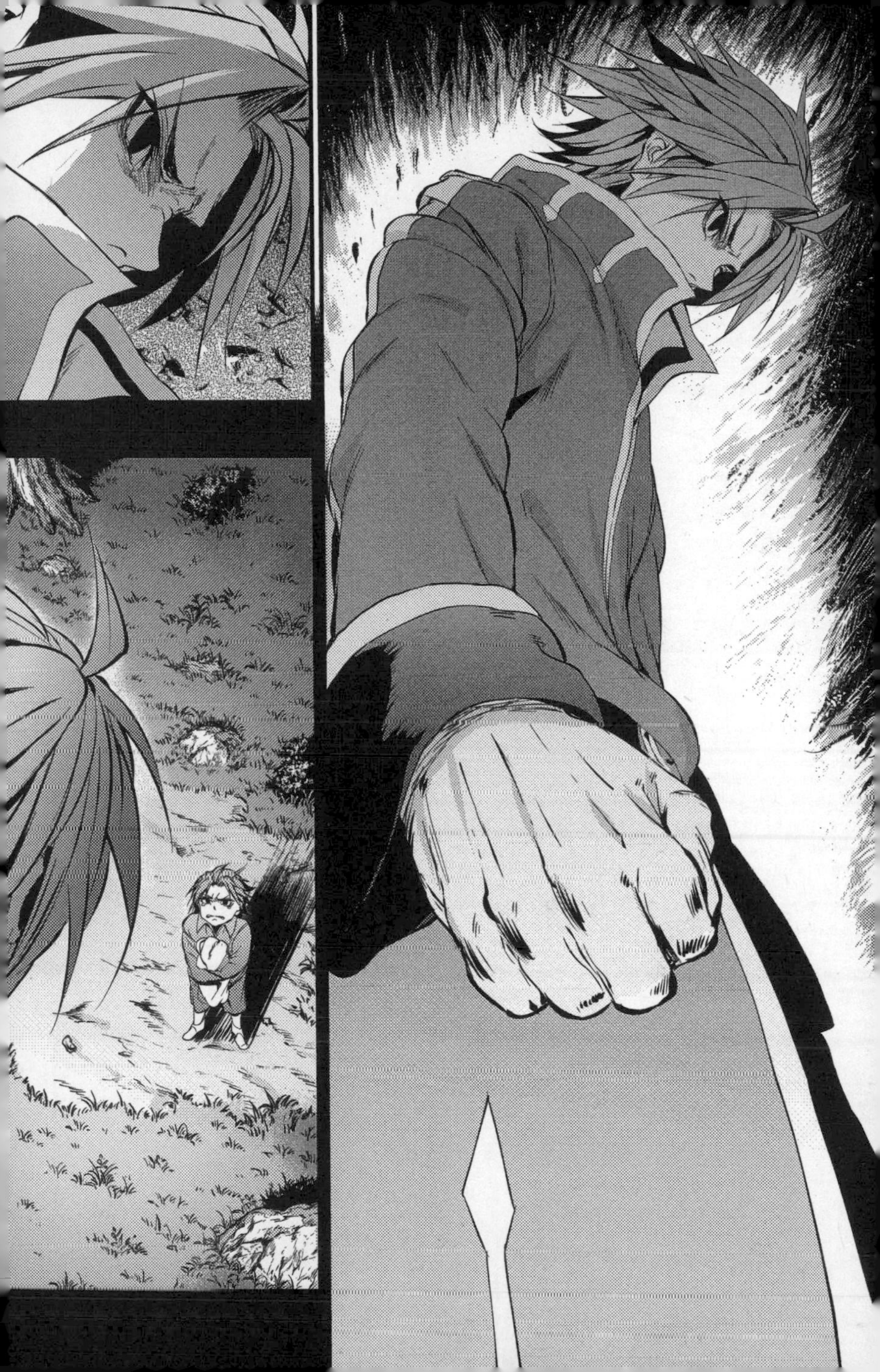

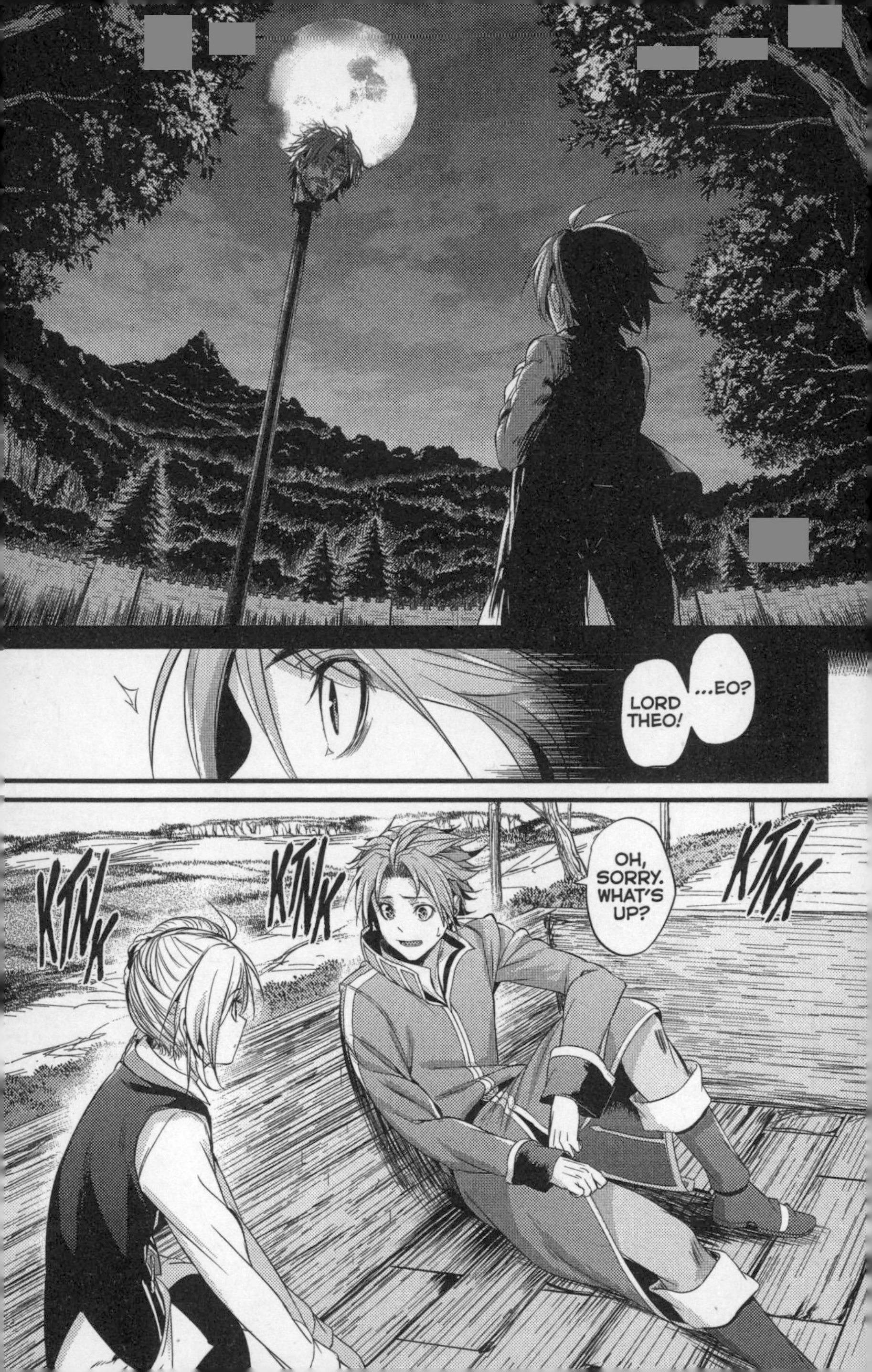
...EO?
LORD THEO!
KTNK
OH, SORRY. WHAT'S UP?
KTNK
KTNK

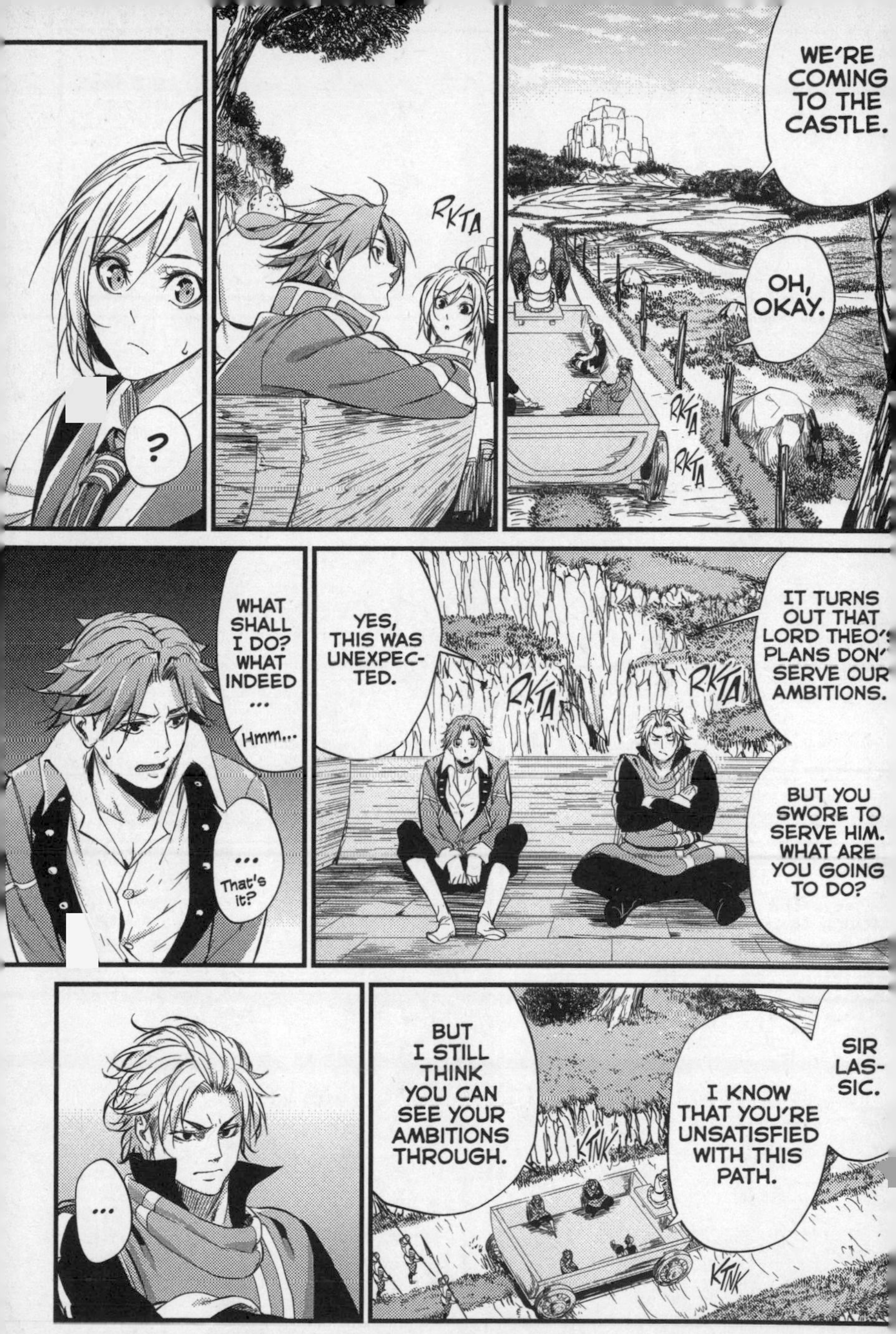

WE'RE COMING TO THE CASTLE.
OH, OKAY.
RKTA
RKTA
RKTA
?
IT TURNS OUT THAT LORD THEO'S PLANS DON'T SERVE OUR AMBITIONS.
BUT YOU SWORE TO SERVE HIM. WHAT ARE YOU GOING TO DO?
RKTA
RKTA
YES, THIS WAS UNEXPECTED.
WHAT SHALL I DO? WHAT INDEED...
Hmm...
... That's it?
SIR LAS-SIC.
I KNOW THAT YOU'RE UNSATISFIED WITH THIS PATH.
BUT I STILL THINK YOU CAN SEE YOUR AMBITIONS THROUGH.
KTNK
KTNK
...

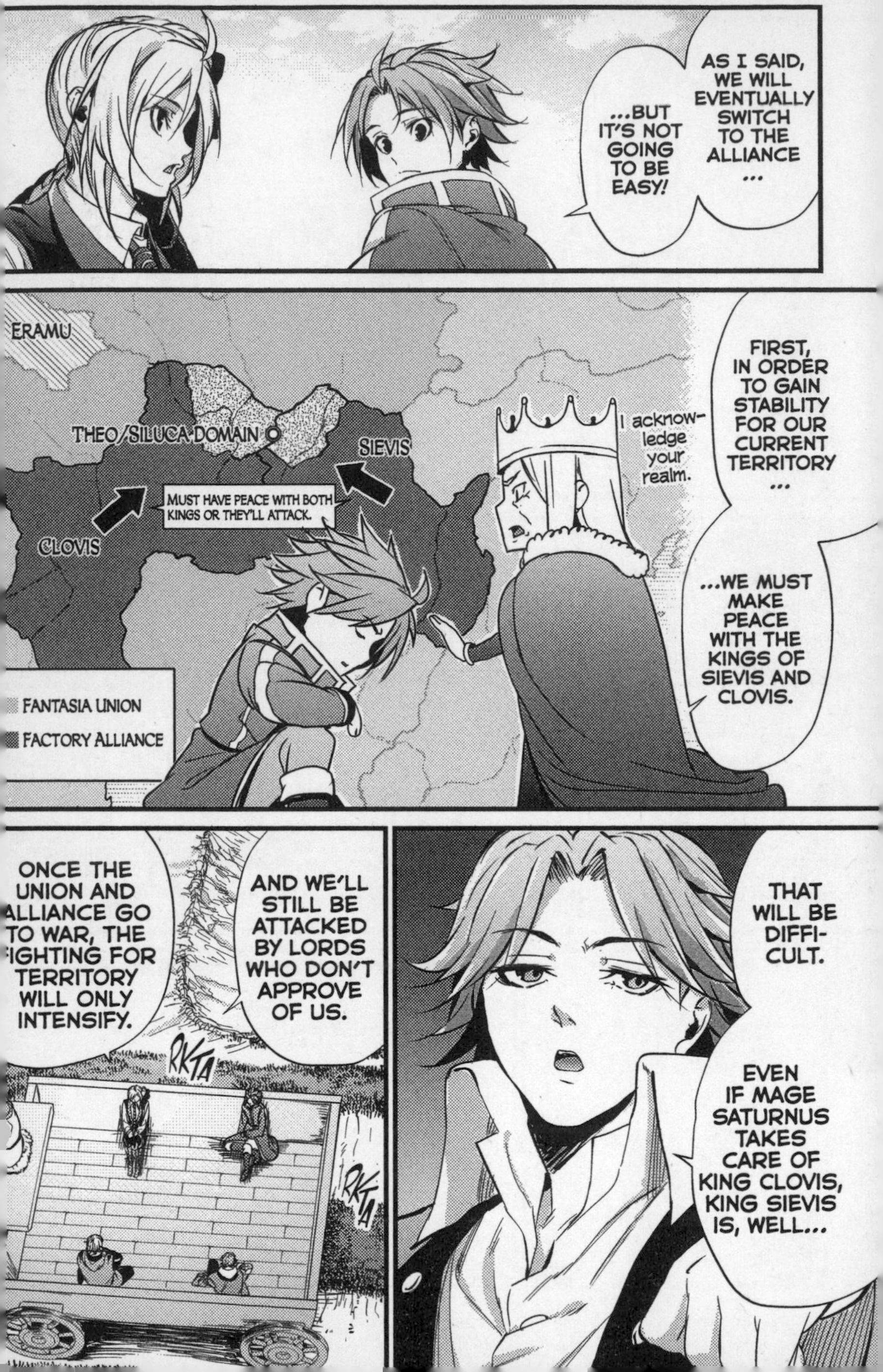
AS I SAID, WE WILL EVENTUALLY SWITCH TO THE ALLIANCE...
...BUT IT'S NOT GOING TO BE EASY!
FIRST, IN ORDER TO GAIN STABILITY FOR OUR CURRENT TERRITORY...
...WE MUST MAKE PEACE WITH THE KINGS OF SIEVIS AND CLOVIS.
I acknowledge your realm.
ERAMU
THEO/SILUCA DOMAIN
SIEVIS
MUST HAVE PEACE WITH BOTH KINGS OR THEY'LL ATTACK.
CLOVIS
FANTASIA UNION
FACTORY ALLIANCE
THAT WILL BE DIFFICULT.
EVEN IF MAGE SATURNUS TAKES CARE OF KING CLOVIS, KING SIEVIS IS, WELL...
ONCE THE UNION AND ALLIANCE GO TO WAR, THE FIGHTING FOR TERRITORY WILL ONLY INTENSIFY.
AND WE'LL STILL BE ATTACKED BY LORDS WHO DON'T APPROVE OF US.
RKTA
RKTA

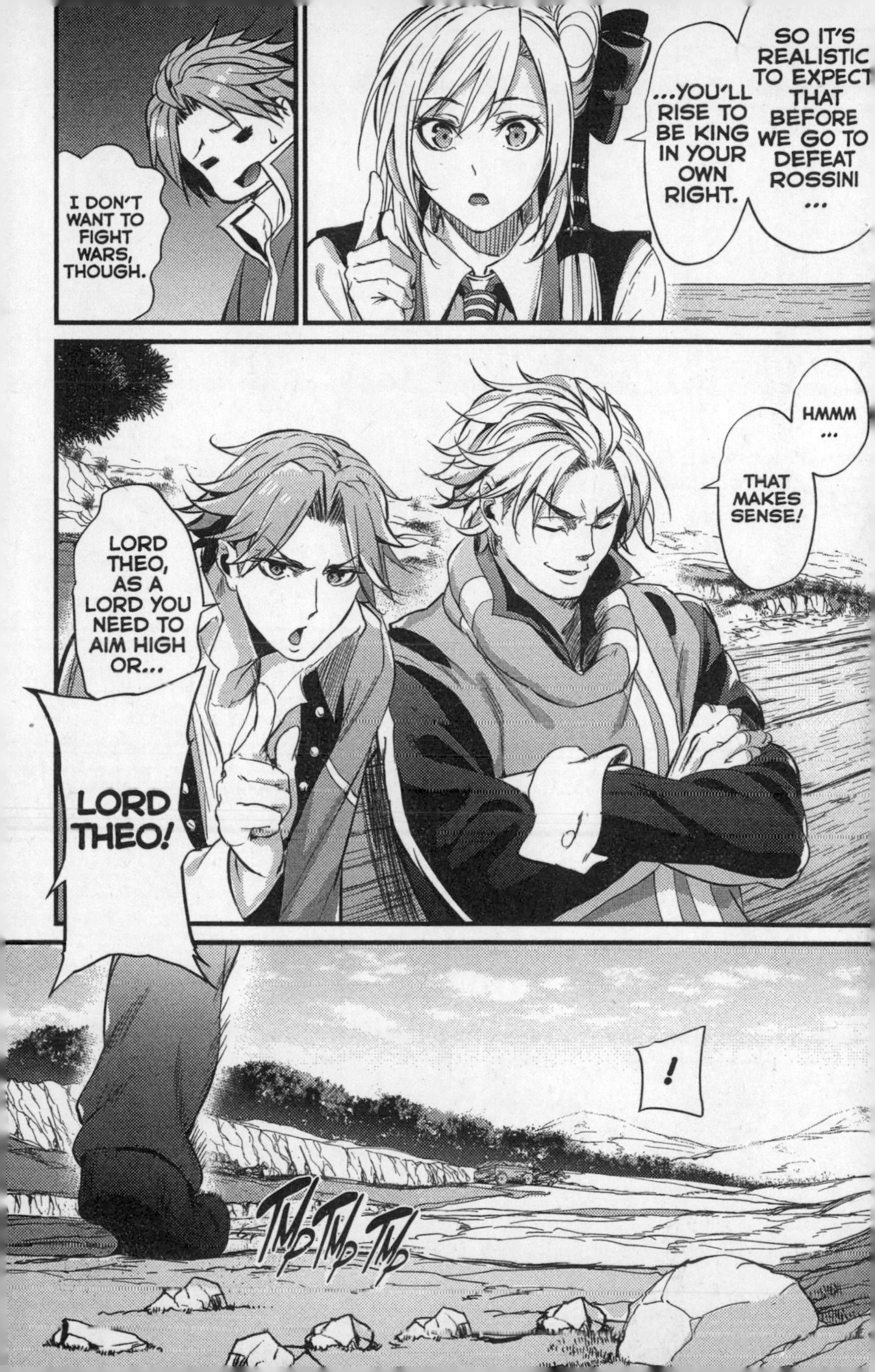
SO IT'S REALISTIC TO EXPECT THAT BEFORE WE GO TO DEFEAT ROSSINI...
...YOU'LL RISE TO BE KING IN YOUR OWN RIGHT.
I DON'T WANT TO FIGHT WARS, THOUGH.
HMMM... THAT MAKES SENSE!
LORD THEO, AS A LORD YOU NEED TO AIM HIGH OR...
LORD THEO!
!
TMP TMP TMP

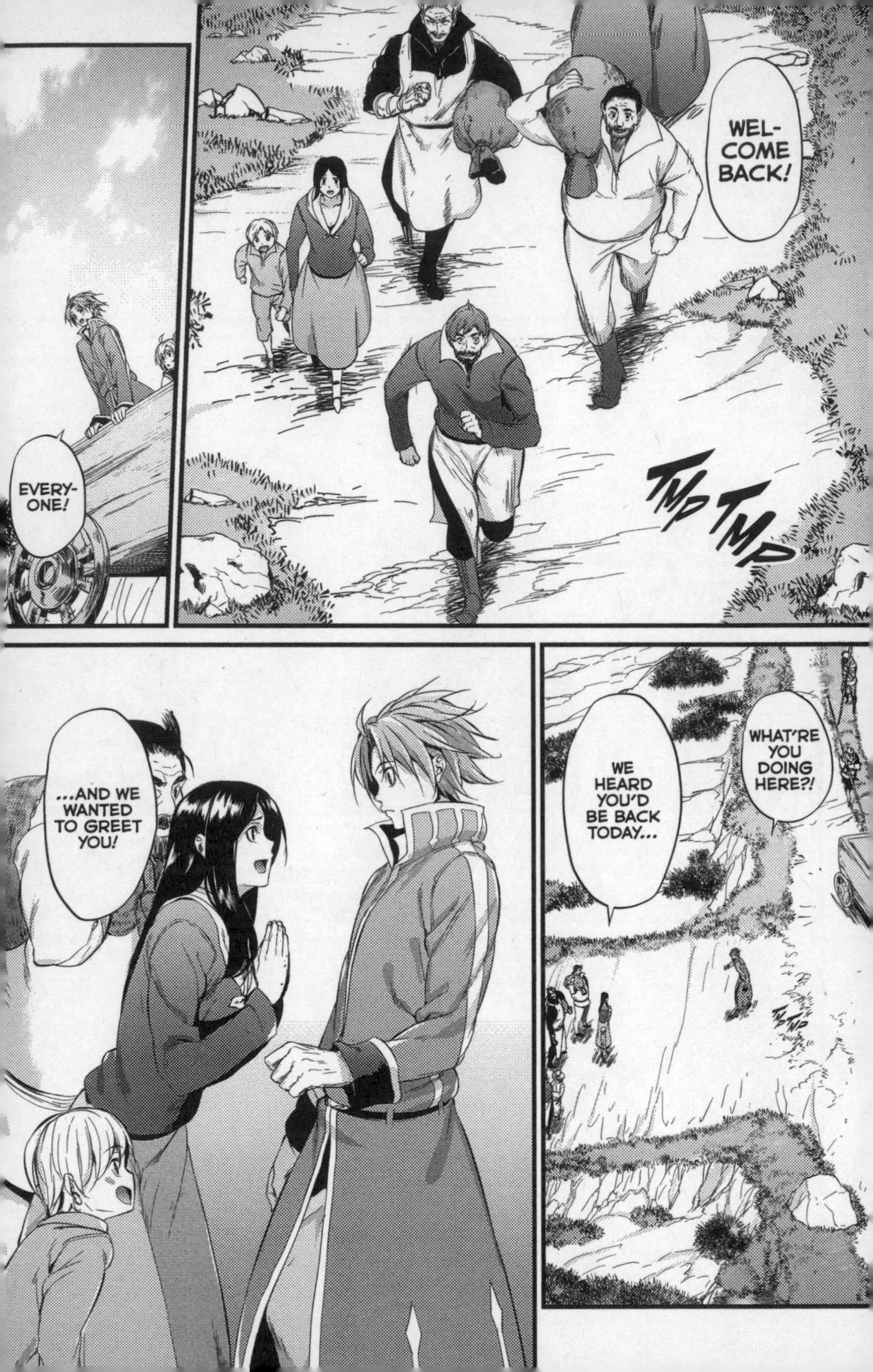
WEL-COME BACK!
TMP TMP
EVERY-ONE!
WHAT'RE YOU DOING HERE?!
WE HEARD YOU'D BE BACK TODAY...
TMP TMP
...AND WE WANTED TO GREET YOU!

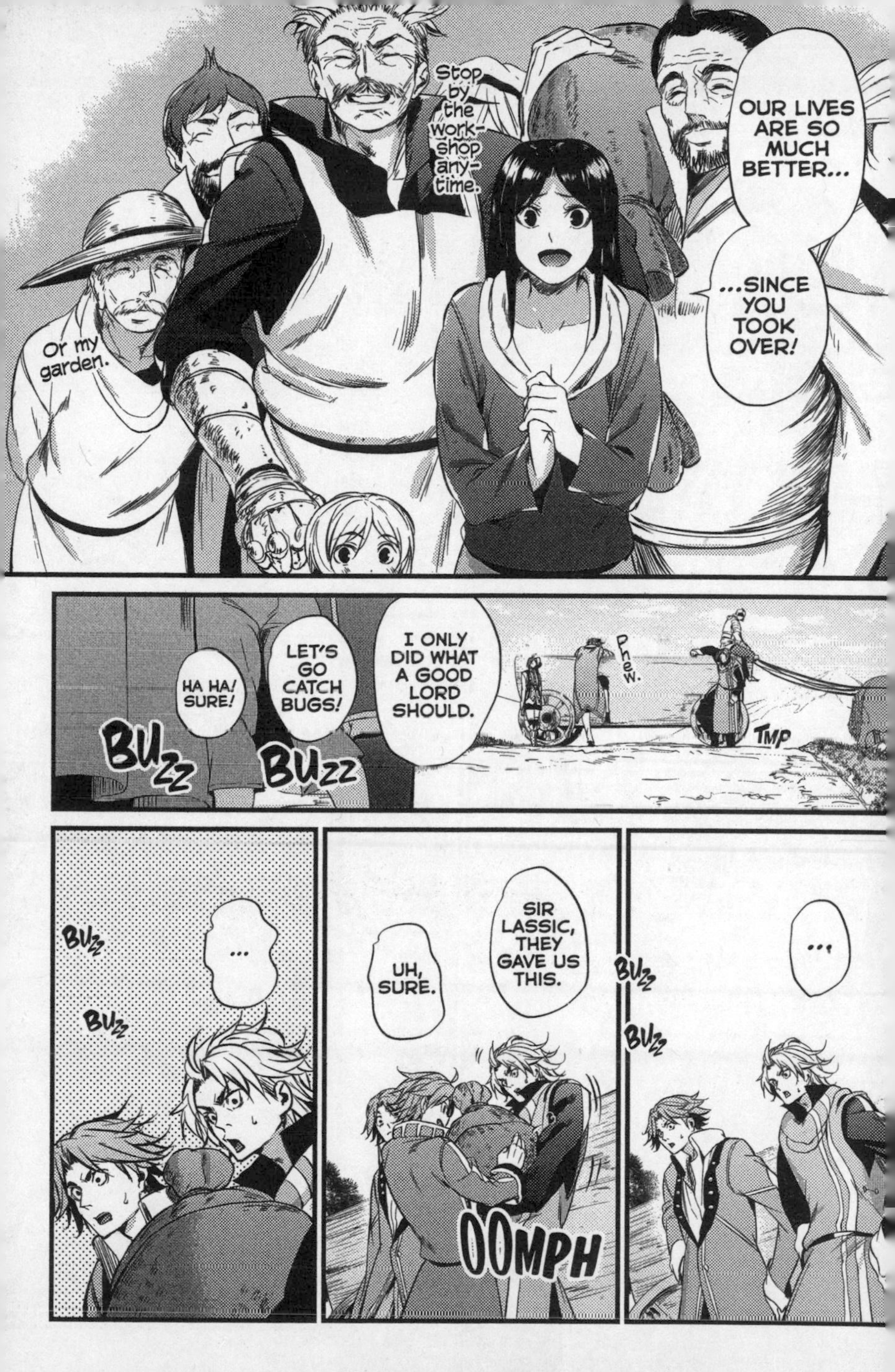
OUR LIVES ARE SO MUCH BETTER...
...SINCE YOU TOOK OVER!
Stop by the work-shop any-time.
Or my garden.
Phew.
TMP
I ONLY DID WHAT A GOOD LORD SHOULD.
LET'S GO CATCH BUGS!
HA HA! SURE!
BUZZ
BUZZ
...
BUZZ
BUZZ
SIR LASSIC, THEY GAVE US THIS.
UH, SURE.
OOMPH
BUZZ
...
BUZZ

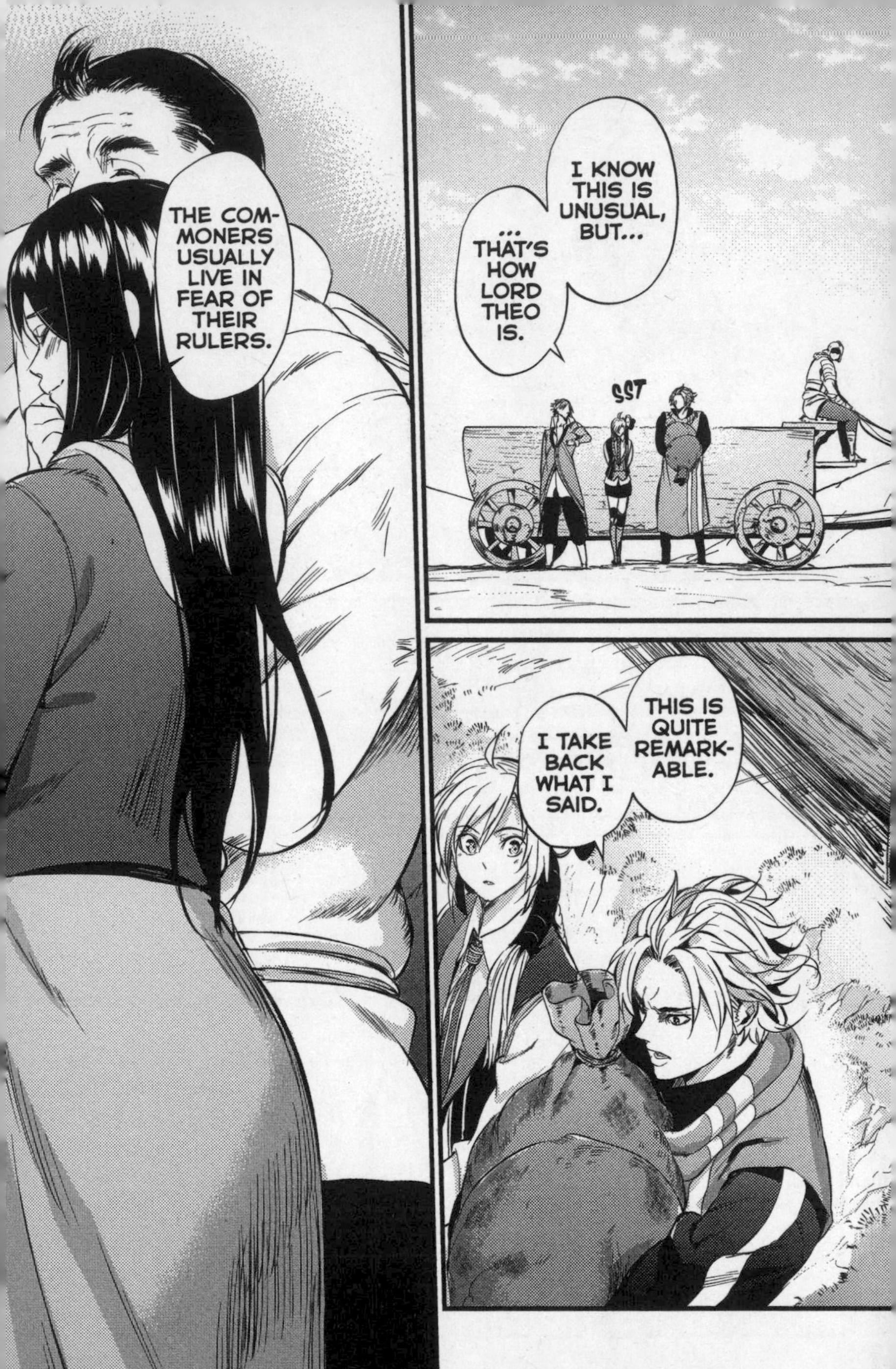
I KNOW THIS IS UNUSUAL, BUT...
...THAT'S HOW LORD THEO IS.
SST
THIS IS QUITE REMARK-ABLE.
I TAKE BACK WHAT I SAID.
THE COM-MONERS USUALLY LIVE IN FEAR OF THEIR RULERS.

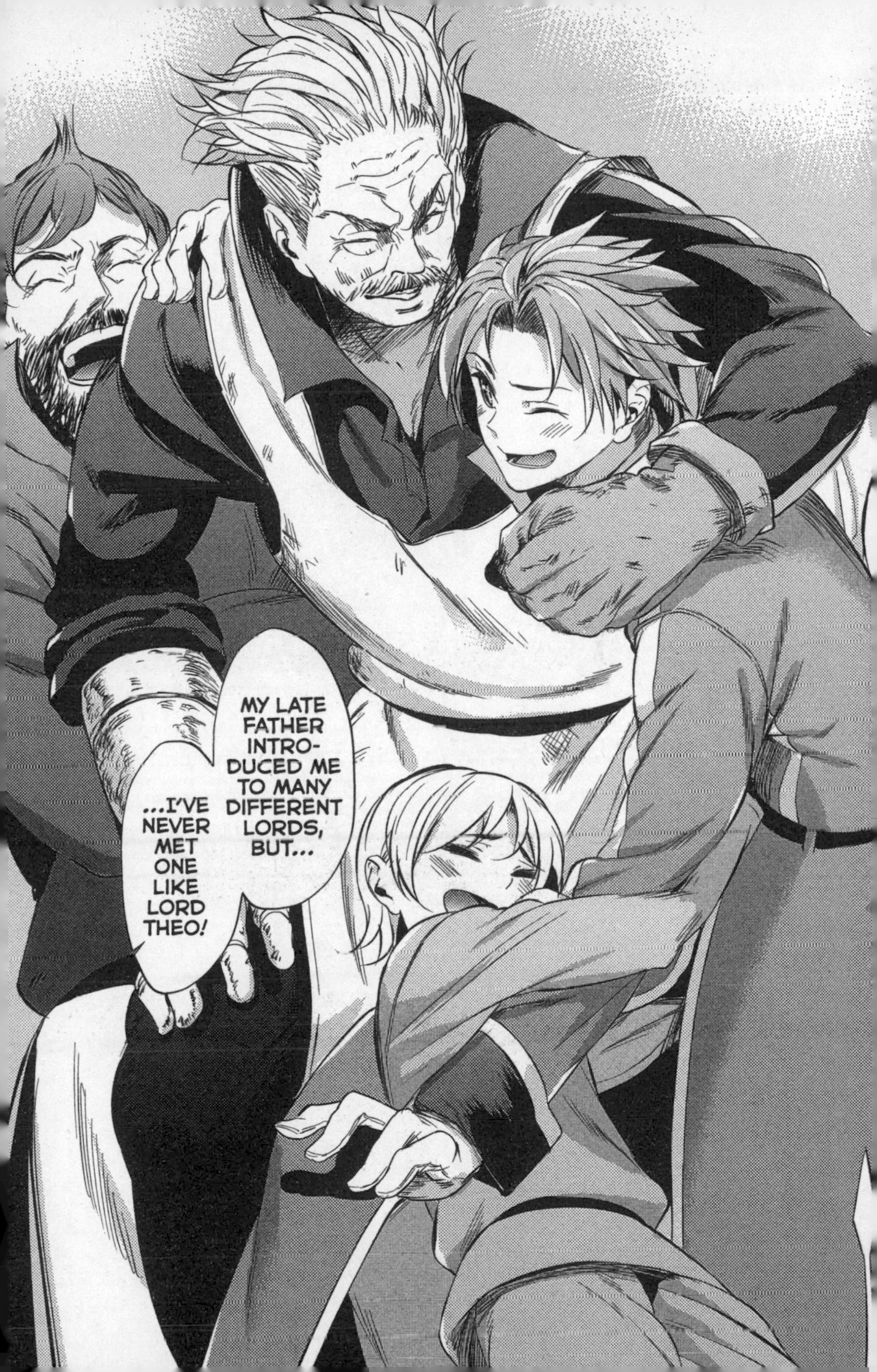
MY LATE FATHER INTRO-DUCED ME TO MANY DIFFERENT LORDS, BUT...
...I'VE NEVER MET ONE LIKE LORD THEO!

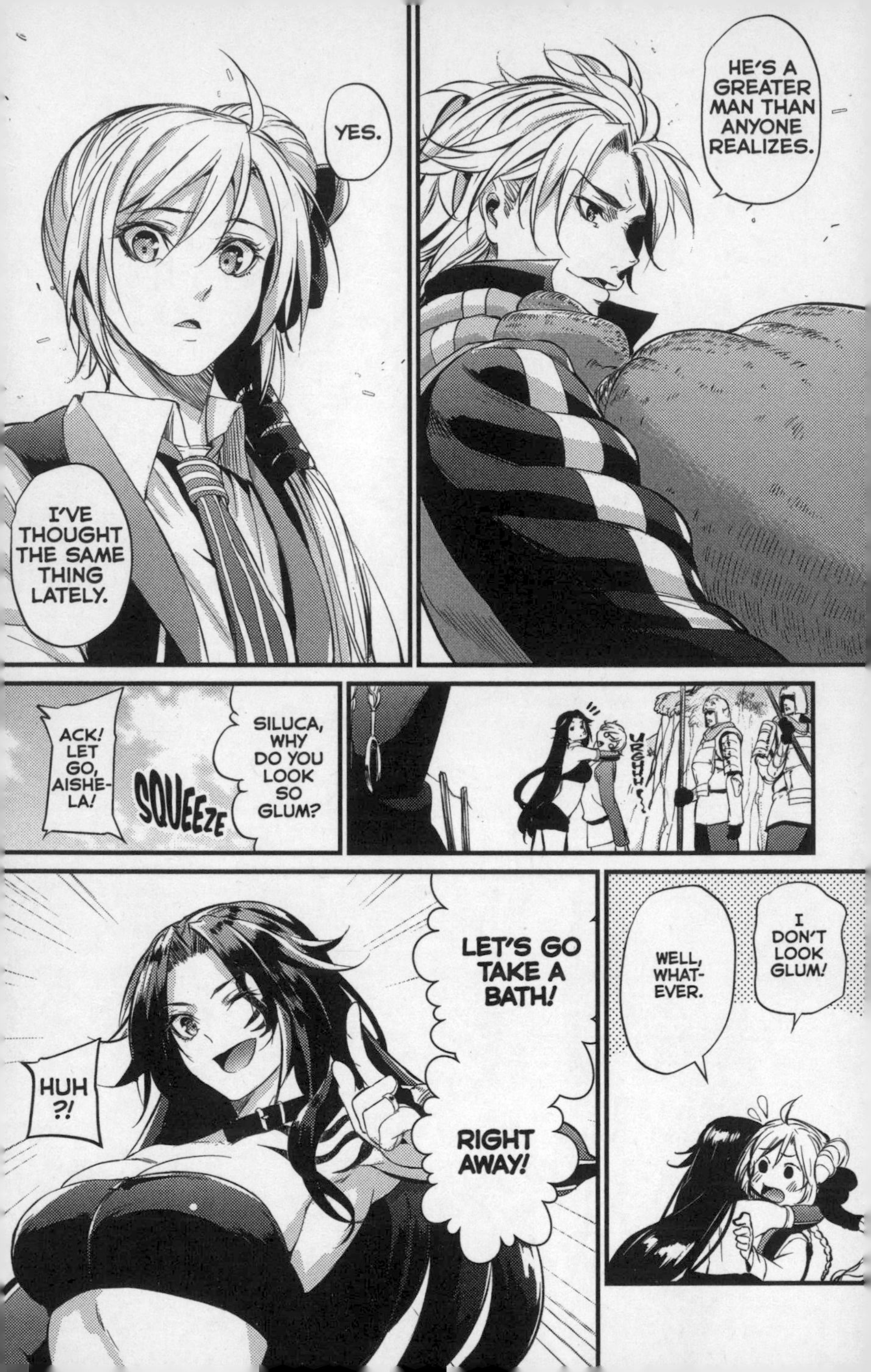
HE'S A GREATER MAN THAN ANYONE REALIZES.
YES.
I'VE THOUGHT THE SAME THING LATELY.
SILUCA, WHY DO YOU LOOK SO GLUM?
SQUEEZE
ACK! LET GO, AISHE-LA!
I DON'T LOOK GLUM!
WELL, WHAT-EVER.
LET'S GO TAKE A BATH!
RIGHT AWAY!
HUH?!

RECORD OF
GRANCREST
WAR

RECORD OF
GRANCREST
—WAR—

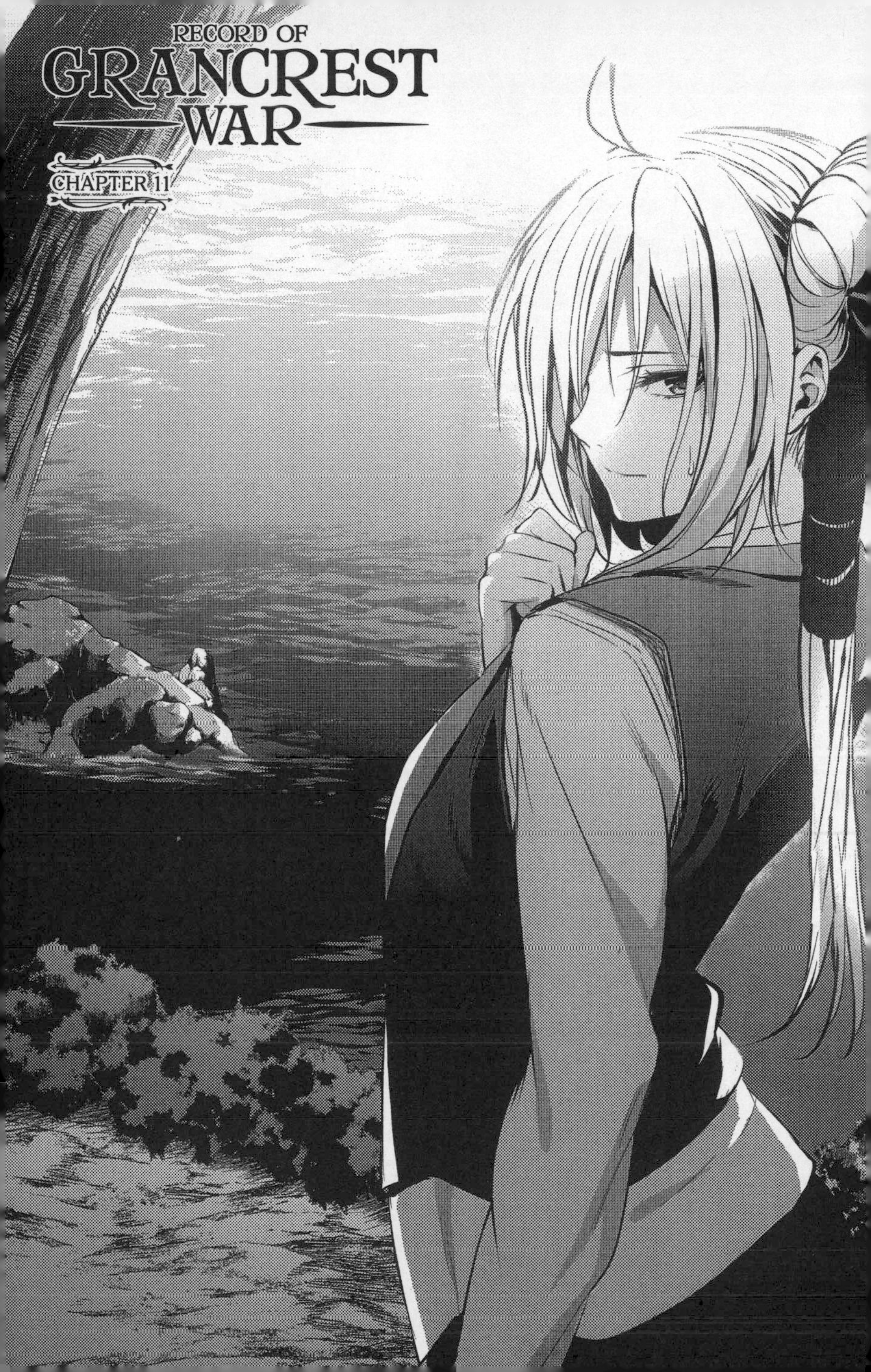
RECORD OF
GRANCREST
WAR
CHAPTER 11

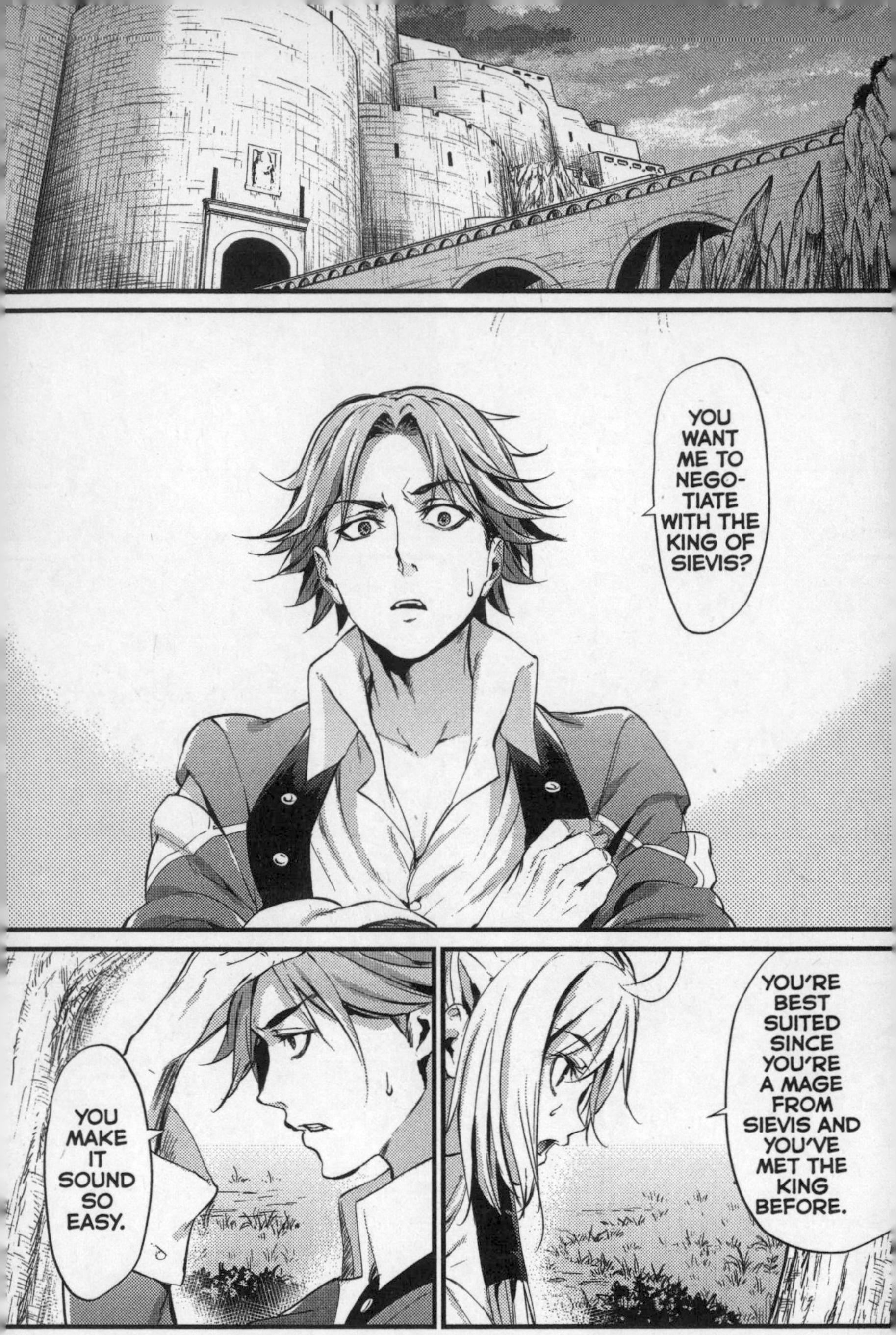
YOU WANT ME TO NEGOTIATE WITH THE KING OF SIEVIS?
YOU'RE BEST SUITED SINCE YOU'RE A MAGE FROM SIEVIS AND YOU'VE MET THE KING BEFORE.
YOU MAKE IT SOUND SO EASY.

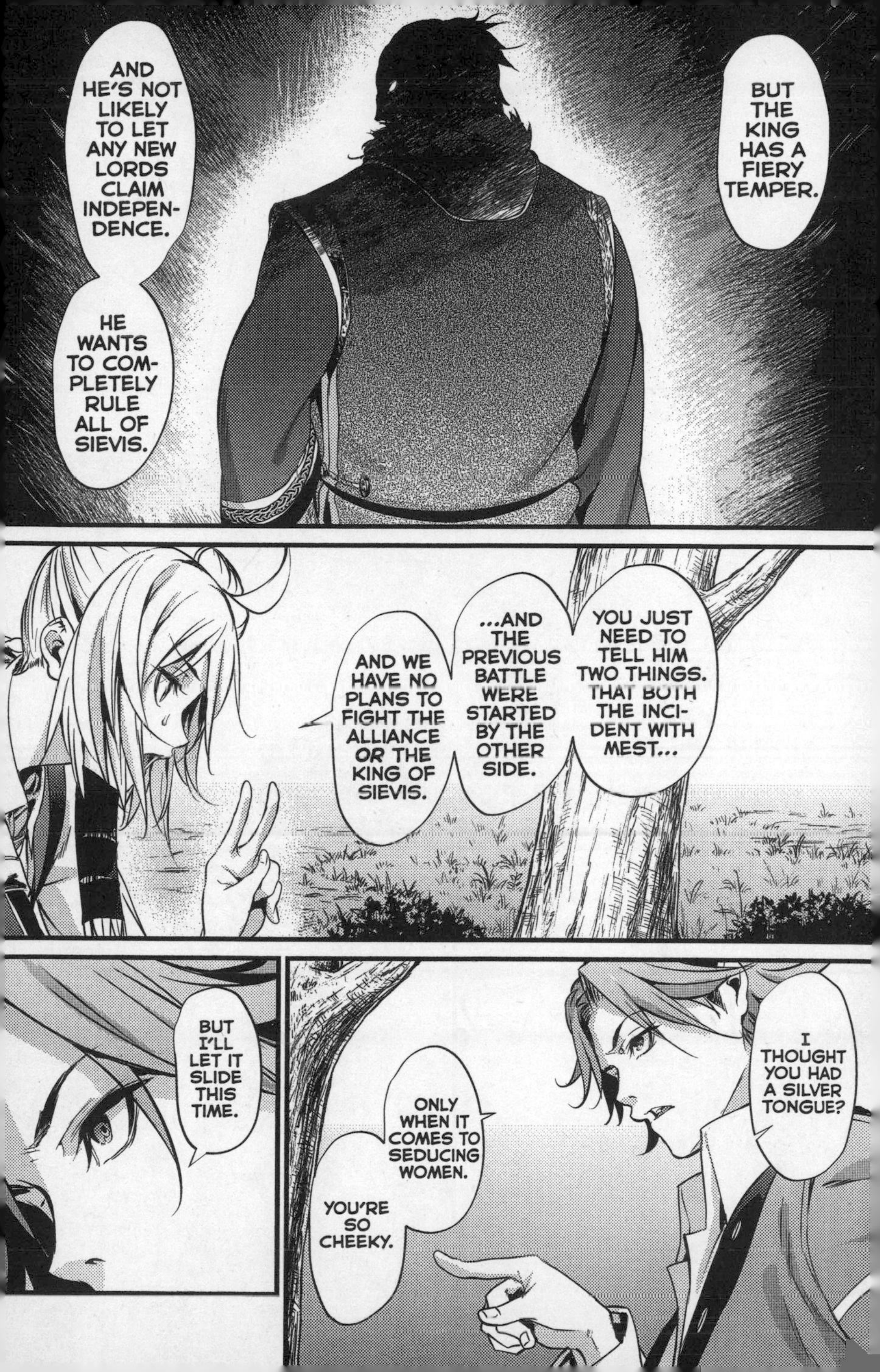
BUT THE KING HAS A FIERY TEMPER.
AND HE'S NOT LIKELY TO LET ANY NEW LORDS CLAIM INDEPENDENCE.
HE WANTS TO COMPLETELY RULE ALL OF SIEVIS.
YOU JUST NEED TO TELL HIM TWO THINGS. THAT BOTH THE INCIDENT WITH MEST...
...AND THE PREVIOUS BATTLE WERE STARTED BY THE OTHER SIDE.
AND WE HAVE NO PLANS TO FIGHT THE ALLIANCE *OR* THE KING OF SIEVIS.
I THOUGHT YOU HAD A SILVER TONGUE?
ONLY WHEN IT COMES TO SEDUCING WOMEN.
YOU'RE SO CHEEKY.
BUT I'LL LET IT SLIDE THIS TIME.

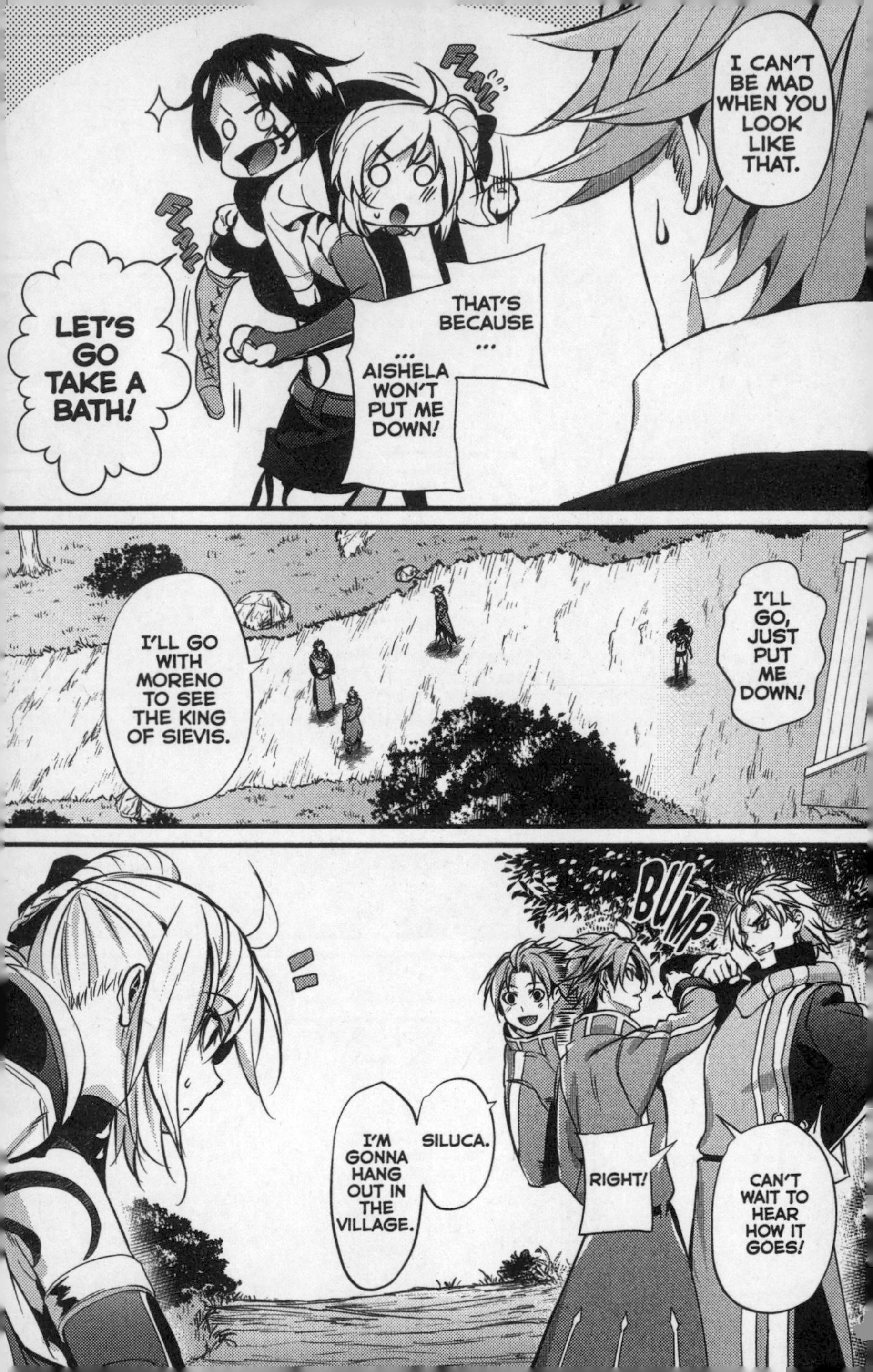
I CAN'T BE MAD WHEN YOU LOOK LIKE THAT.
FLAIL
THAT'S BECAUSE ...
... AISHELA WON'T PUT ME DOWN!
FLAIL
LET'S GO TAKE A BATH!
I'LL GO, JUST PUT ME DOWN!
I'LL GO WITH MORENO TO SEE THE KING OF SIEVIS.
BUMP
CAN'T WAIT TO HEAR HOW IT GOES!
RIGHT!
SILUCA.
I'M GONNA HANG OUT IN THE VILLAGE.

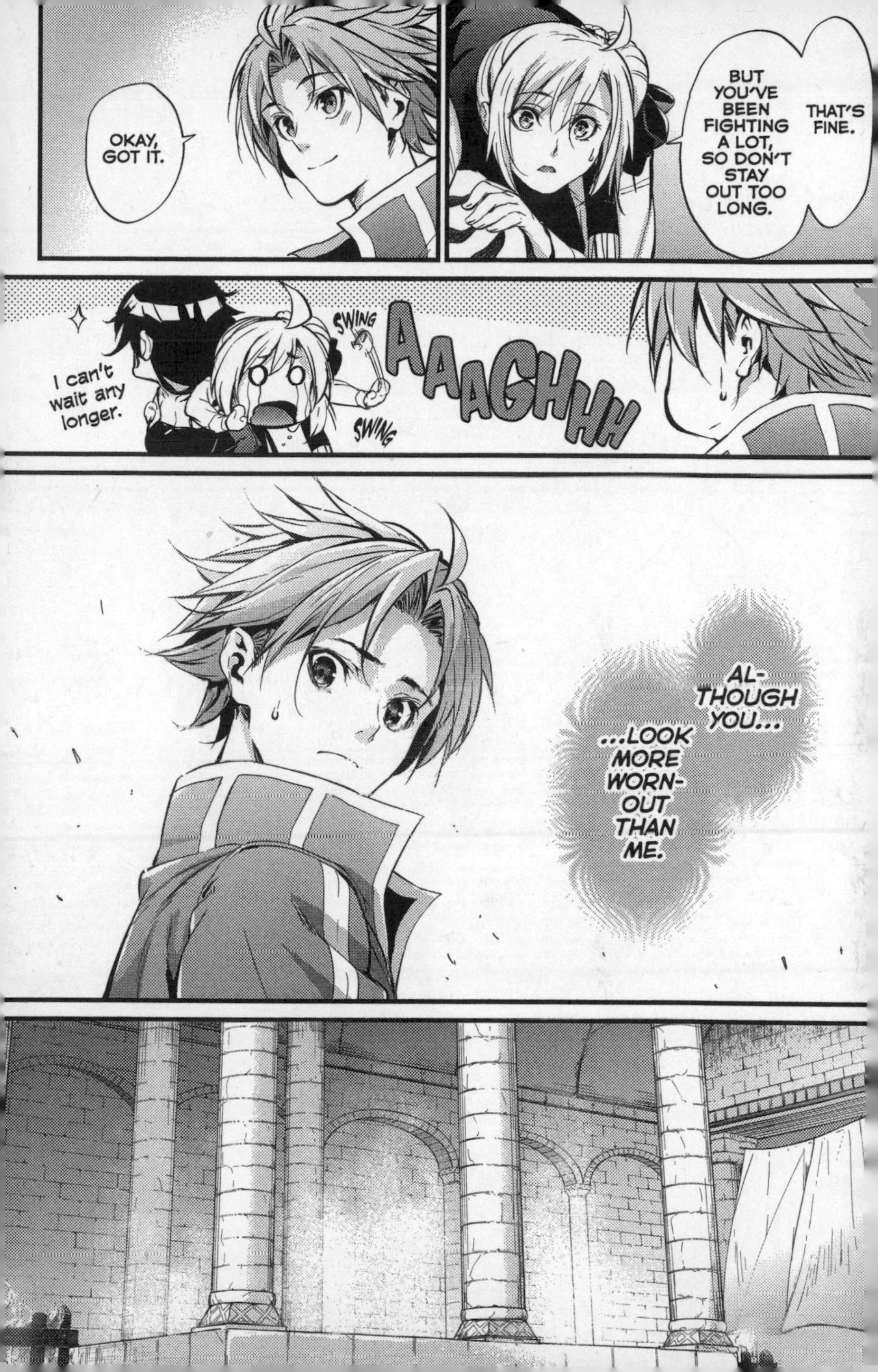
THAT'S FINE.
BUT YOU'VE BEEN FIGHTING A LOT, SO DON'T STAY OUT TOO LONG.
OKAY, GOT IT.
SWING
AAAGHHH
SWING
I can't wait any longer.
AL-THOUGH YOU...
...LOOK MORE WORN-OUT THAN ME.

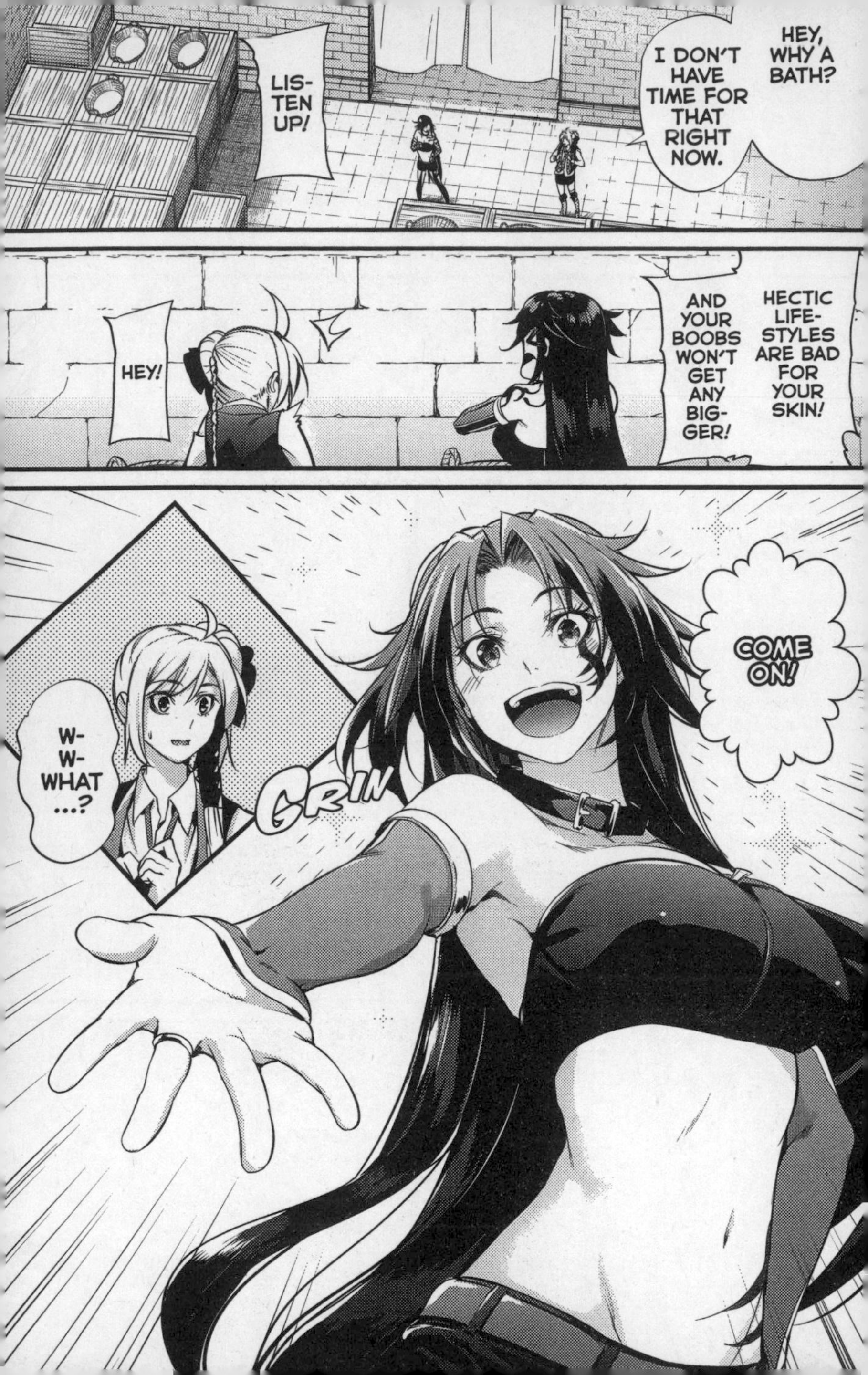

HEY, WHY A BATH?
I DON'T HAVE TIME FOR THAT RIGHT NOW.
LIS-TEN UP!
HECTIC LIFE-STYLES ARE BAD FOR YOUR SKIN!
AND YOUR BOOBS WON'T GET ANY BIG-GER!
HEY!
COME ON!
GRIN
W-W-WHAT ...?

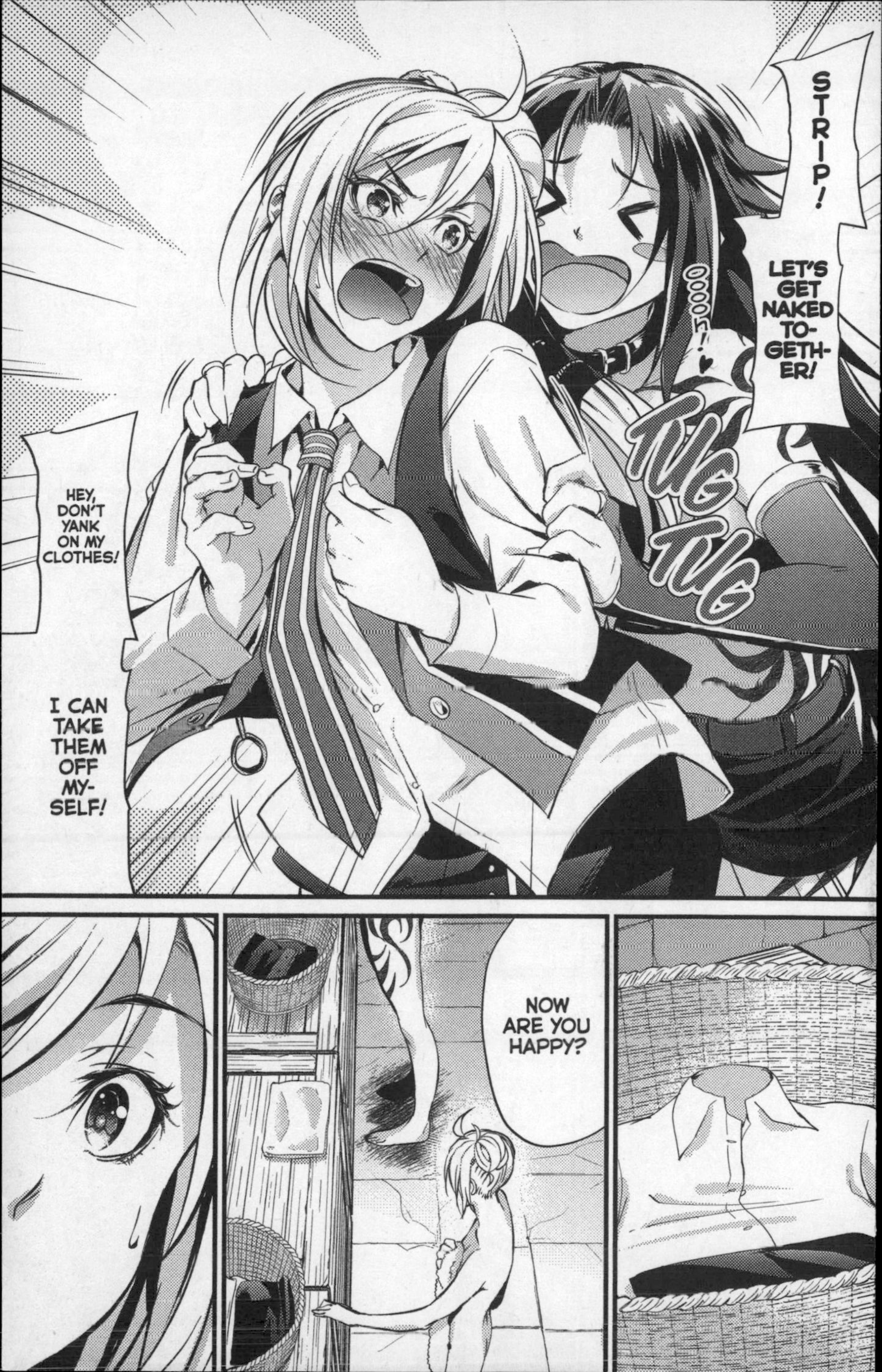
STRIP!
LET'S GET NAKED TO-GETH-ER!
Ooooh!♥
TUG TUG
HEY, DON'T YANK ON MY CLOTHES!
I CAN TAKE THEM OFF MY-SELF!
NOW ARE YOU HAPPY?

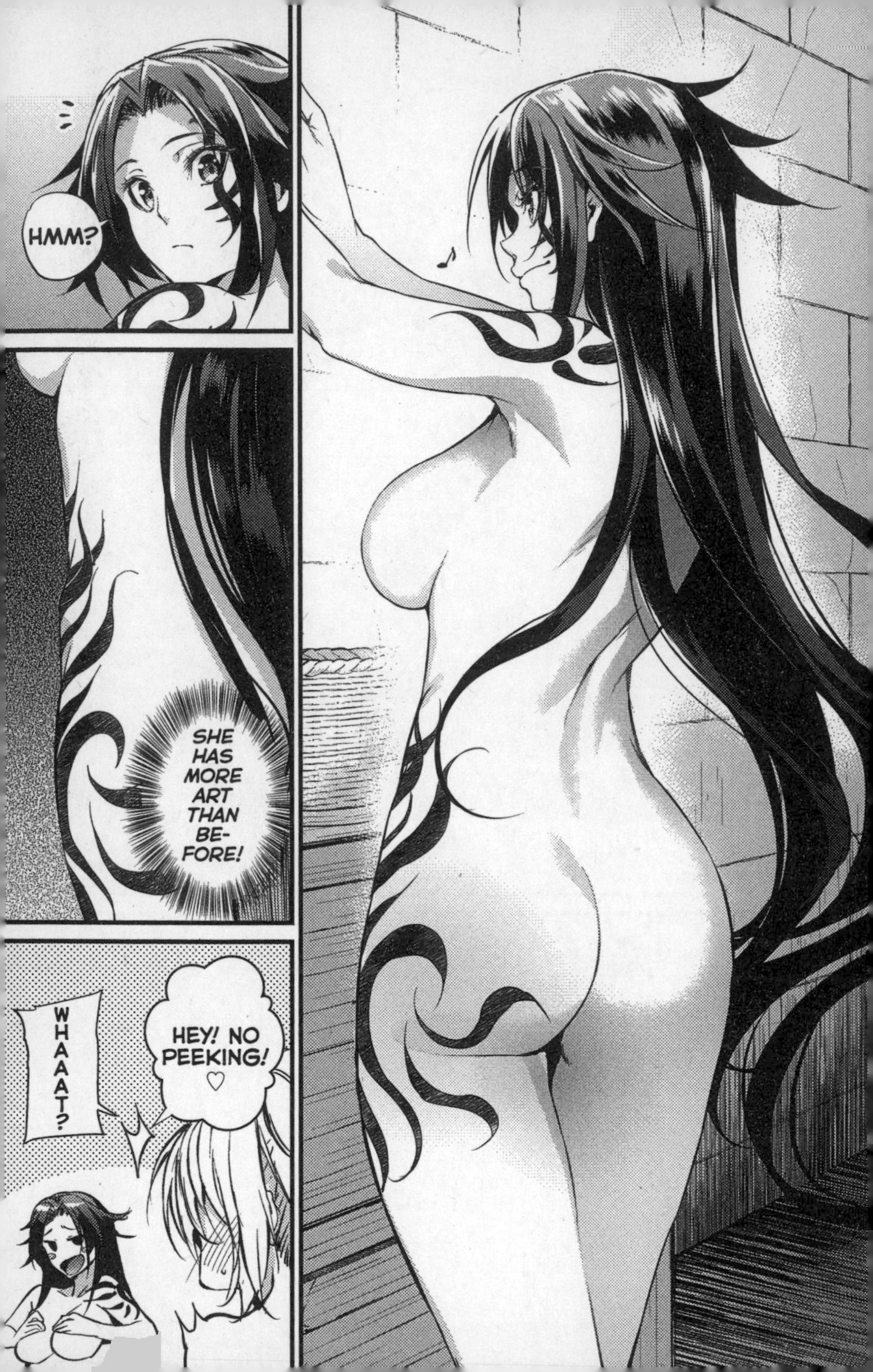
HMM?
SHE HAS MORE ART THAN BE-FORE!
HEY! NO PEEKING! ♡
WHAAAT?!

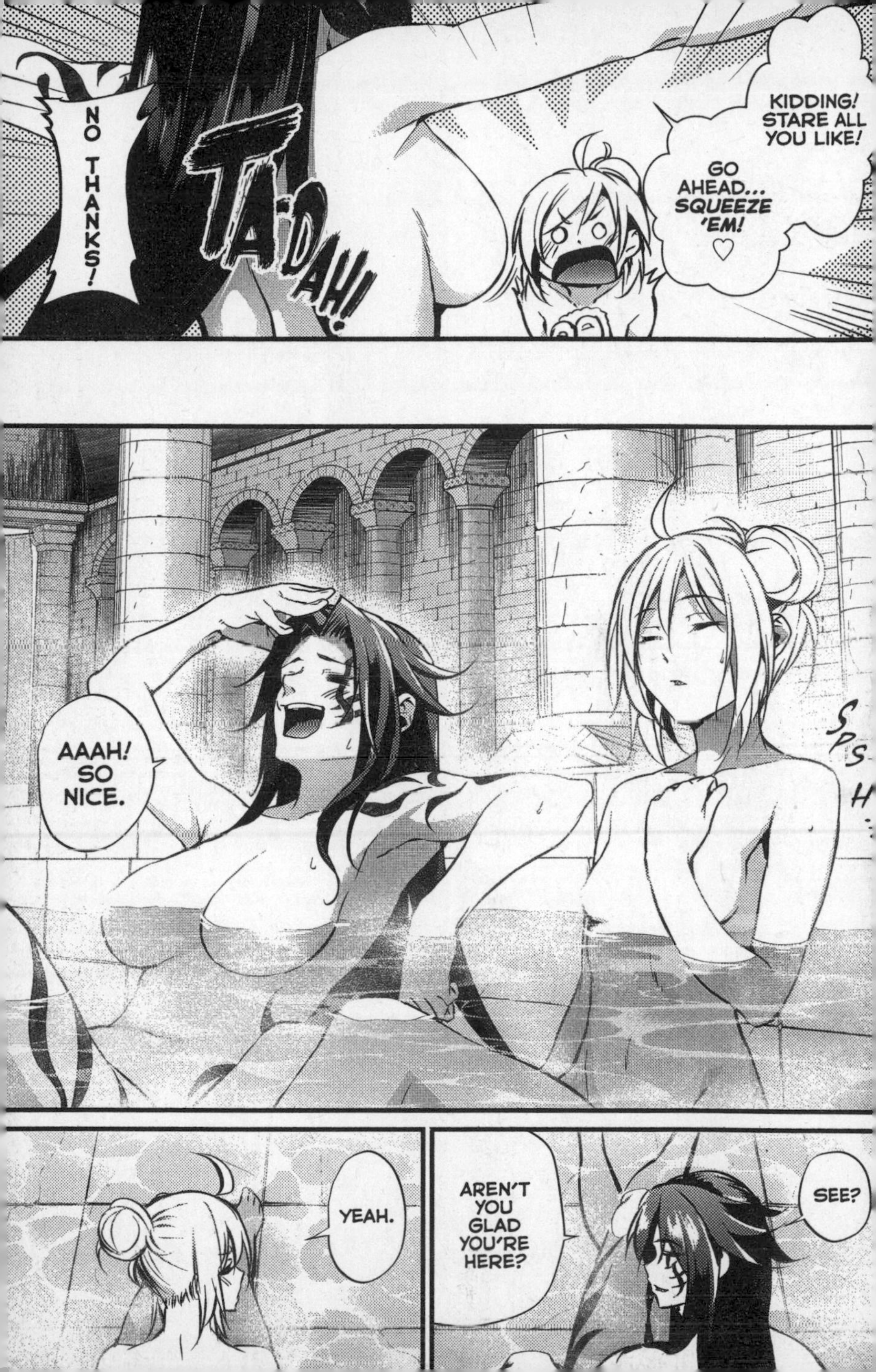
KIDDING! STARE ALL YOU LIKE!
GO AHEAD... SQUEEZE 'EM! ♡
TA-DAH!
NO THANKS!
SPSH
AAAH! SO NICE.
SEE?
AREN'T YOU GLAD YOU'RE HERE?
YEAH.

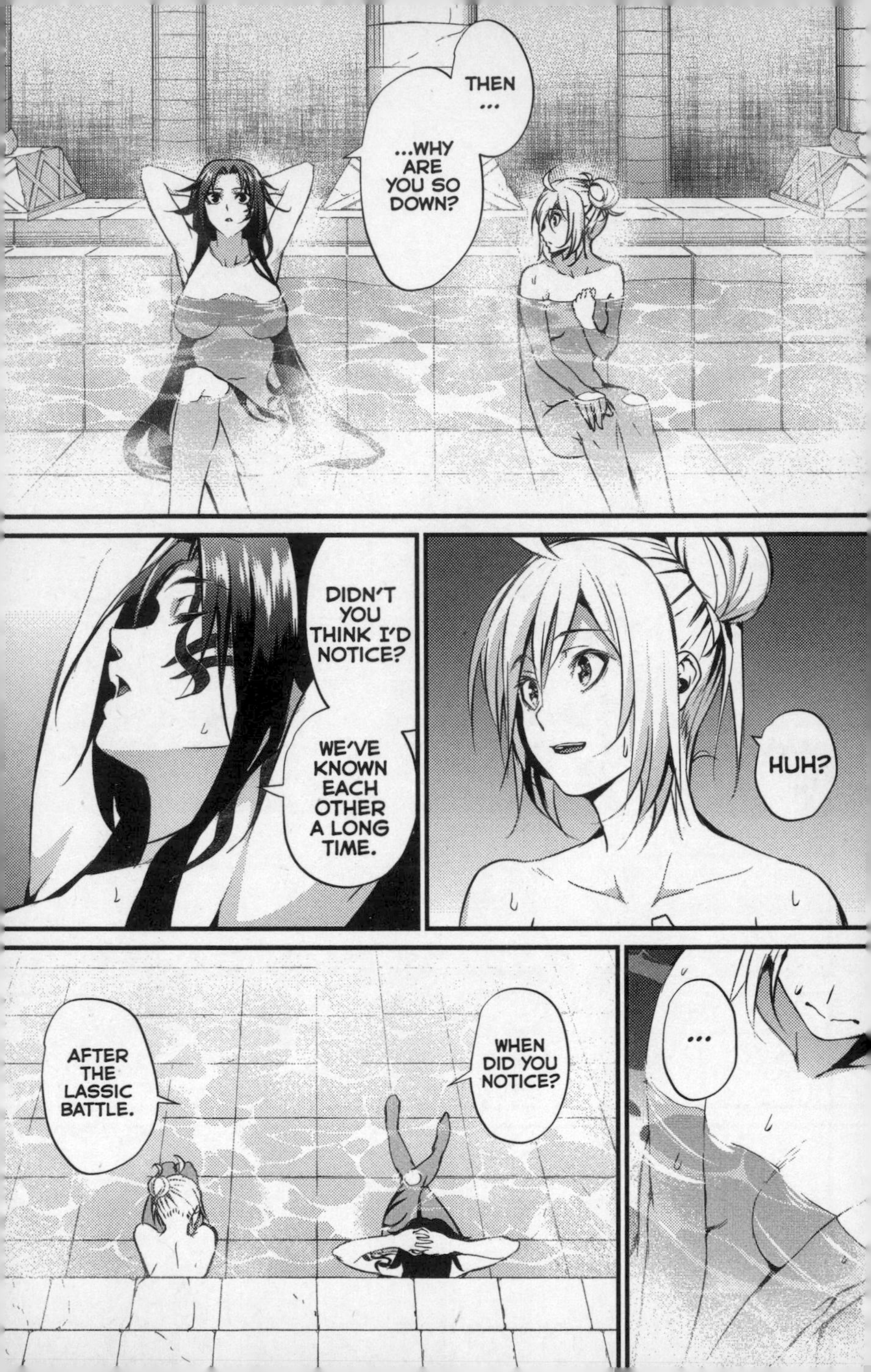
THEN ...
...WHY ARE YOU SO DOWN?
HUH?
DIDN'T YOU THINK I'D NOTICE?
WE'VE KNOWN EACH OTHER A LONG TIME.
...
WHEN DID YOU NOTICE?
AFTER THE LASSIC BATTLE.

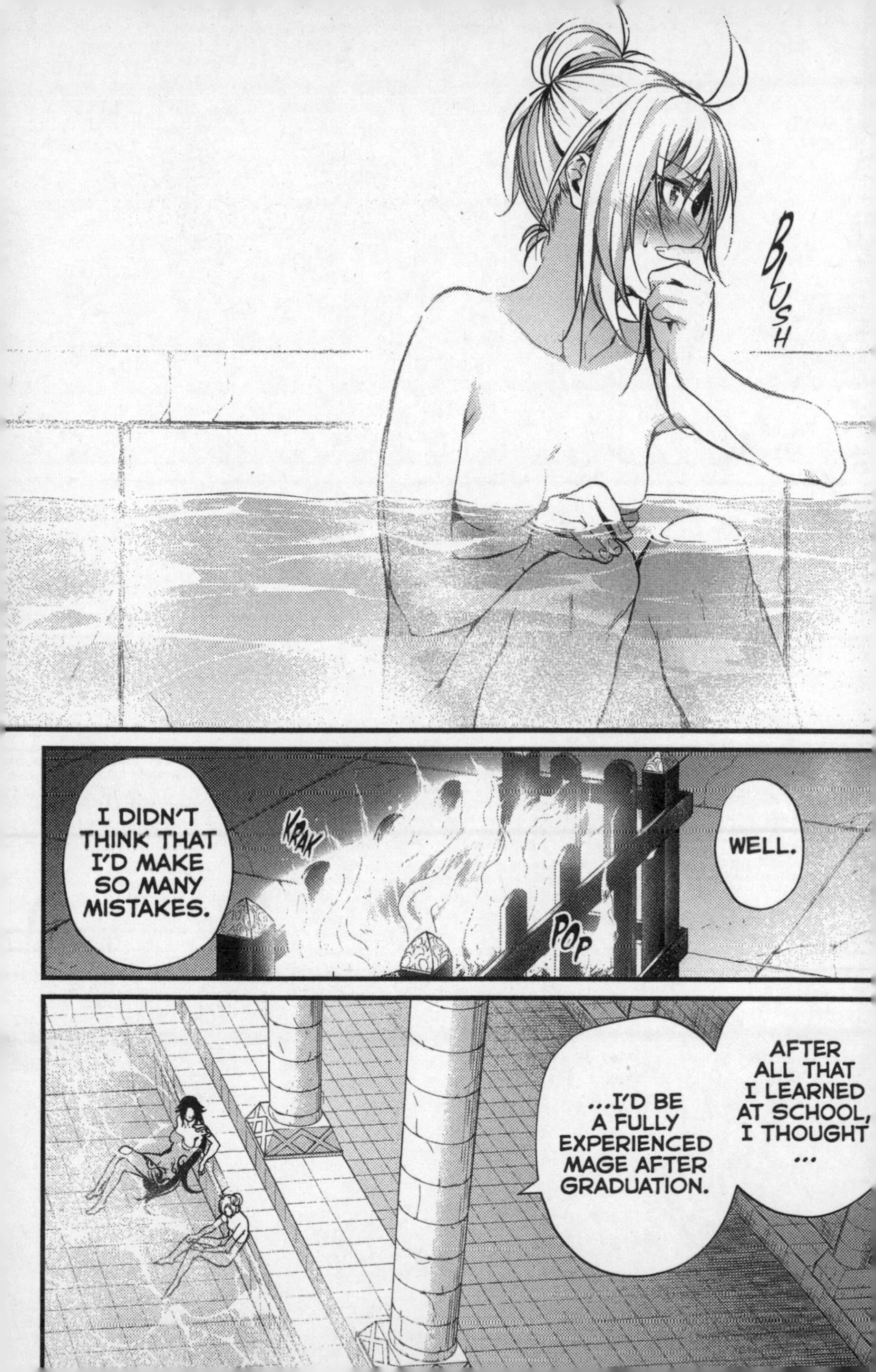
BLUSH
WELL.
I DIDN'T THINK THAT I'D MAKE SO MANY MISTAKES.
KRAK
POP
AFTER ALL THAT I LEARNED AT SCHOOL, I THOUGHT ...
...I'D BE A FULLY EXPERIENCED MAGE AFTER GRADUATION.

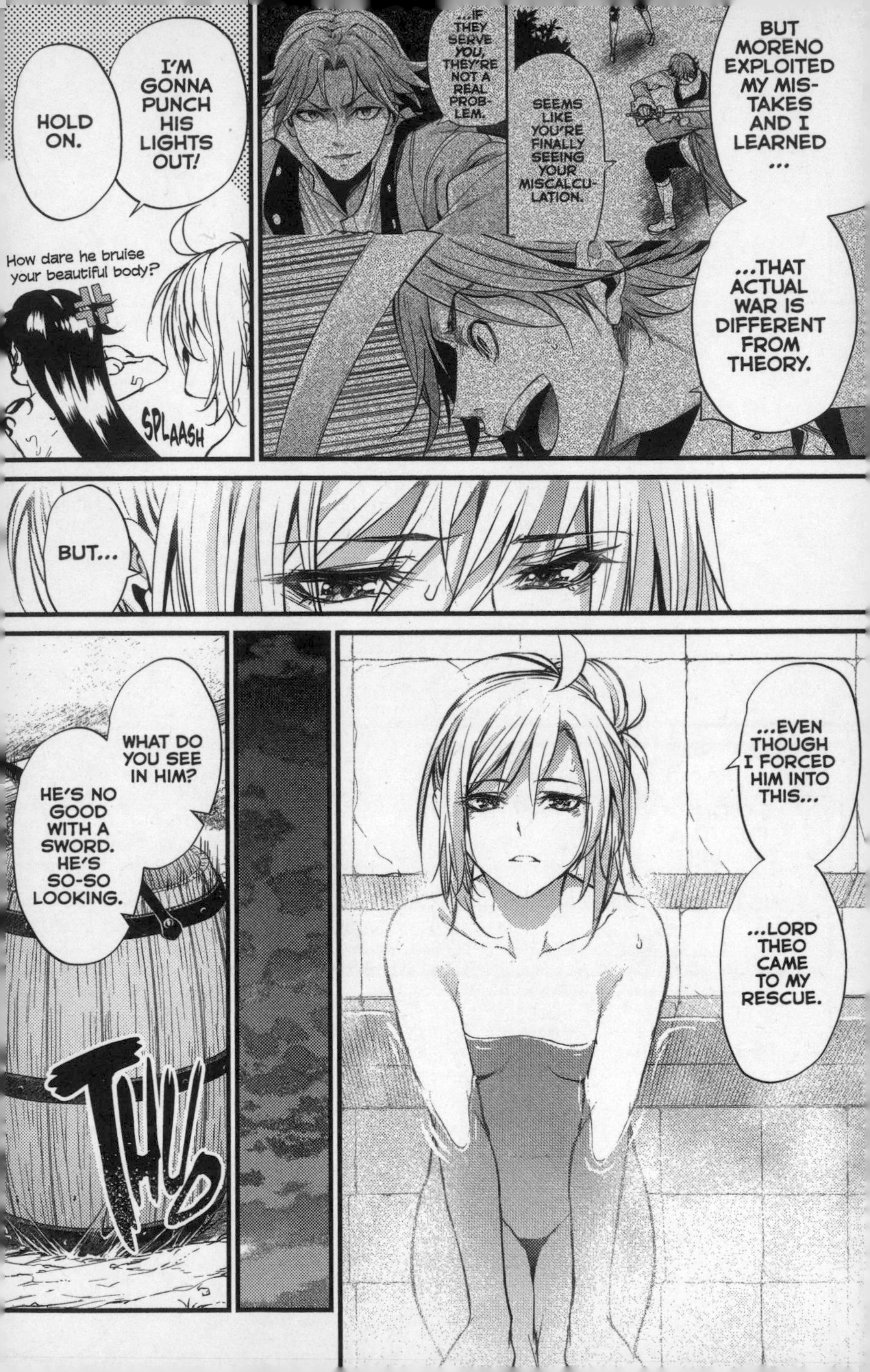
BUT MORENO EXPLOITED MY MISTAKES AND I LEARNED...
...THAT ACTUAL WAR IS DIFFERENT FROM THEORY.
SEEMS LIKE YOU'RE FINALLY SEEING YOUR MISCALCULATION.
...IF THEY SERVE *YOU*, THEY'RE NOT A REAL PROBLEM.
I'M GONNA PUNCH HIS LIGHTS OUT!
HOLD ON.
How dare he bruise your beautiful body?
SPLAASH
BUT...
...EVEN THOUGH I FORCED HIM INTO THIS...
...LORD THEO CAME TO MY RESCUE.
WHAT DO YOU SEE IN HIM?
HE'S NO GOOD WITH A SWORD. HE'S SO-SO LOOKING.
THUD

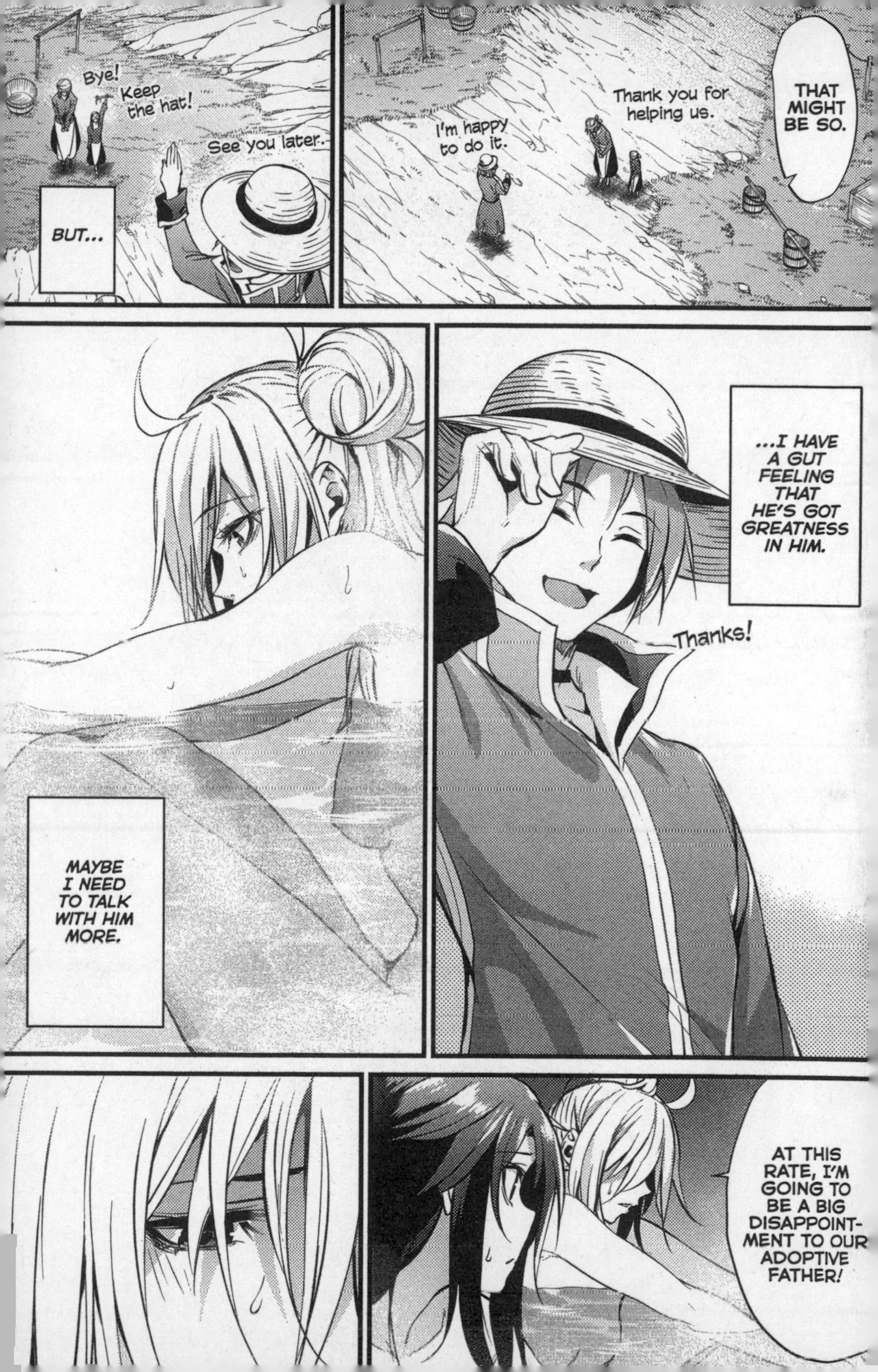
THAT MIGHT BE SO.
Thank you for helping us.
I'm happy to do it.
See you later.
Keep the hat!
Bye!
BUT...
...I HAVE A GUT FEELING THAT HE'S GOT GREATNESS IN HIM.
Thanks!
MAYBE I NEED TO TALK WITH HIM MORE.
AT THIS RATE, I'M GOING TO BE A BIG DISAPPOINTMENT TO OUR ADOPTIVE FATHER!

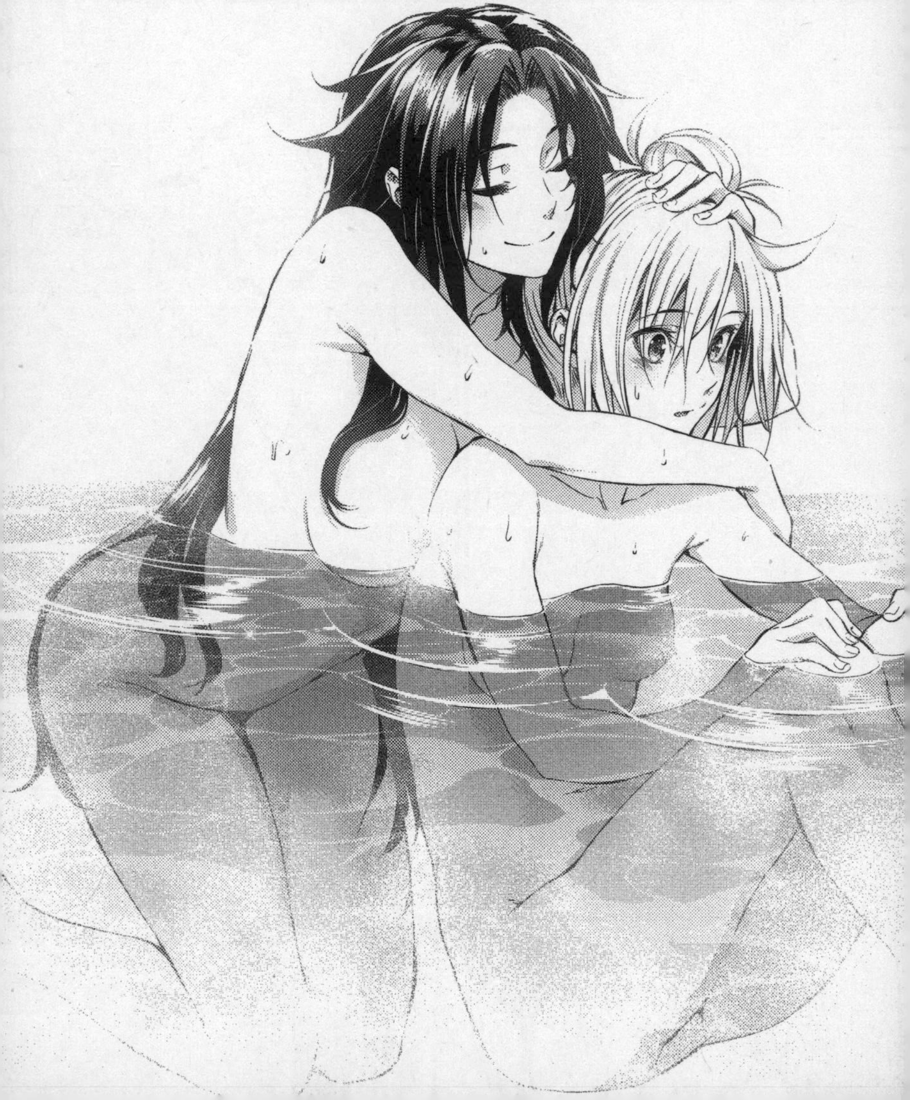

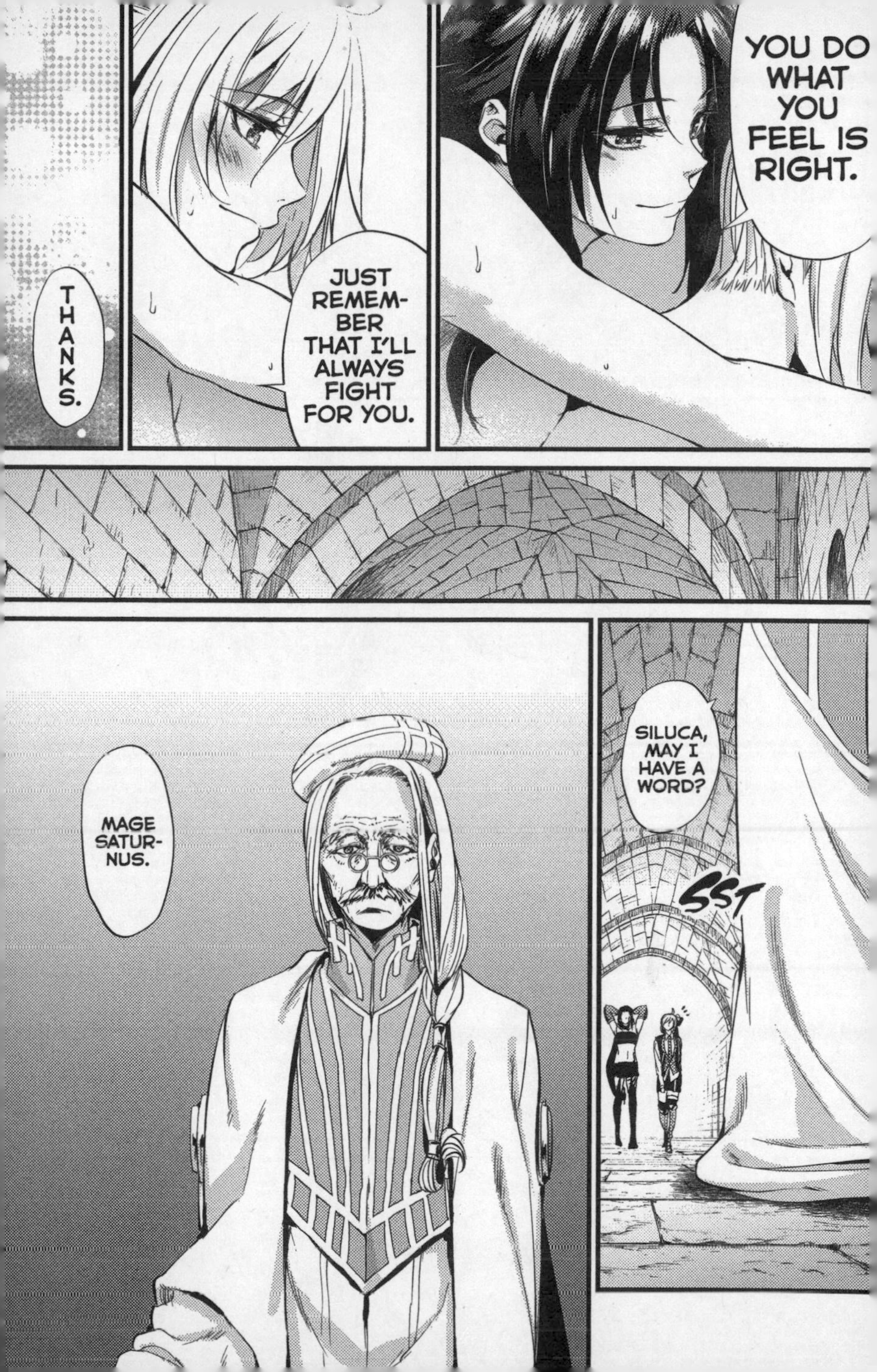
YOU DO WHAT YOU FEEL IS RIGHT.
JUST REMEMBER THAT I'LL ALWAYS FIGHT FOR YOU.
THANKS.
SILUCA, MAY I HAVE A WORD?
SST
MAGE SATURNUS.

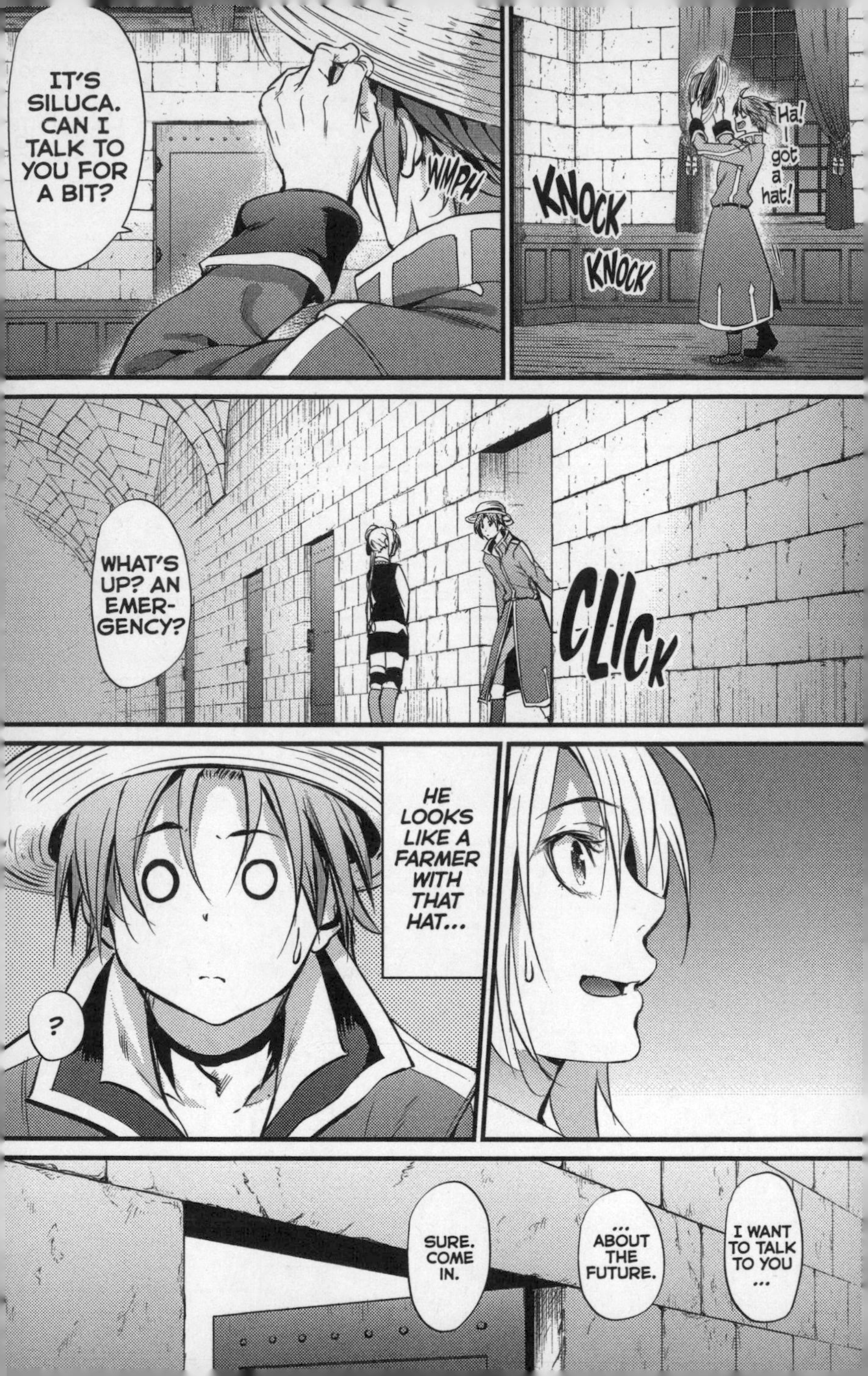
Ha! I got a hat!
KNOCK
KNOCK
WMPH
IT'S SILUCA. CAN I TALK TO YOU FOR A BIT?
CLICK
WHAT'S UP? AN EMER-GENCY?
HE LOOKS LIKE A FARMER WITH THAT HAT...
?
I WANT TO TALK TO YOU ...
... ABOUT THE FUTURE.
SURE. COME IN.

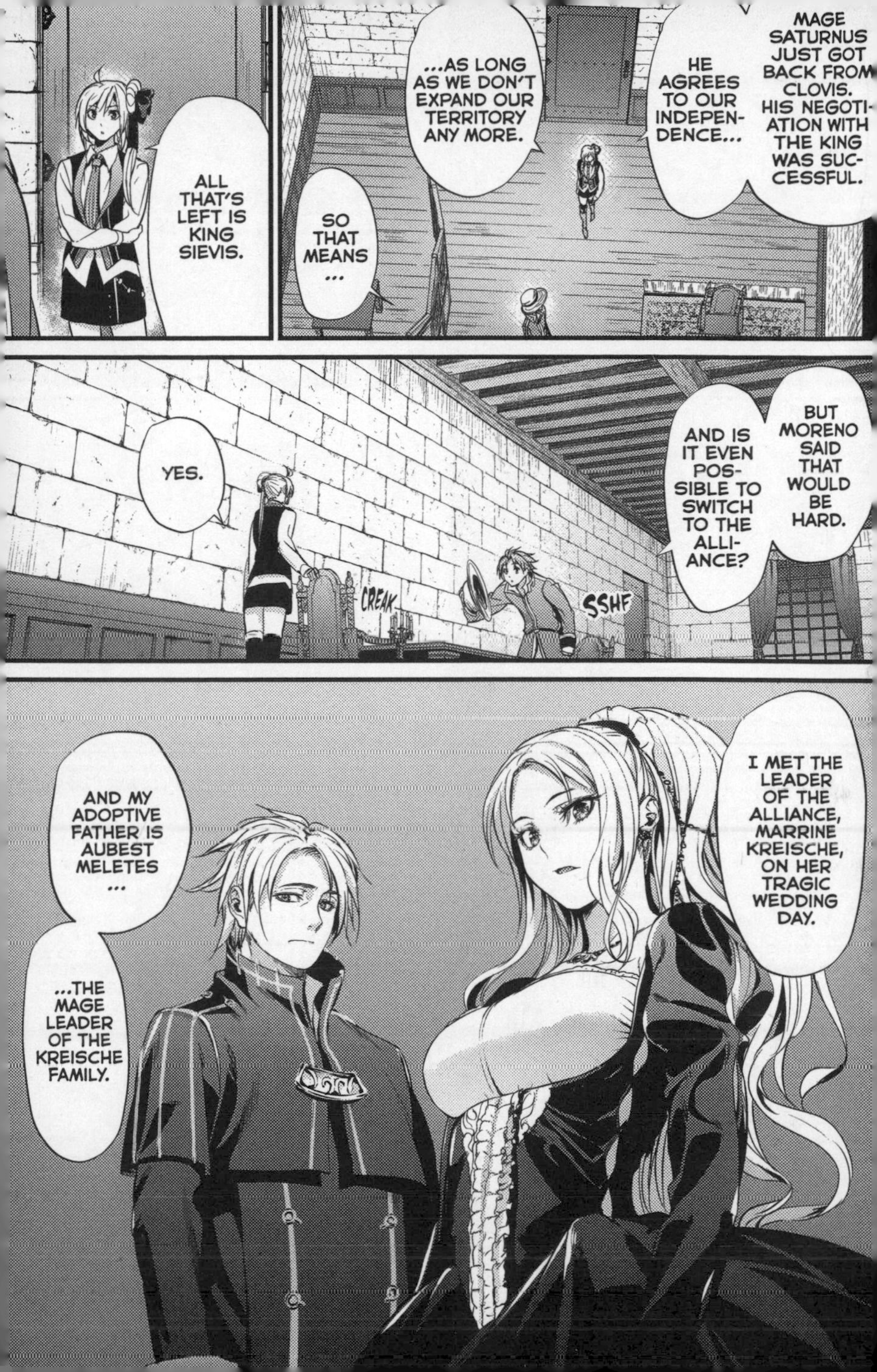
MAGE SATURNUS JUST GOT BACK FROM CLOVIS. HIS NEGOTIATION WITH THE KING WAS SUCCESSFUL.
HE AGREES TO OUR INDEPENDENCE...
...AS LONG AS WE DON'T EXPAND OUR TERRITORY ANY MORE.
SO THAT MEANS...
ALL THAT'S LEFT IS KING SIEVIS.
BUT MORENO SAID THAT WOULD BE HARD.
AND IS IT EVEN POSSIBLE TO SWITCH TO THE ALLIANCE?
SSHF
CREAK
YES.
I MET THE LEADER OF THE ALLIANCE, MARRINE KREISCHE, ON HER TRAGIC WEDDING DAY.
AND MY ADOPTIVE FATHER IS AUBEST MELETES...
...THE MAGE LEADER OF THE KREISCHE FAMILY.

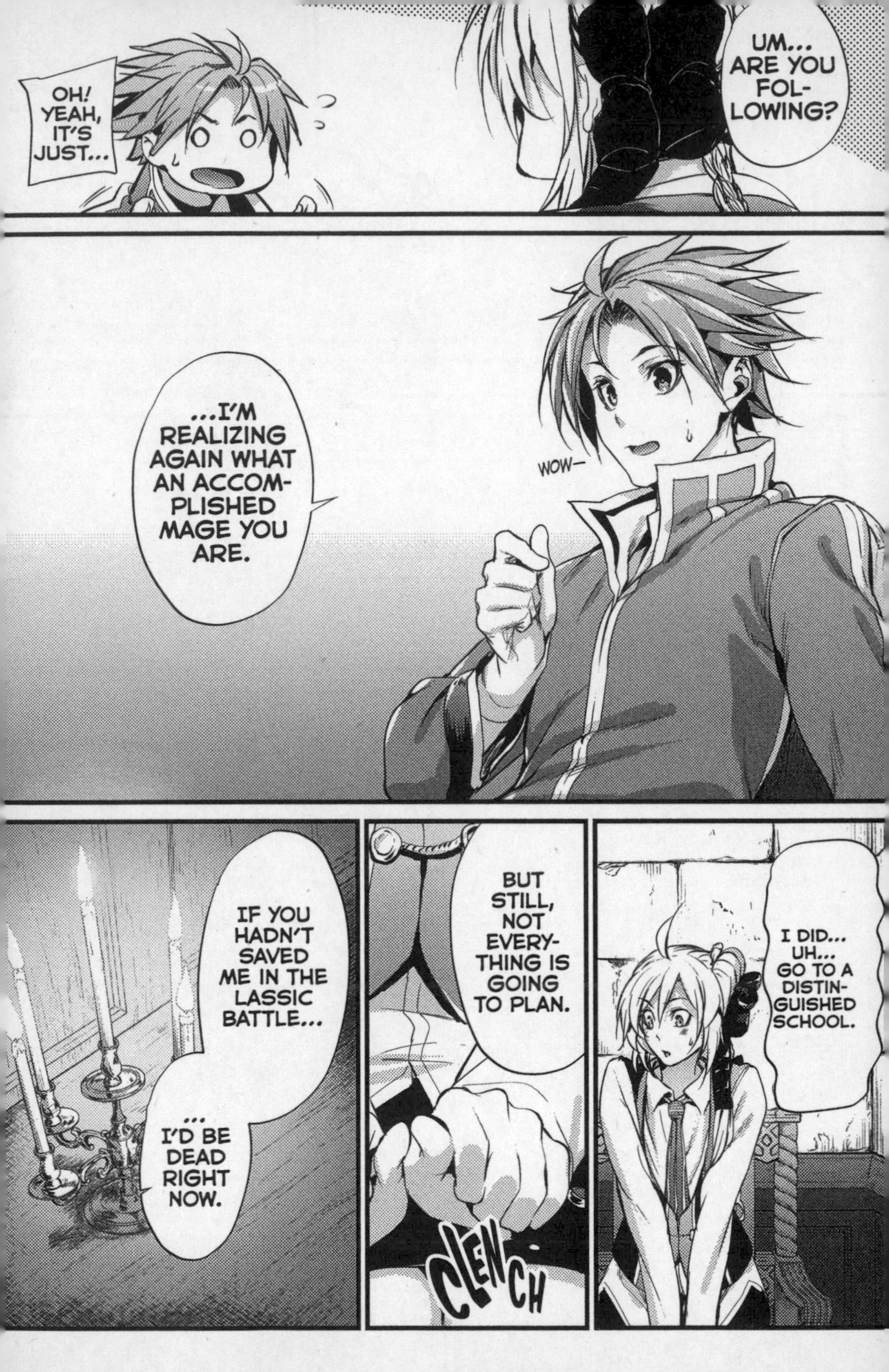
UM... ARE YOU FOL-LOWING?
OH! YEAH, IT'S JUST...
WOW—
...I'M REALIZING AGAIN WHAT AN ACCOM-PLISHED MAGE YOU ARE.
I DID... UH... GO TO A DISTIN-GUISHED SCHOOL.
BUT STILL, NOT EVERY-THING IS GOING TO PLAN.
CLENCH
IF YOU HADN'T SAVED ME IN THE LASSIC BATTLE...
...I'D BE DEAD RIGHT NOW.

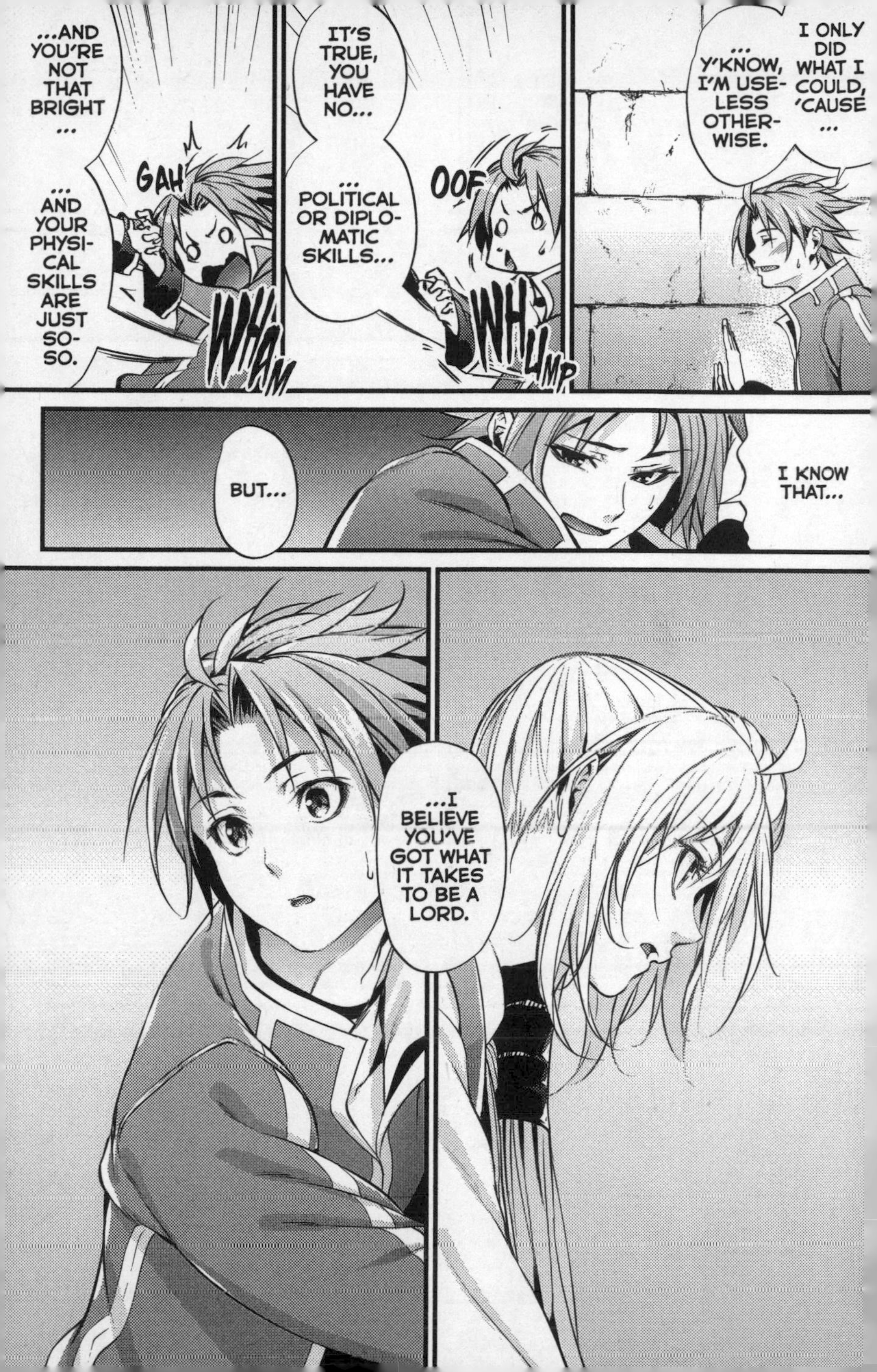
I ONLY DID WHAT I COULD, 'CAUSE...
...Y'KNOW, I'M USELESS OTHERWISE.
IT'S TRUE, YOU HAVE NO...
...POLITICAL OR DIPLOMATIC SKILLS...
OOF
WHUMP
...AND YOU'RE NOT THAT BRIGHT...
...AND YOUR PHYSICAL SKILLS ARE JUST SO-SO.
GAH
WHAM
I KNOW THAT...
BUT...
...I BELIEVE YOU'VE GOT WHAT IT TAKES TO BE A LORD.

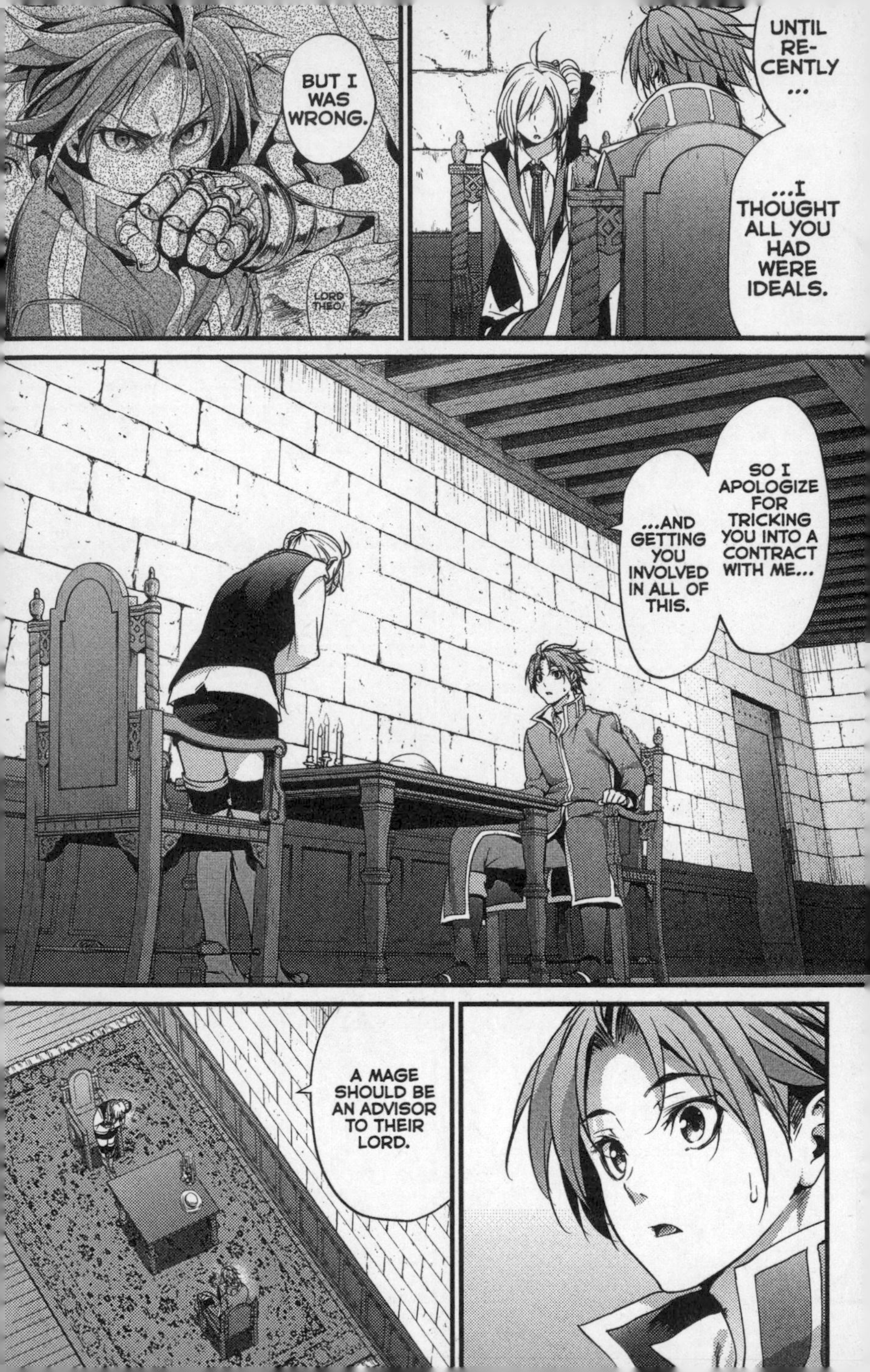
UNTIL RE-CENTLY ...
...I THOUGHT ALL YOU HAD WERE IDEALS.
BUT I WAS WRONG.
LORD THEO!
SO I APOLOGIZE FOR TRICKING YOU INTO A CONTRACT WITH ME...
...AND GETTING YOU INVOLVED IN ALL OF THIS.
A MAGE SHOULD BE AN ADVISOR TO THEIR LORD.

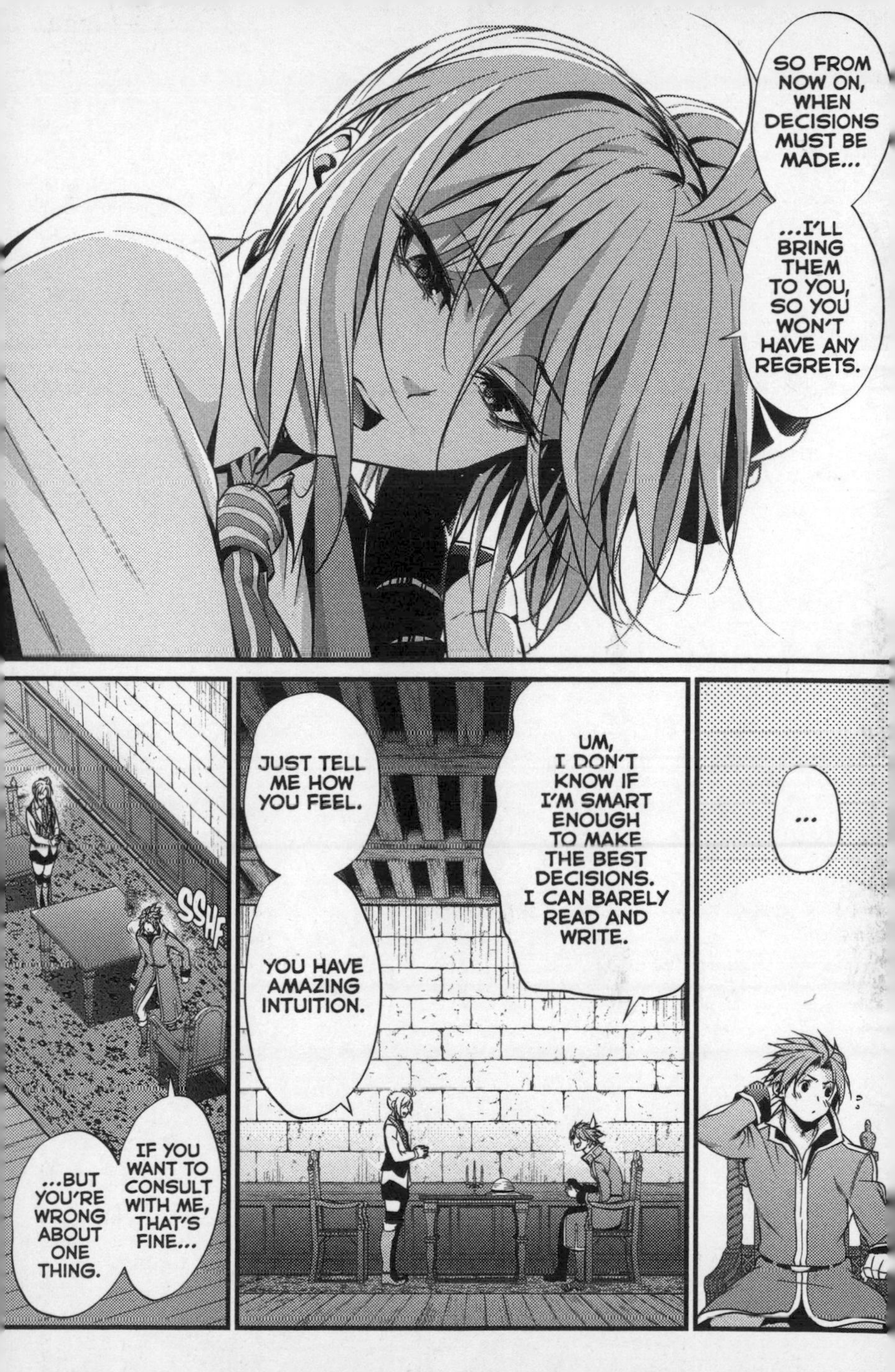
SO FROM NOW ON, WHEN DECISIONS MUST BE MADE...
...I'LL BRING THEM TO YOU, SO YOU WON'T HAVE ANY REGRETS.
...
UM, I DON'T KNOW IF I'M SMART ENOUGH TO MAKE THE BEST DECISIONS. I CAN BARELY READ AND WRITE.
JUST TELL ME HOW YOU FEEL.
YOU HAVE AMAZING INTUITION.
SSHF
IF YOU WANT TO CONSULT WITH ME, THAT'S FINE...
...BUT YOU'RE WRONG ABOUT ONE THING.

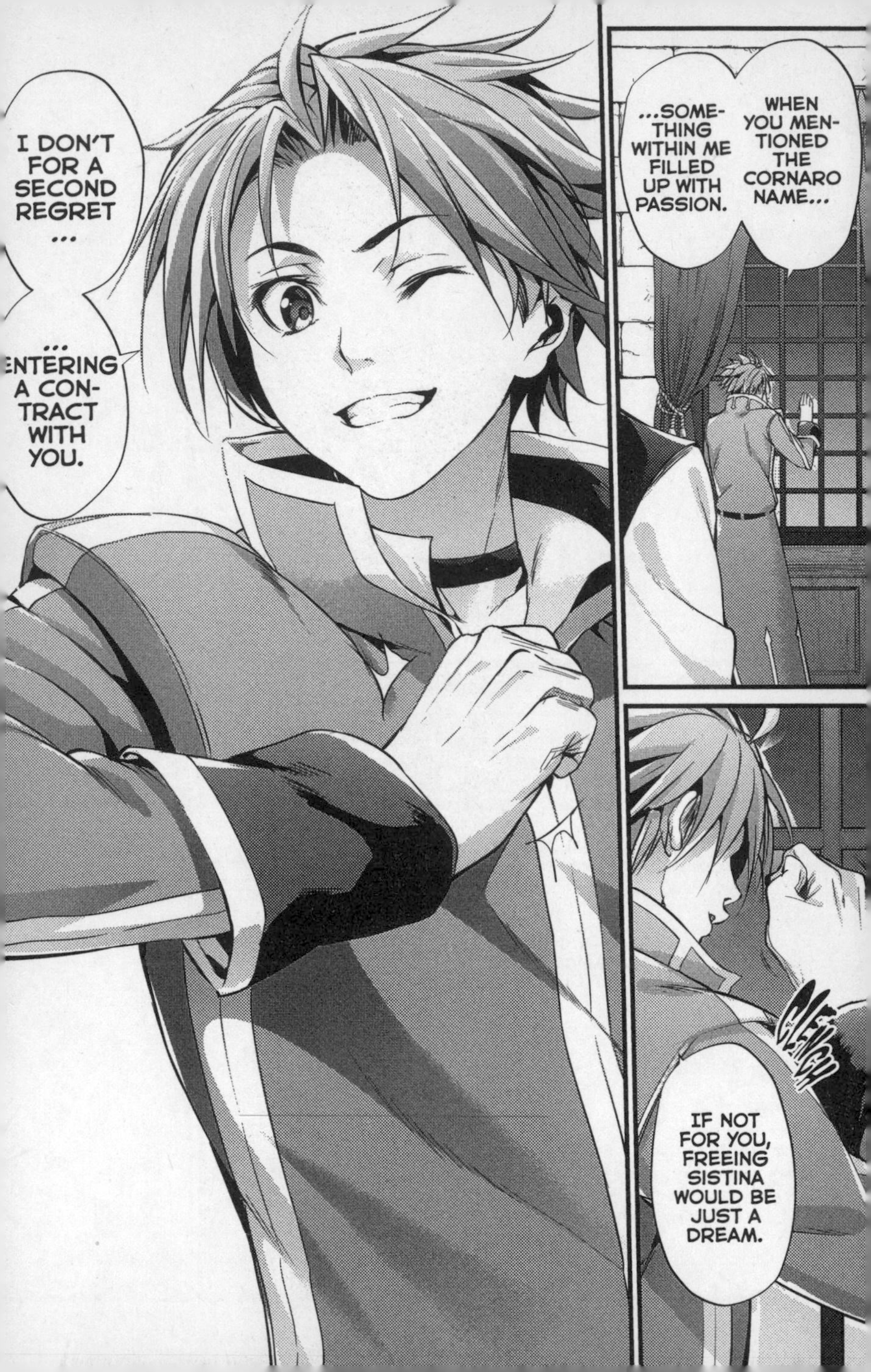
WHEN YOU MENTIONED THE CORNARO NAME...
...SOMETHING WITHIN ME FILLED UP WITH PASSION.
CLENCH
IF NOT FOR YOU, FREEING SISTINA WOULD BE JUST A DREAM.
I DON'T FOR A SECOND REGRET...
...ENTERING A CONTRACT WITH YOU.

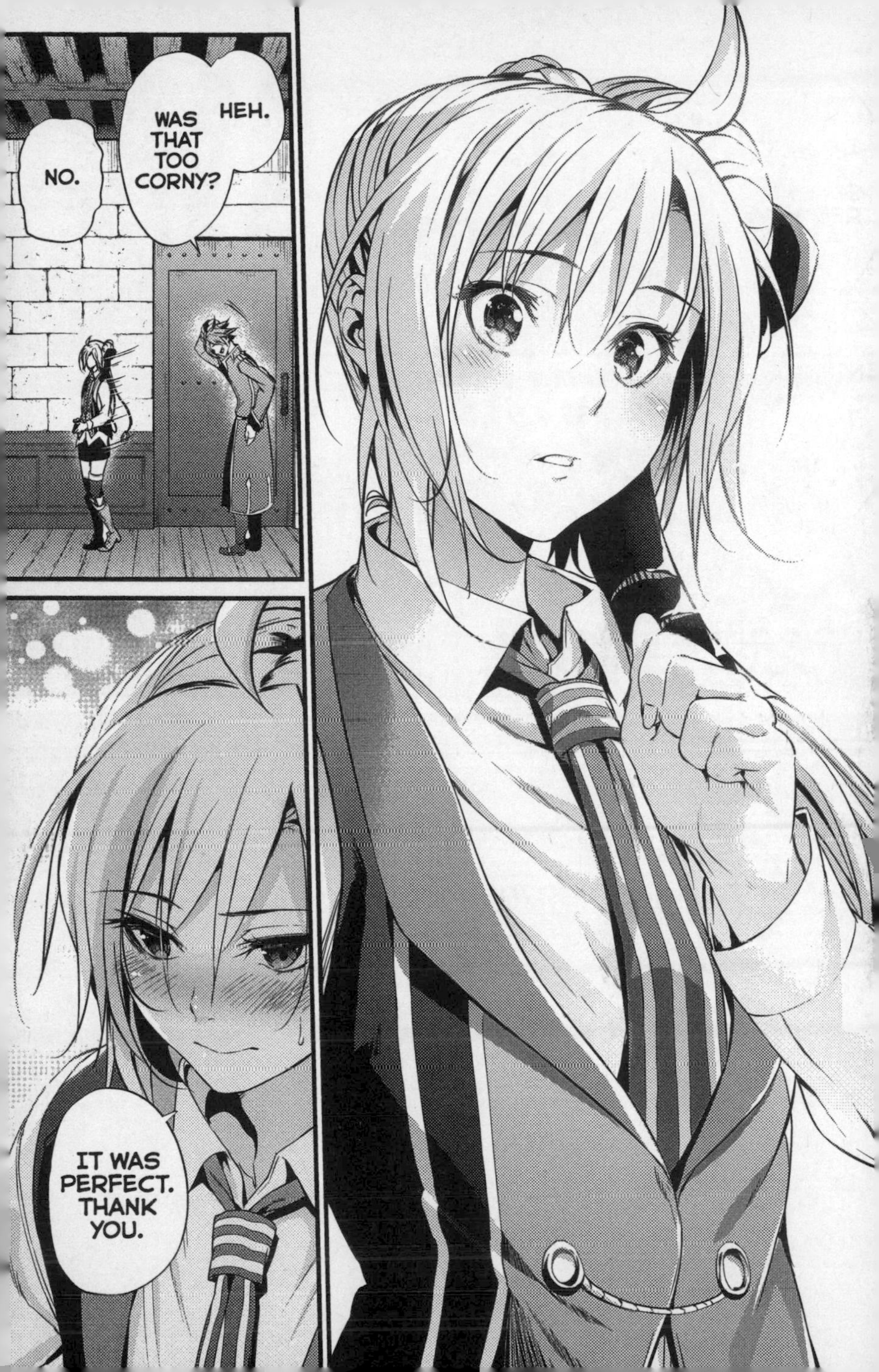
HEH.
WAS THAT TOO CORNY?
NO.
IT WAS PERFECT. THANK YOU.

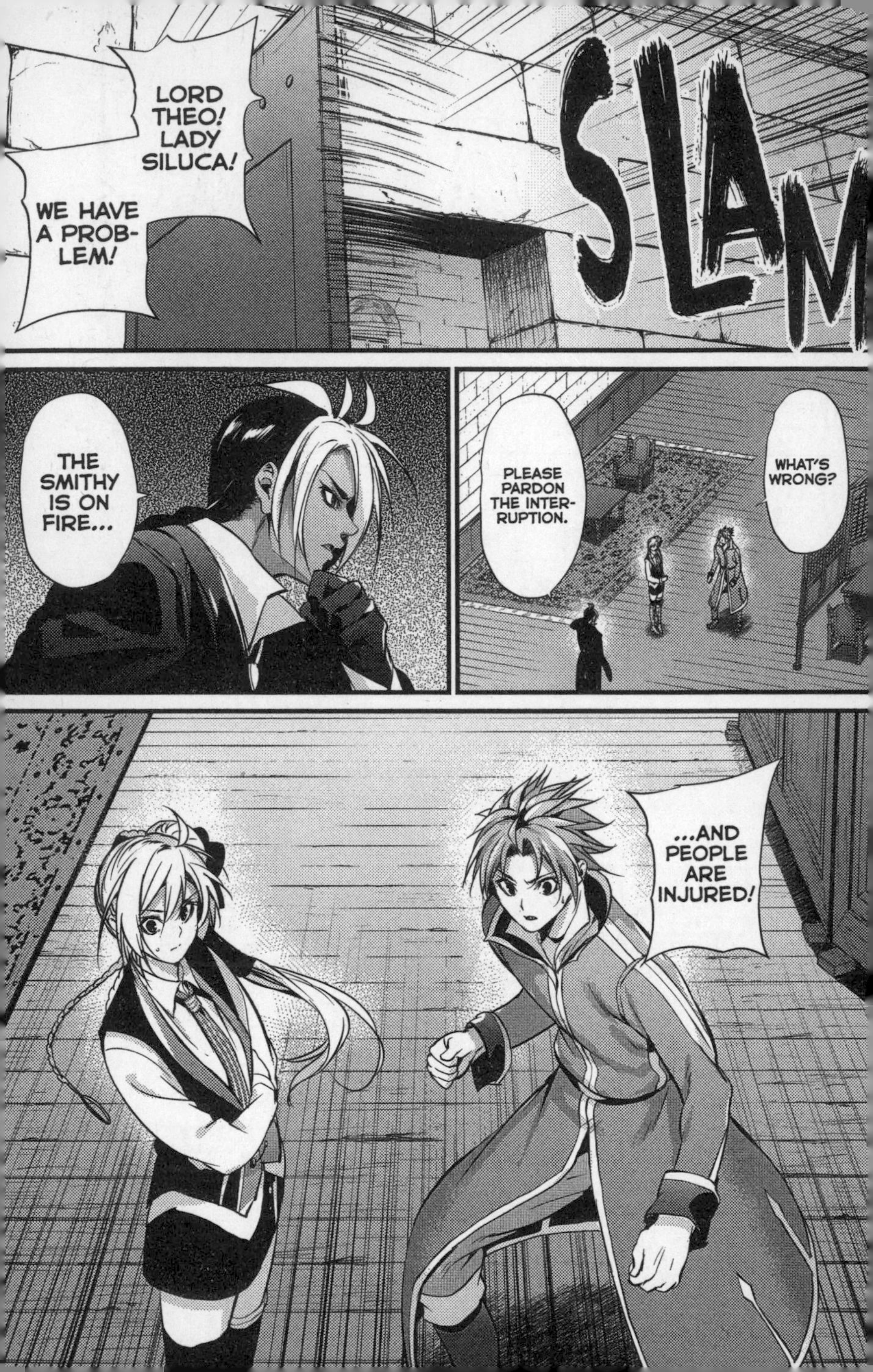
SLAM
LORD THEO! LADY SILUCA!
WE HAVE A PROB-LEM!
WHAT'S WRONG?
PLEASE PARDON THE INTER-RUPTION.
THE SMITHY IS ON FIRE...
...AND PEOPLE ARE INJURED!

RECORD OF
GRANCREST
WAR

RECORD OF
GRANCREST
WAR

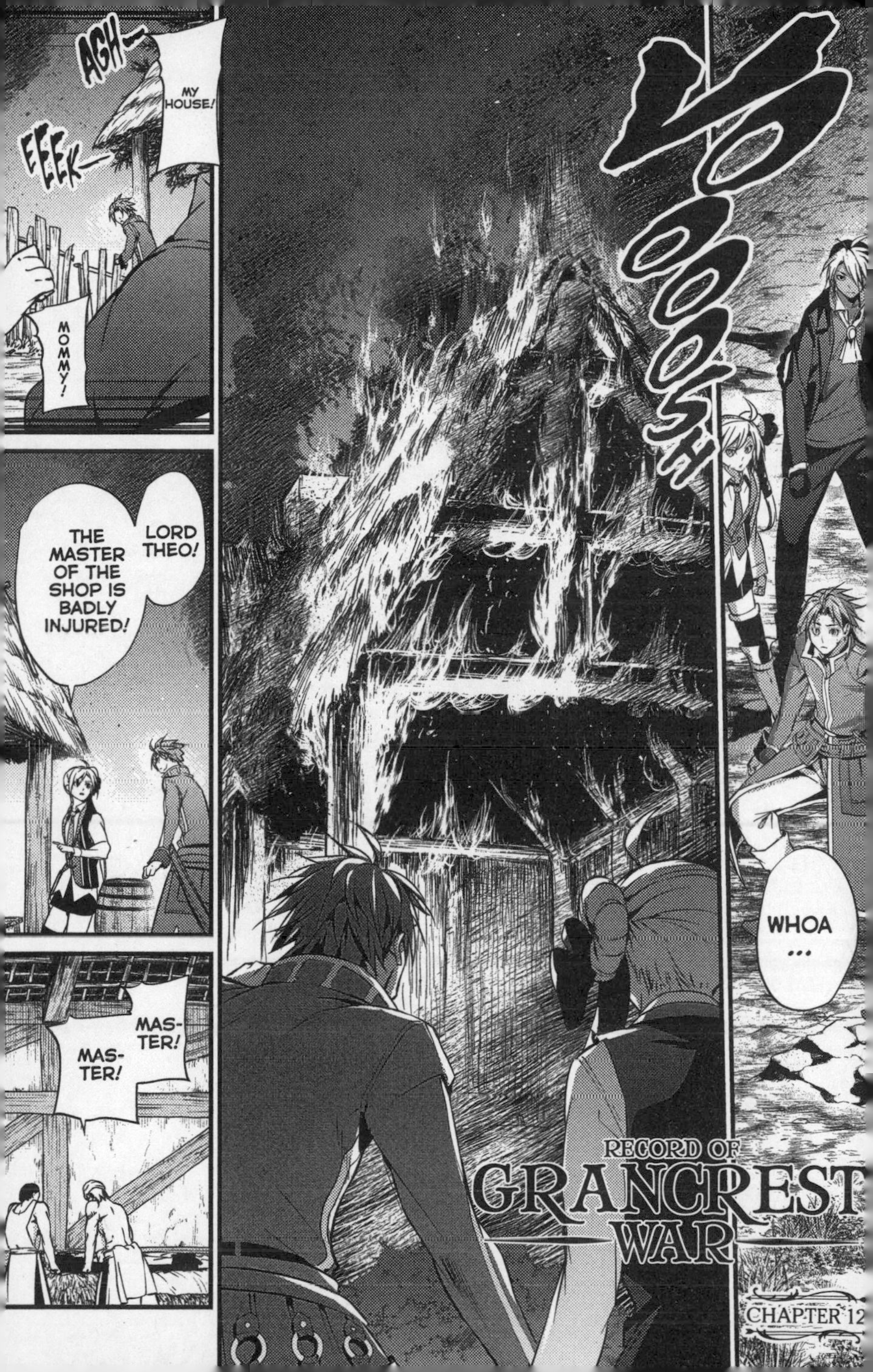
VOOOOSH
WHOA ...
RECORD OF GRANCREST WAR
CHAPTER 12
AGH—
MY HOUSE!
EEEEK—
MOMMY!
LORD THEO!
THE MASTER OF THE SHOP IS BADLY INJURED!
MASTER!
MASTER!

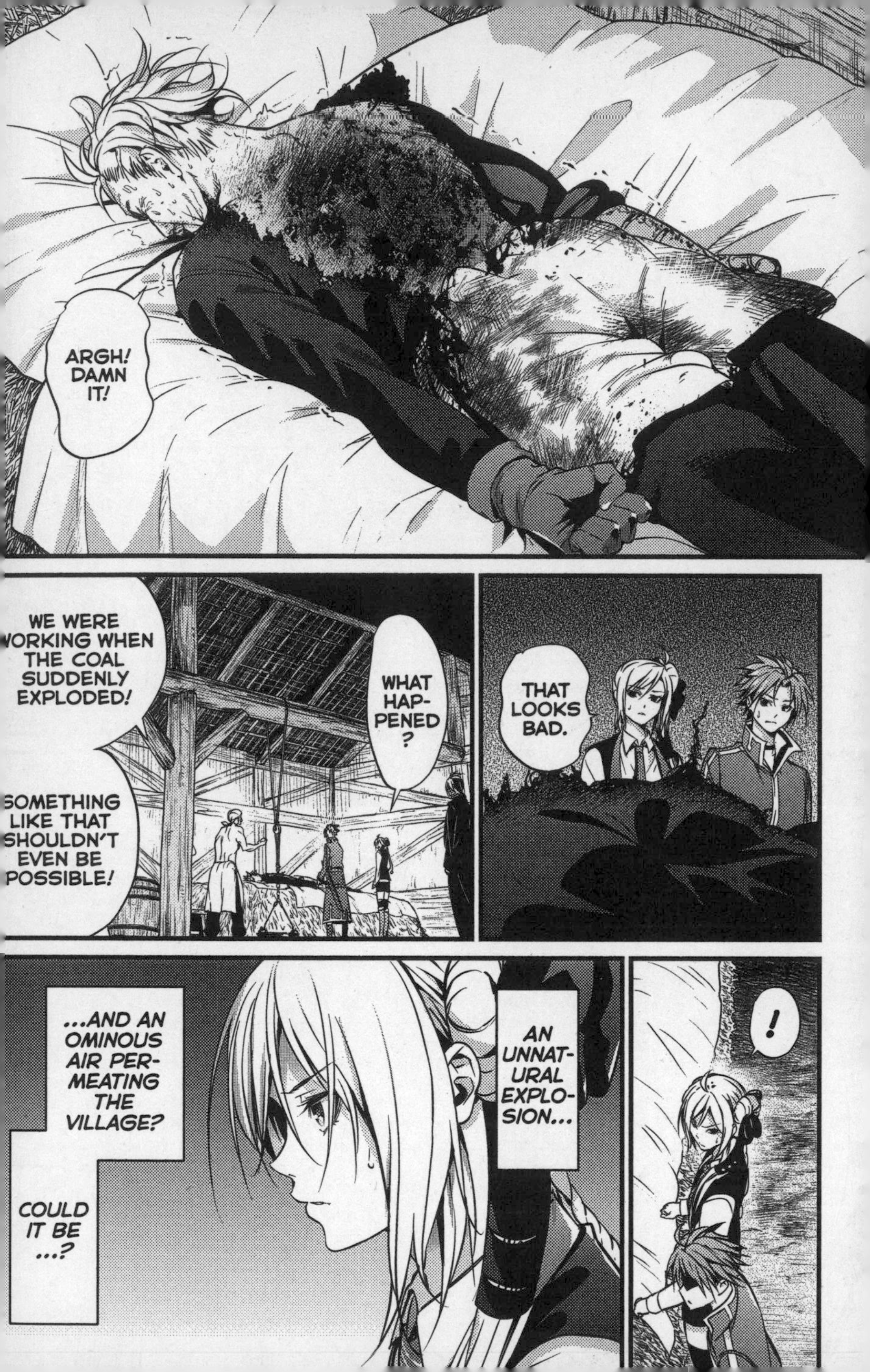
ARGH! DAMN IT!
THAT LOOKS BAD.
WHAT HAPPENED?
WE WERE WORKING WHEN THE COAL SUDDENLY EXPLODED!
SOMETHING LIKE THAT SHOULDN'T EVEN BE POSSIBLE!
!
AN UNNATURAL EXPLOSION...
...AND AN OMINOUS AIR PERMEATING THE VILLAGE?
COULD IT BE ...?

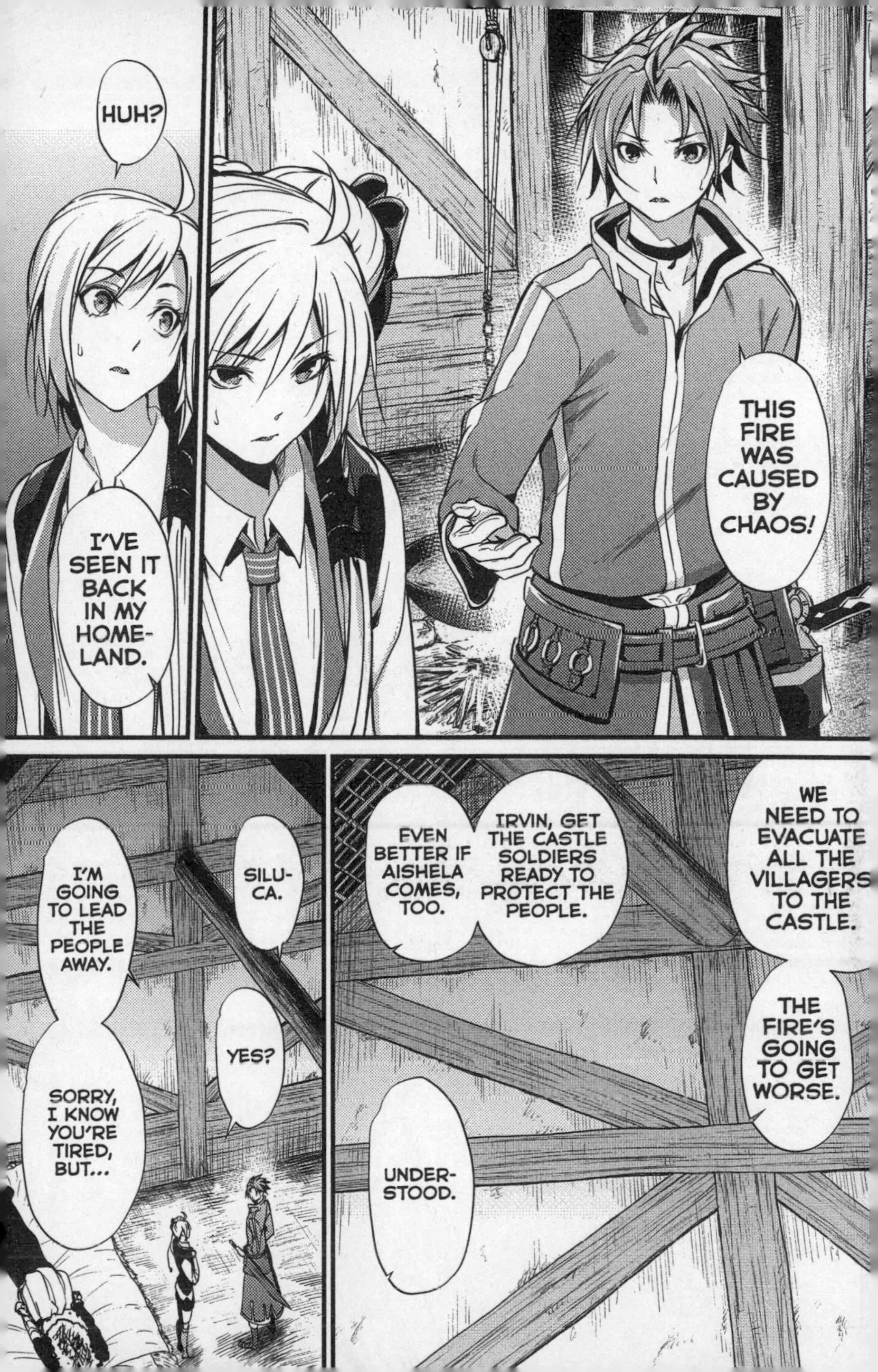
THIS FIRE WAS CAUSED BY CHAOS!
HUH?
I'VE SEEN IT BACK IN MY HOMELAND.
WE NEED TO EVACUATE ALL THE VILLAGERS TO THE CASTLE.
IRVIN, GET THE CASTLE SOLDIERS READY TO PROTECT THE PEOPLE.
EVEN BETTER IF AISHELA COMES, TOO.
THE FIRE'S GOING TO GET WORSE.
UNDER-STOOD.
SILU-CA.
I'M GOING TO LEAD THE PEOPLE AWAY.
YES?
SORRY, I KNOW YOU'RE TIRED, BUT...

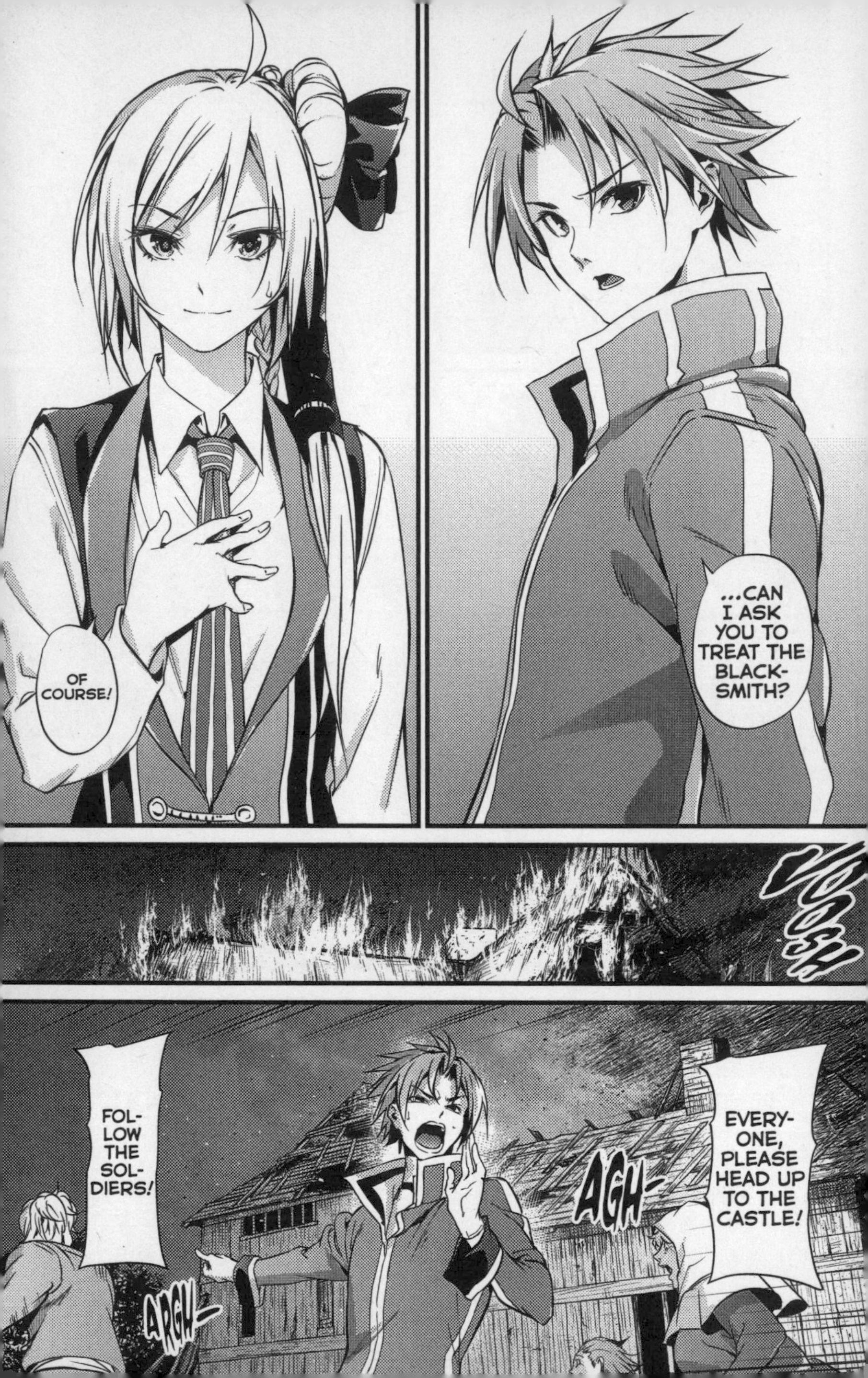
...CAN I ASK YOU TO TREAT THE BLACK-SMITH?
OF COURSE!
VOOSH!
EVERY-ONE, PLEASE HEAD UP TO THE CASTLE!
AGH-
FOL-LOW THE SOL-DIERS!
ARGH-

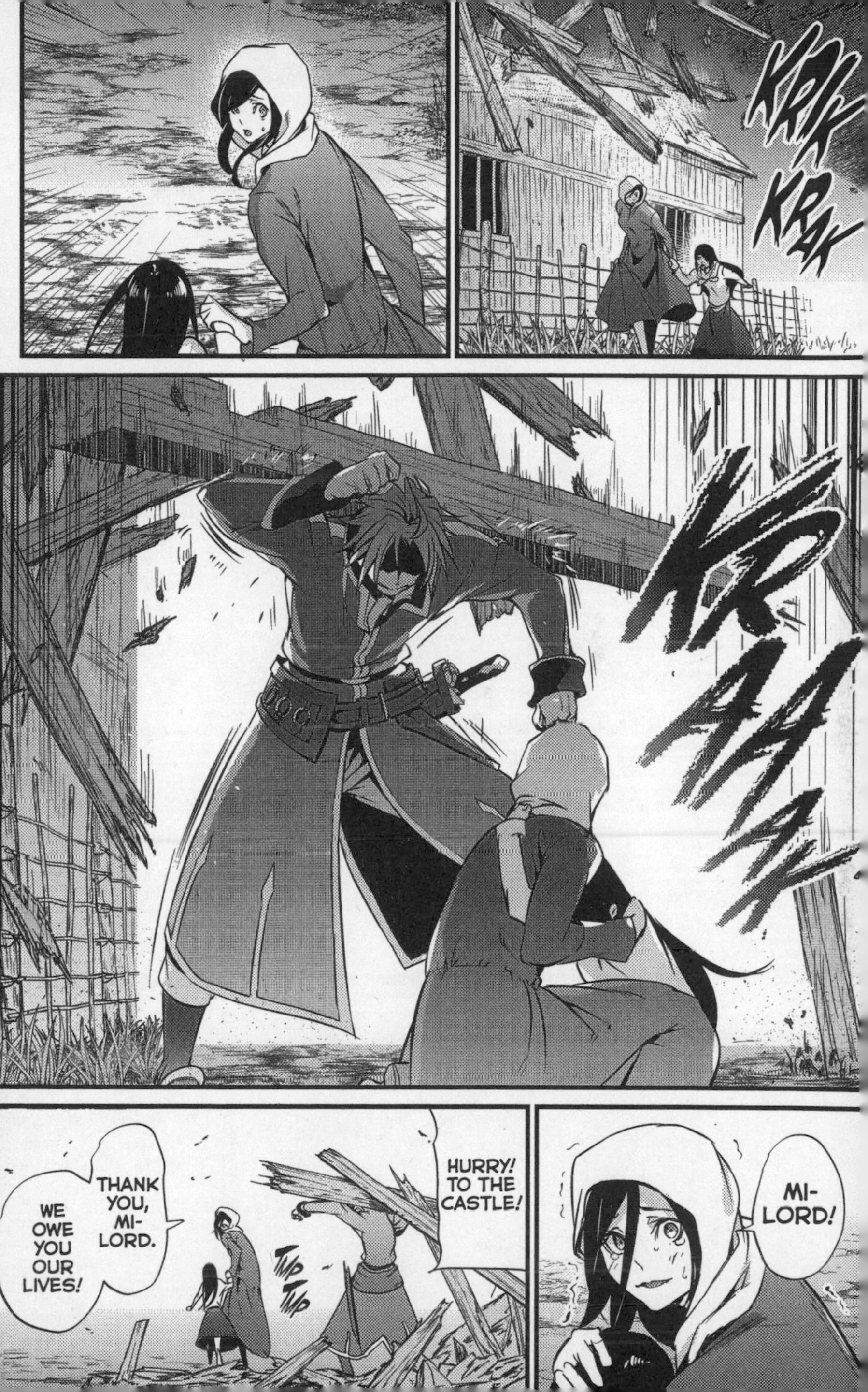
KRAK KRAK
KRAAAAK
MI-LORD!
HURRY! TO THE CASTLE!
TMP TMP
THANK YOU, MI-LORD.
WE OWE YOU OUR LIVES!

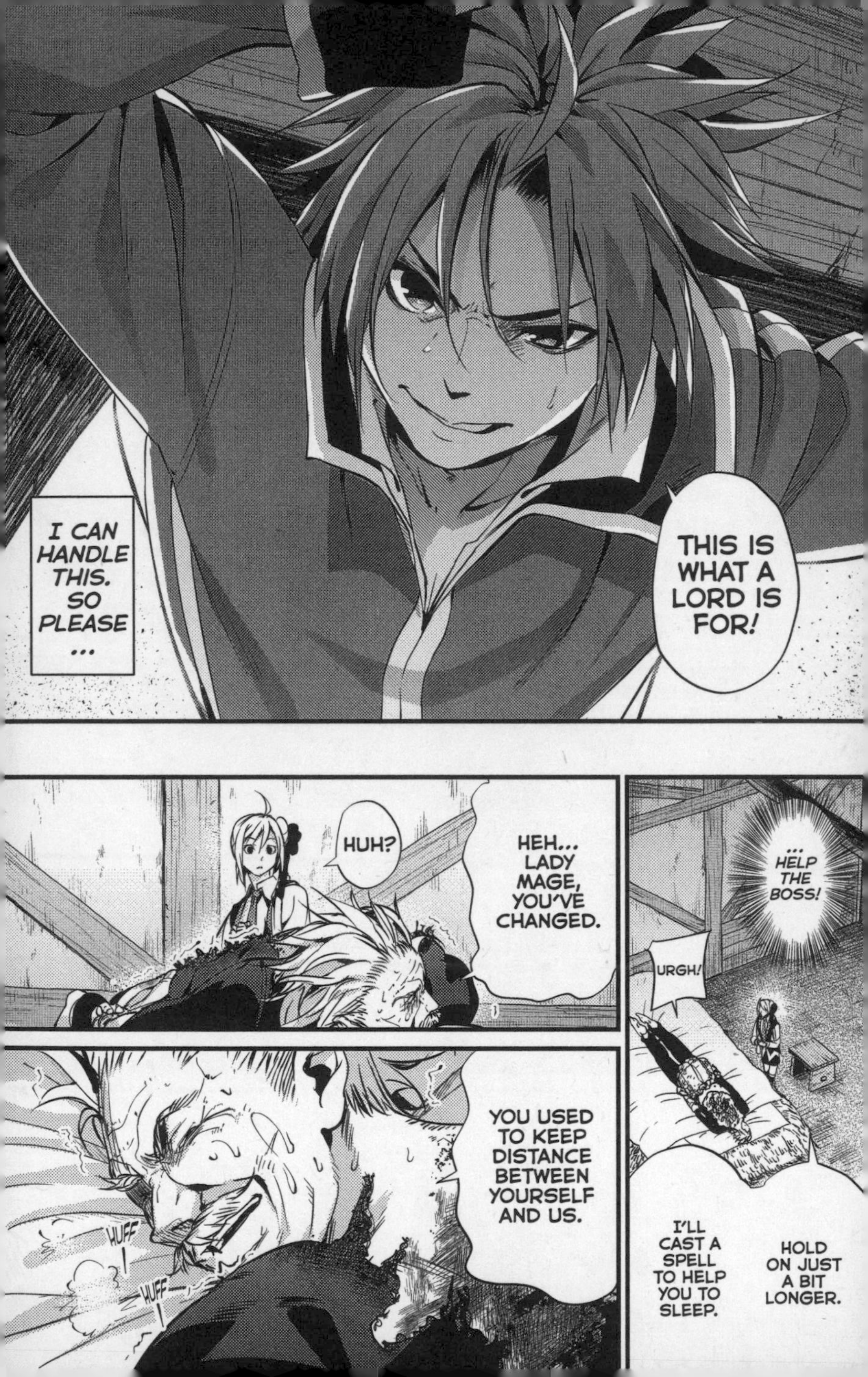
THIS IS WHAT A LORD IS FOR!
I CAN HANDLE THIS. SO PLEASE ...
... HELP THE BOSS!
URGH!
HOLD ON JUST A BIT LONGER.
I'LL CAST A SPELL TO HELP YOU TO SLEEP.
HEH... LADY MAGE, YOU'VE CHANGED.
HUH?
YOU USED TO KEEP DISTANCE BETWEEN YOURSELF AND US.
HUFF!
HUFF!

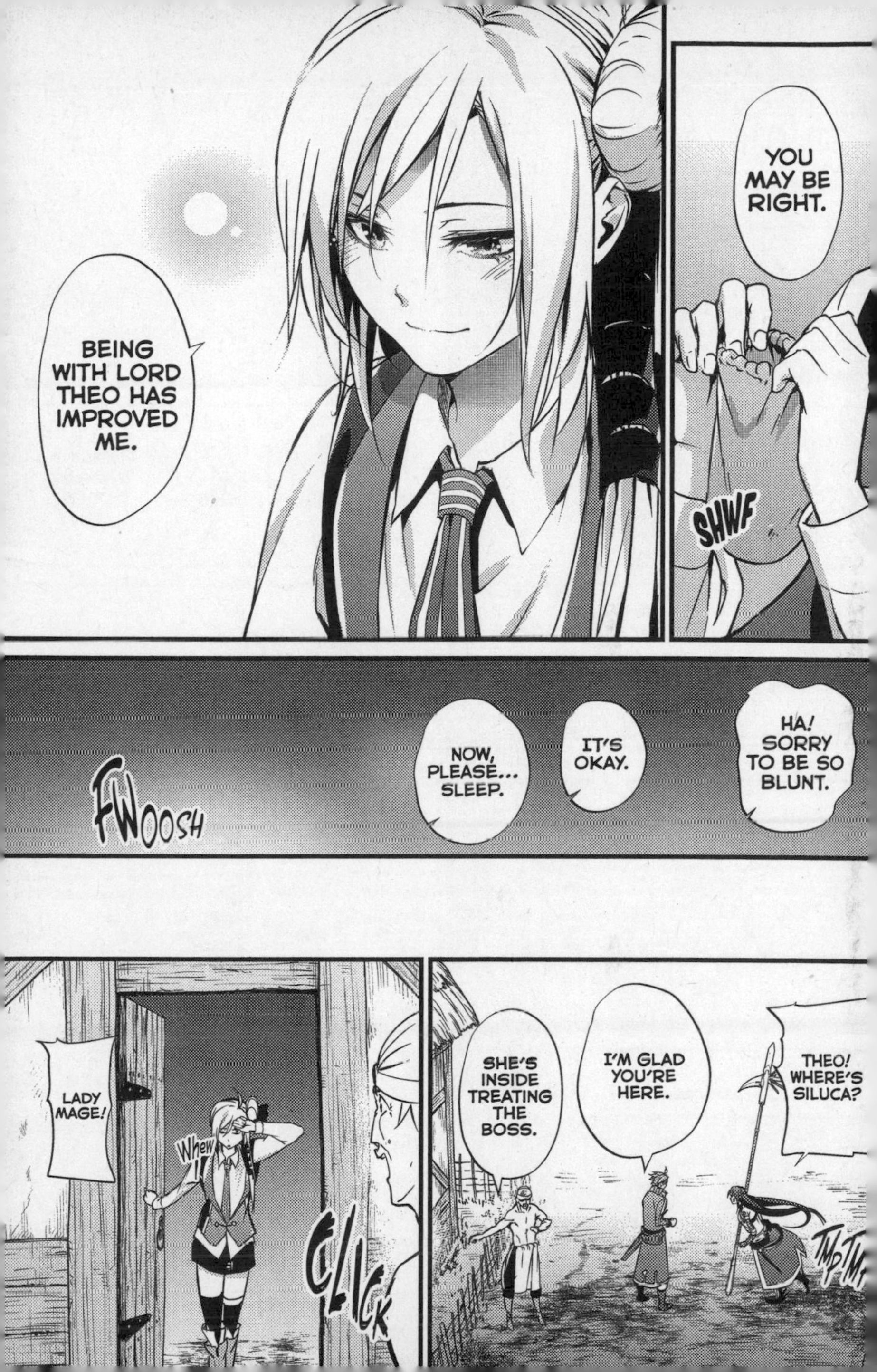
YOU MAY BE RIGHT.
SHWF
BEING WITH LORD THEO HAS IMPROVED ME.
HA! SORRY TO BE SO BLUNT.
IT'S OKAY.
NOW, PLEASE... SLEEP.
FWOOSH
THEO! WHERE'S SILUCA?
TMP-TM
I'M GLAD YOU'RE HERE.
SHE'S INSIDE TREATING THE BOSS.
CLICK
LADY MAGE!
Whew

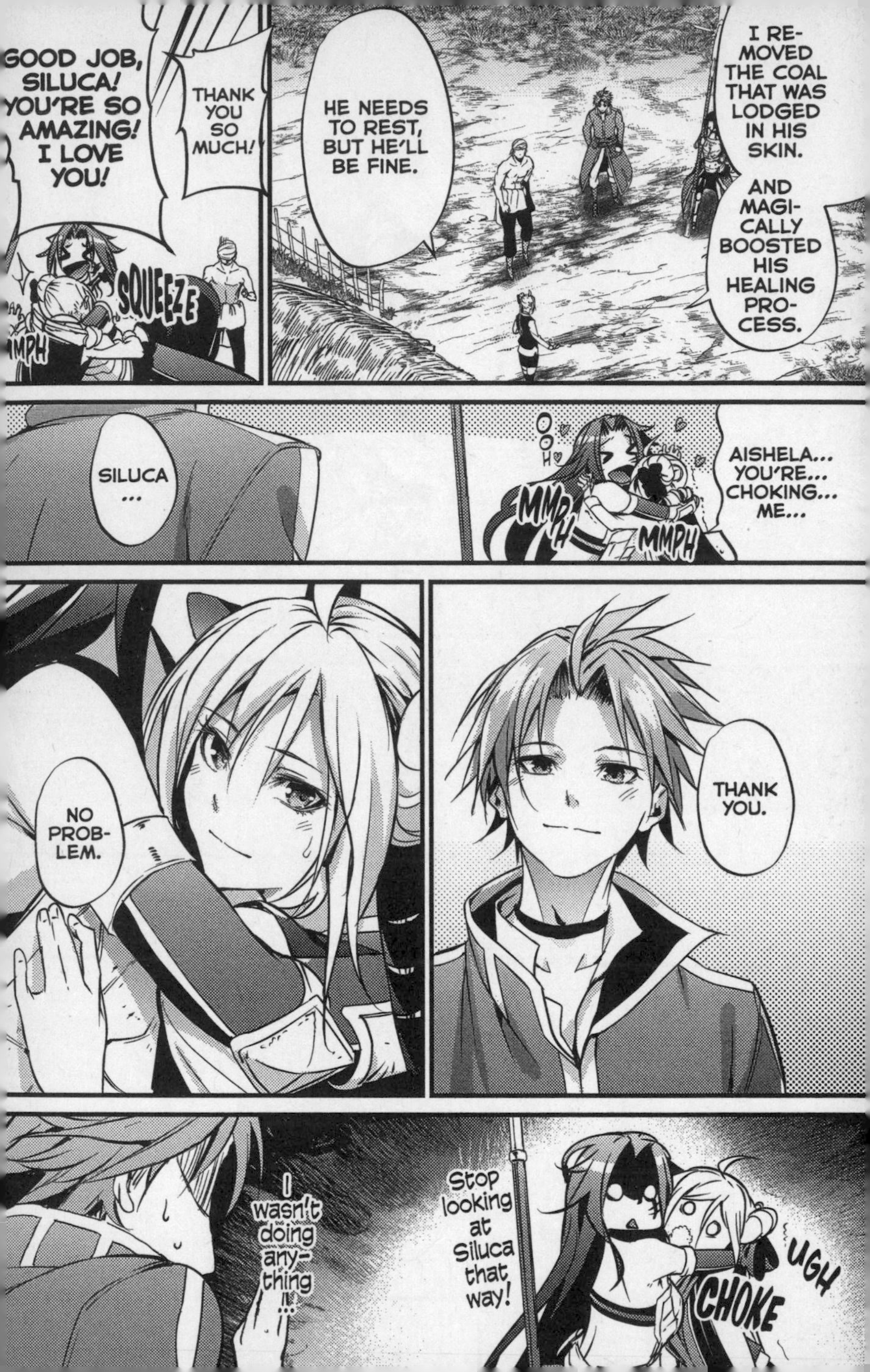
I RE-MOVED THE COAL THAT WAS LODGED IN HIS SKIN.
AND MAGI-CALLY BOOSTED HIS HEALING PRO-CESS.
HE NEEDS TO REST, BUT HE'LL BE FINE.
THANK YOU SO MUCH!
GOOD JOB, SILUCA! YOU'RE SO AMAZING! I LOVE YOU!
SQUEEZE
MMPH
OOH
AISHELA... YOU'RE... CHOKING... ME...
MMPH
MMPH
SILUCA...
THANK YOU.
NO PROB-LEM.
UGH
CHOKE
Stop looking at Siluca that way!
I wasn't doing any-thing!!

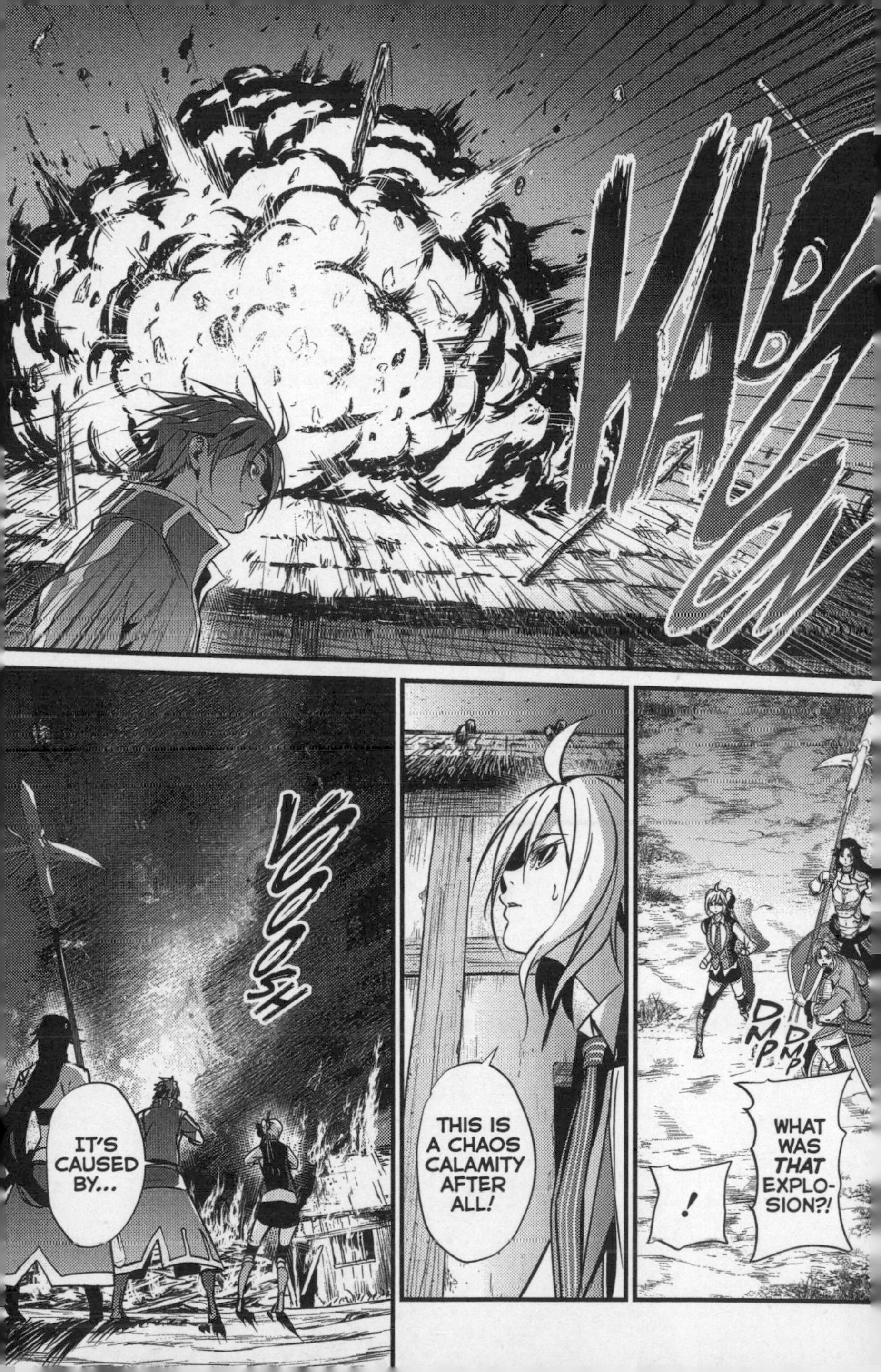
!
WHAT WAS THAT EXPLOSION?!
DMP DMP
THIS IS A CHAOS CALAMITY AFTER ALL!
VWOOSH
IT'S CAUSED BY...

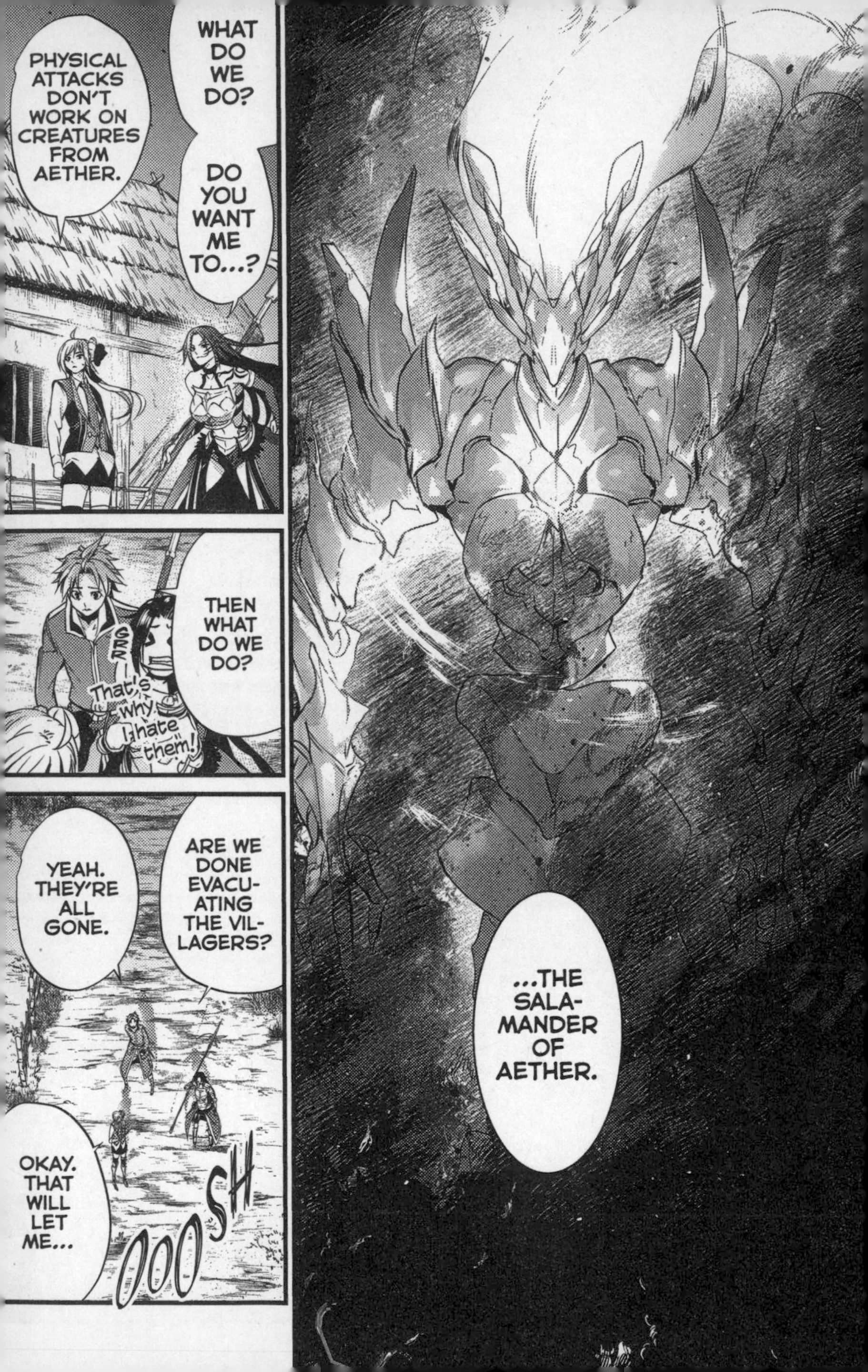
WHAT DO WE DO?
DO YOU WANT ME TO...?
PHYSICAL ATTACKS DON'T WORK ON CREATURES FROM AETHER.
THEN WHAT DO WE DO?
GRR
That's why I hate them!
ARE WE DONE EVACU-ATING THE VIL-LAGERS?
YEAH. THEY'RE ALL GONE.
OKAY. THAT WILL LET ME...
OOOSH
...THE SALA-MANDER OF AETHER.

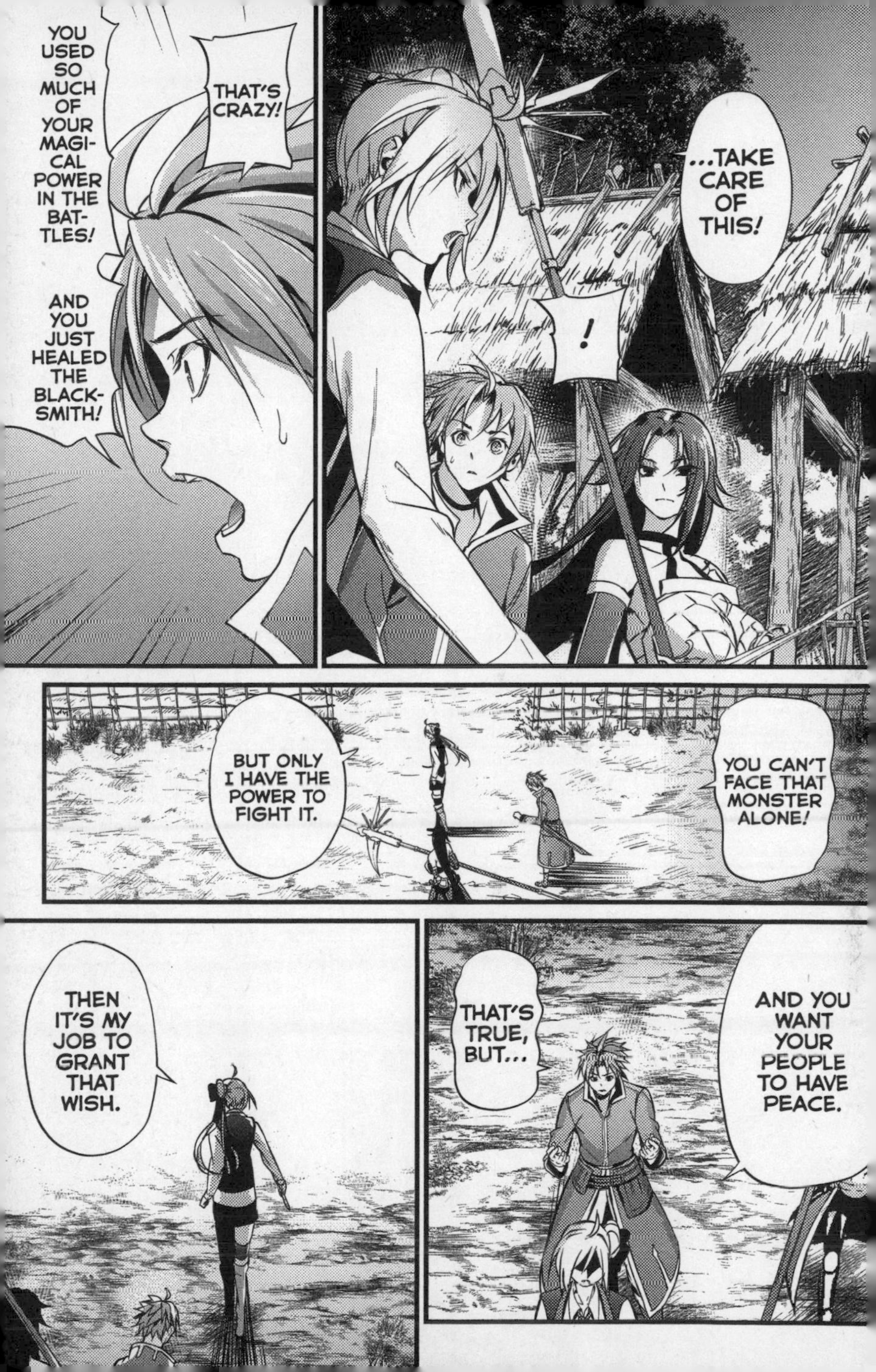
...TAKE CARE OF THIS!
!
THAT'S CRAZY!
YOU USED SO MUCH OF YOUR MAGICAL POWER IN THE BATTLES!
AND YOU JUST HEALED THE BLACKSMITH!
YOU CAN'T FACE THAT MONSTER ALONE!
BUT ONLY I HAVE THE POWER TO FIGHT IT.
AND YOU WANT YOUR PEOPLE TO HAVE PEACE.
THAT'S TRUE, BUT...
THEN IT'S MY JOB TO GRANT THAT WISH.

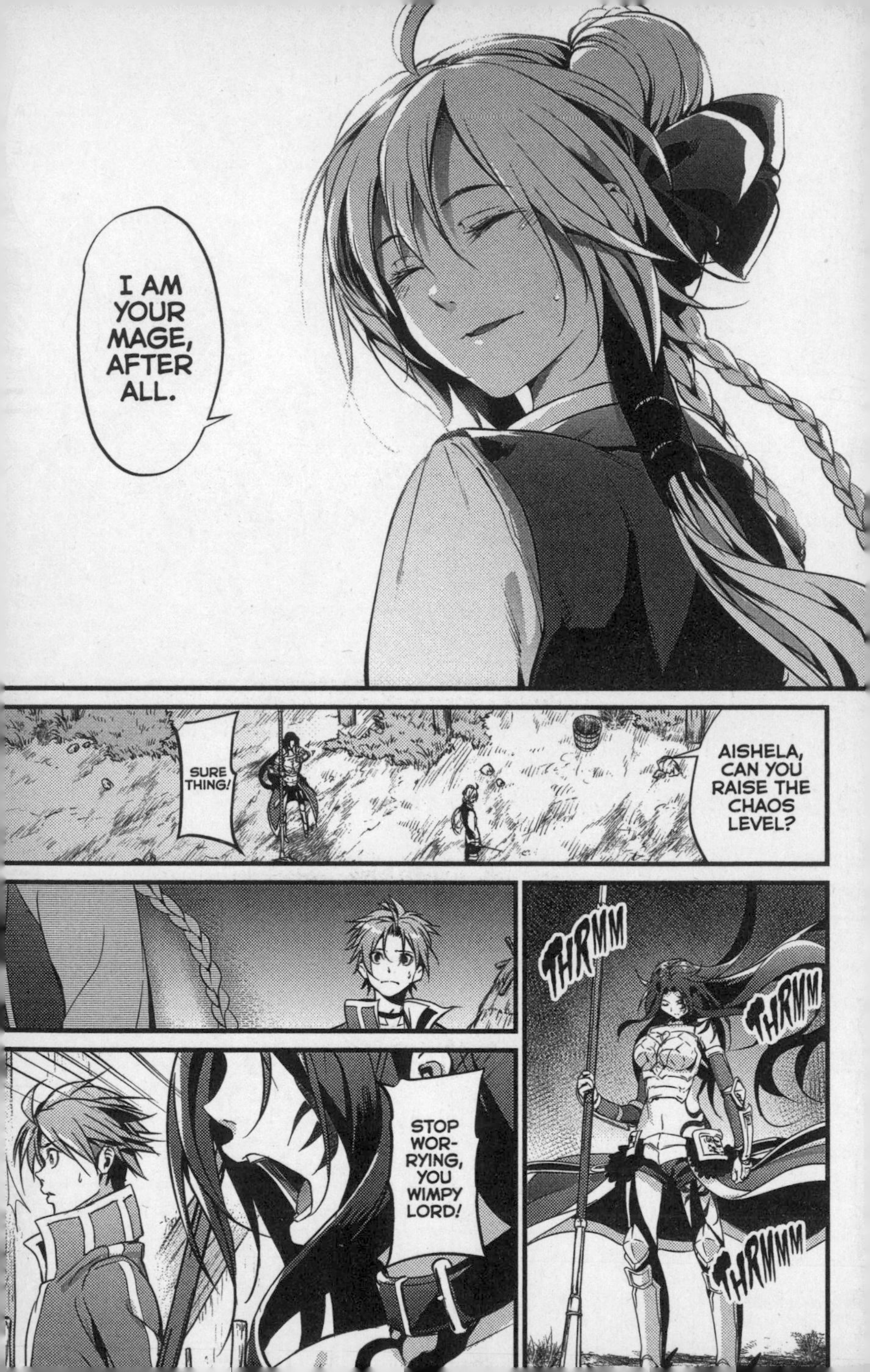
I AM YOUR MAGE, AFTER ALL.
AISHELA, CAN YOU RAISE THE CHAOS LEVEL?
SURE THING!
THRMM
THRMM
THRMMM
STOP WOR-RYING, YOU WIMPY LORD!

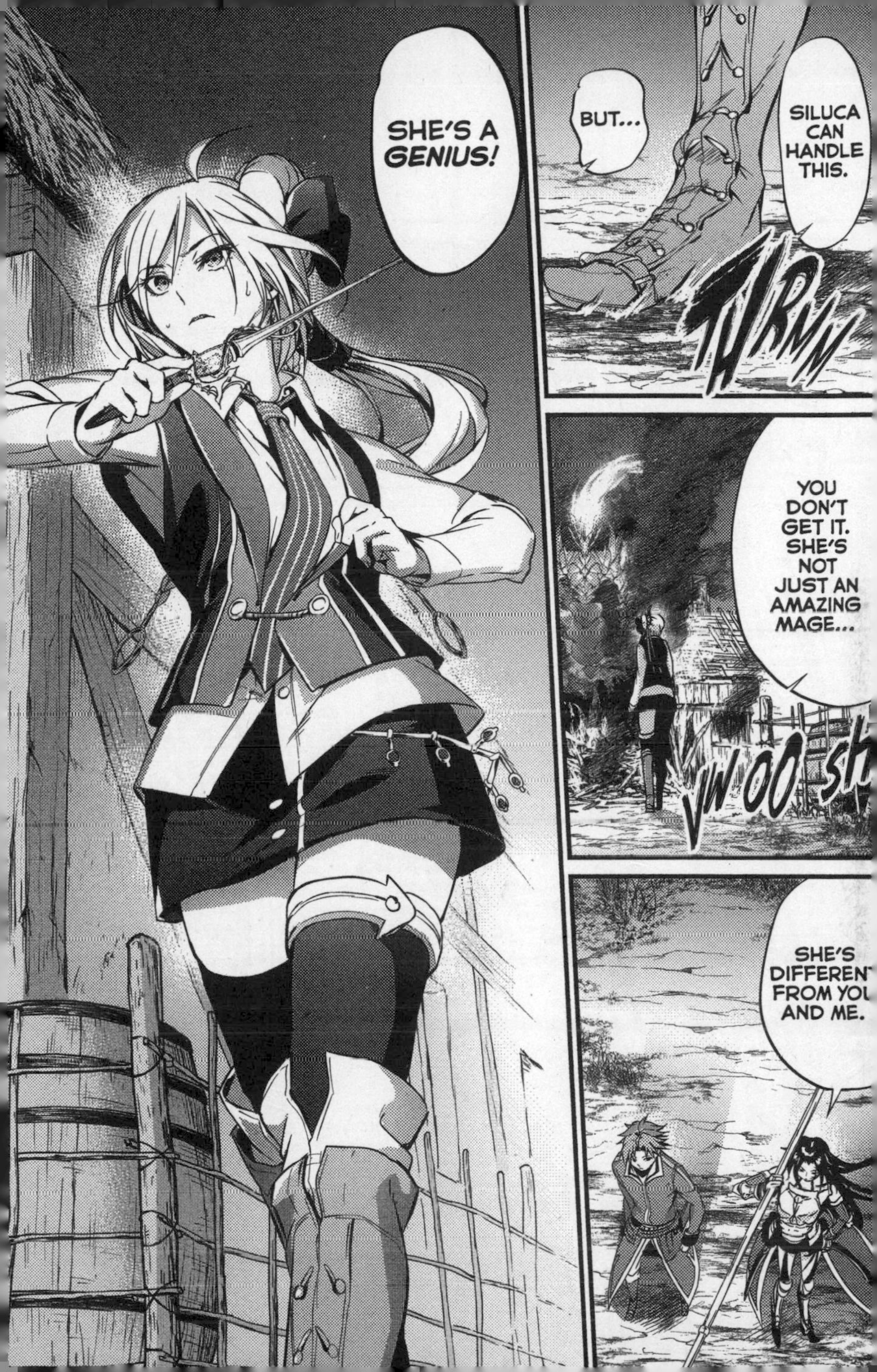
SILUCA CAN HANDLE THIS.
BUT...
YOU DON'T GET IT. SHE'S NOT JUST AN AMAZING MAGE...
SHE'S DIFFERENT FROM YOU AND ME.
SHE'S A GENIUS!

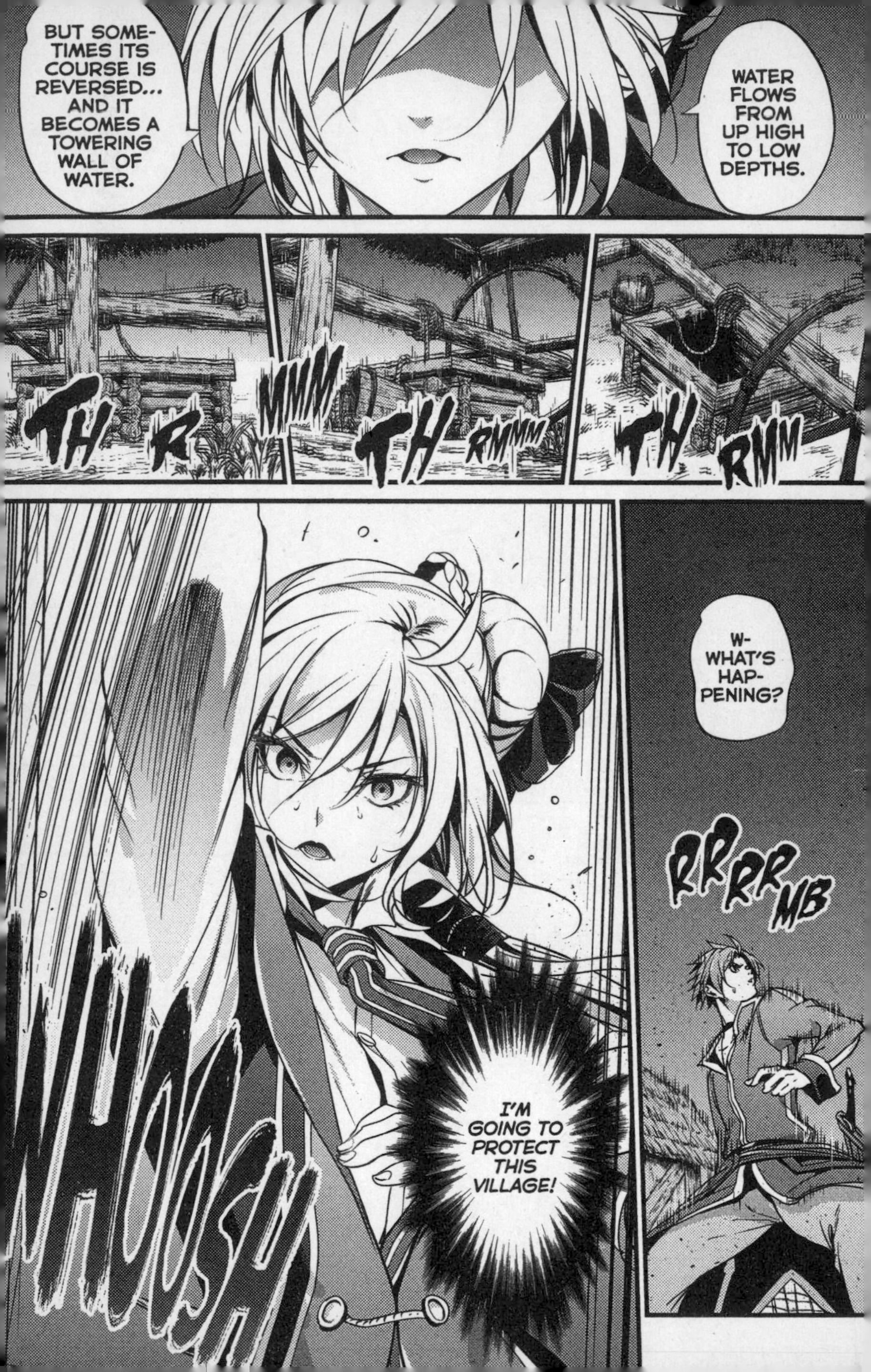
WATER FLOWS FROM UP HIGH TO LOW DEPTHS.
BUT SOMETIMES ITS COURSE IS REVERSED... AND IT BECOMES A TOWERING WALL OF WATER.
TH RMM
TH RMMM
TH R MMM
W-WHAT'S HAPPENING?
RRRRRMB
I'M GOING TO PROTECT THIS VILLAGE!
WHOOSH

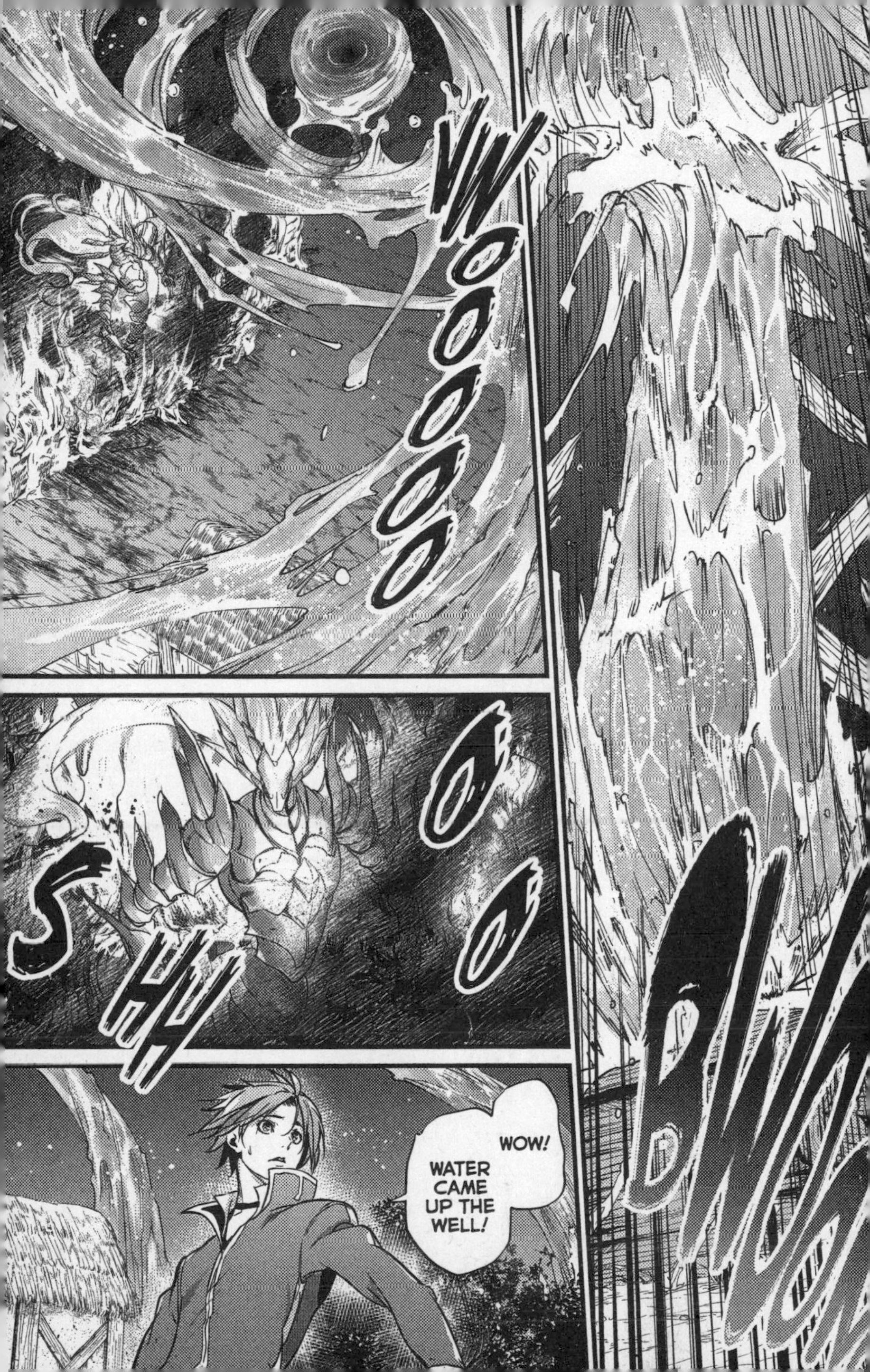
WOW!
WATER CAME UP THE WELL!

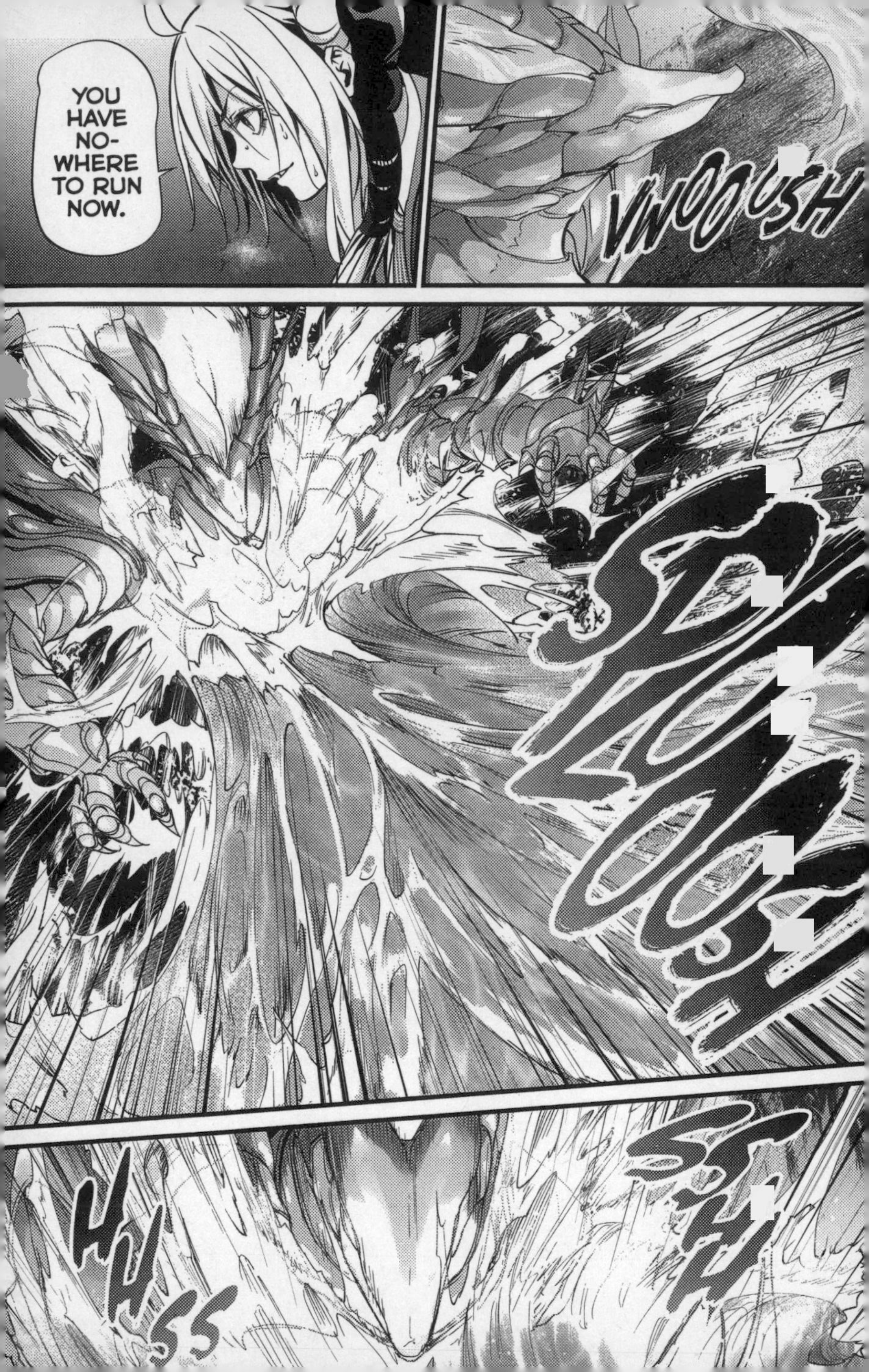
VWOOOSH
YOU HAVE NO-WHERE TO RUN NOW.

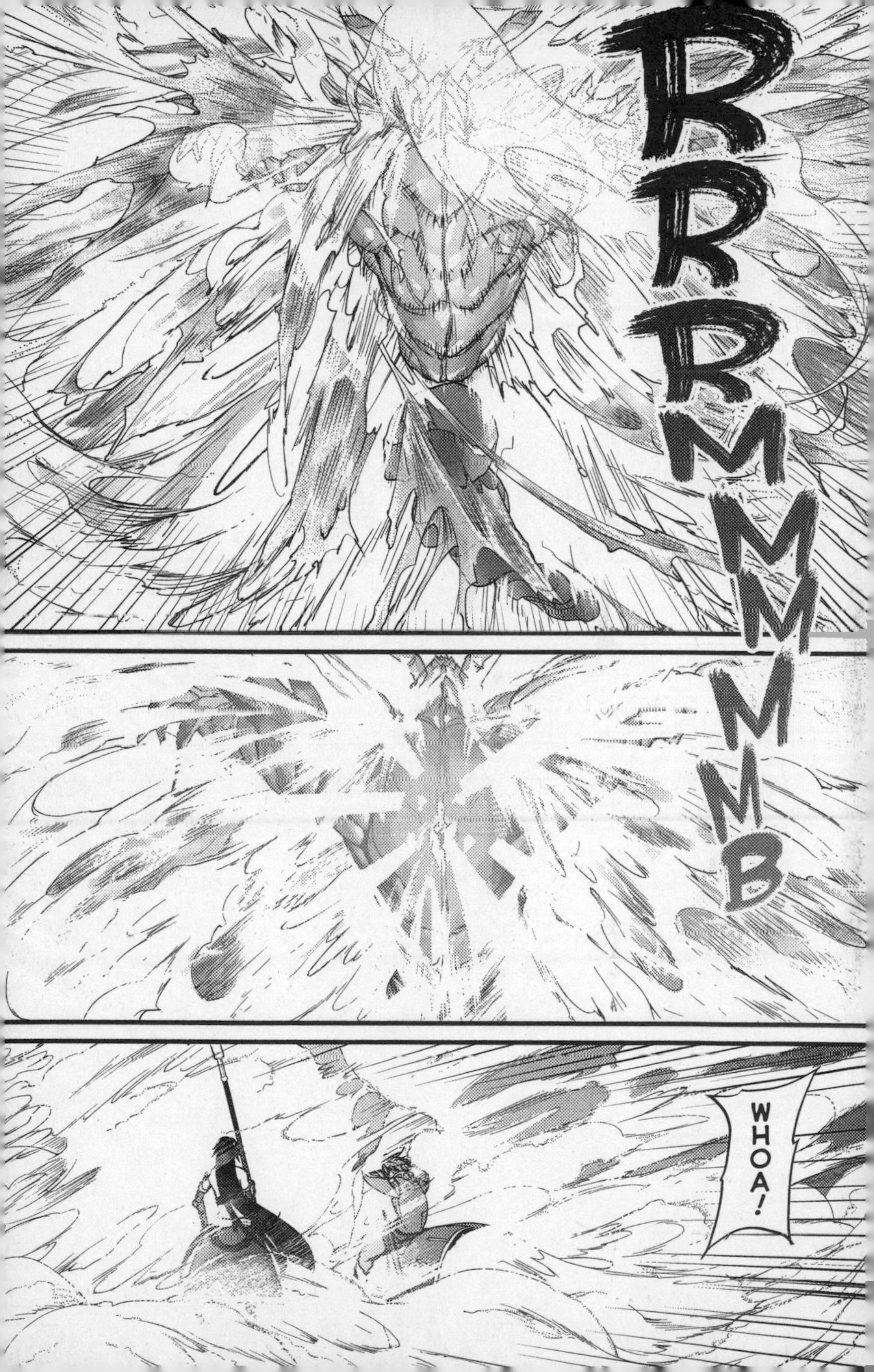
RRRMMMMMB
WHOA!

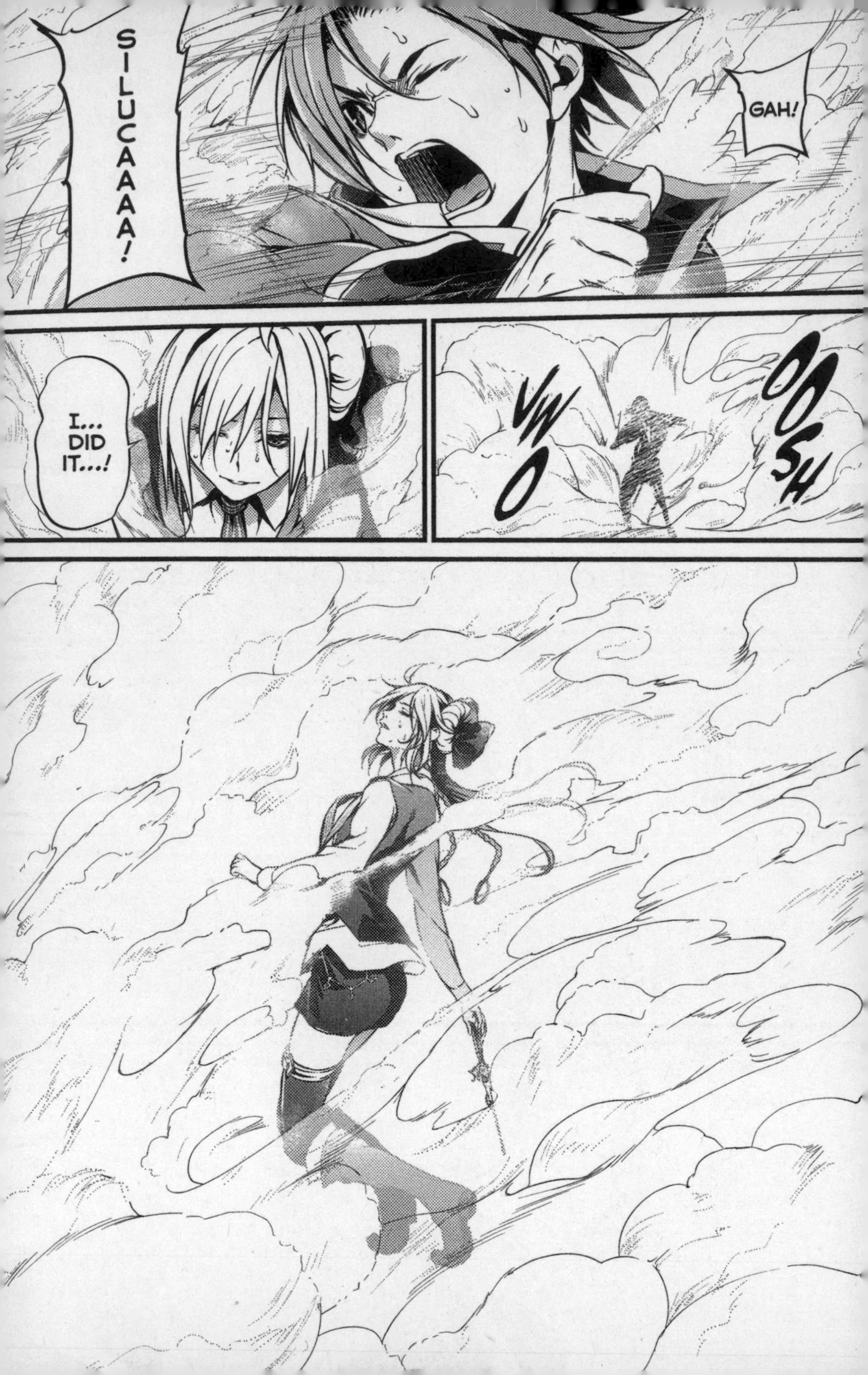
GAH!
SILUCAAAA!
VWO
OOSH
I... DID IT...!

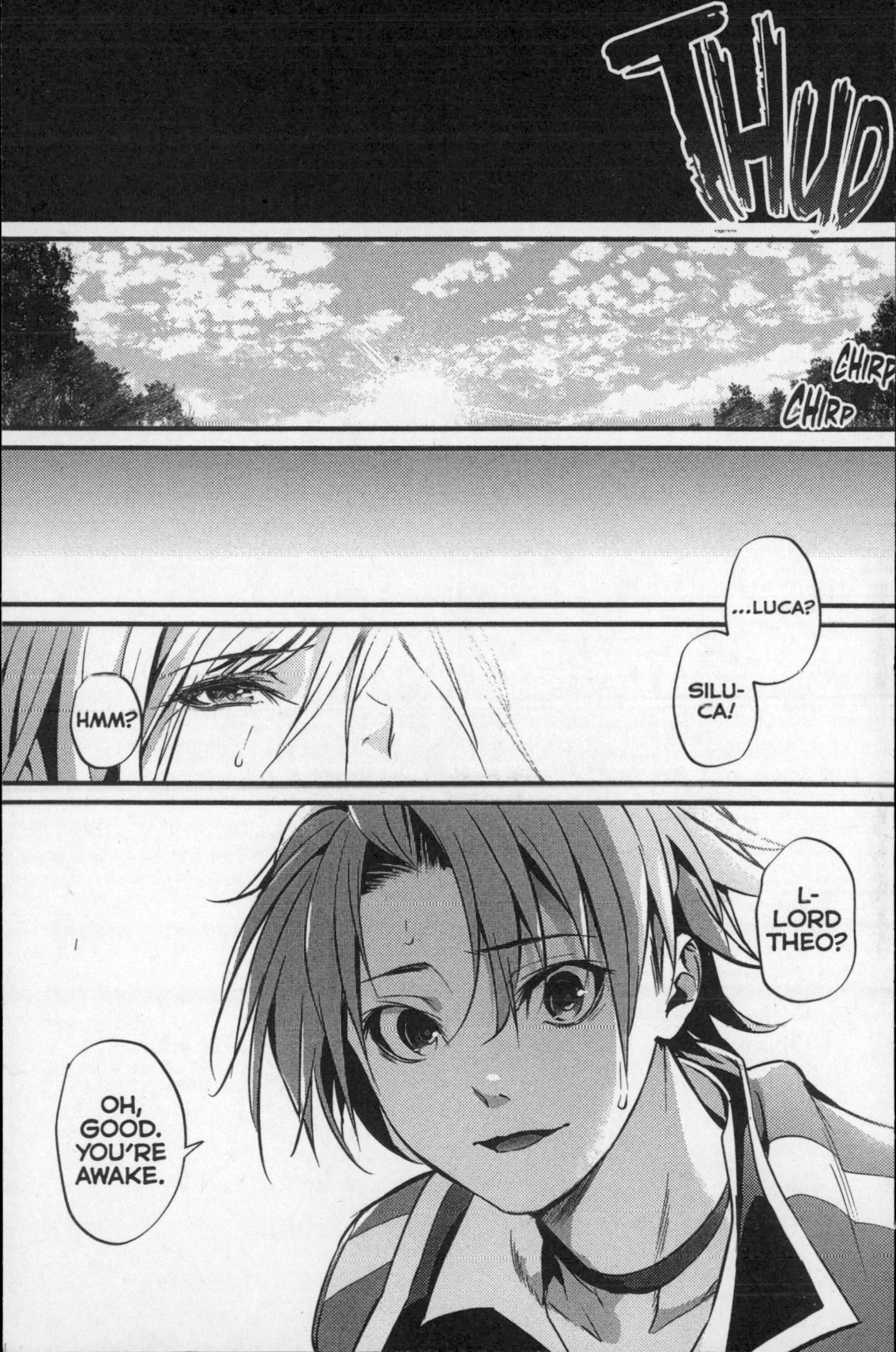
THUD
CHIRP
CHIRP
...LUCA?
SILU-CA!
HMM?
L-LORD THEO?
OH, GOOD. YOU'RE AWAKE.

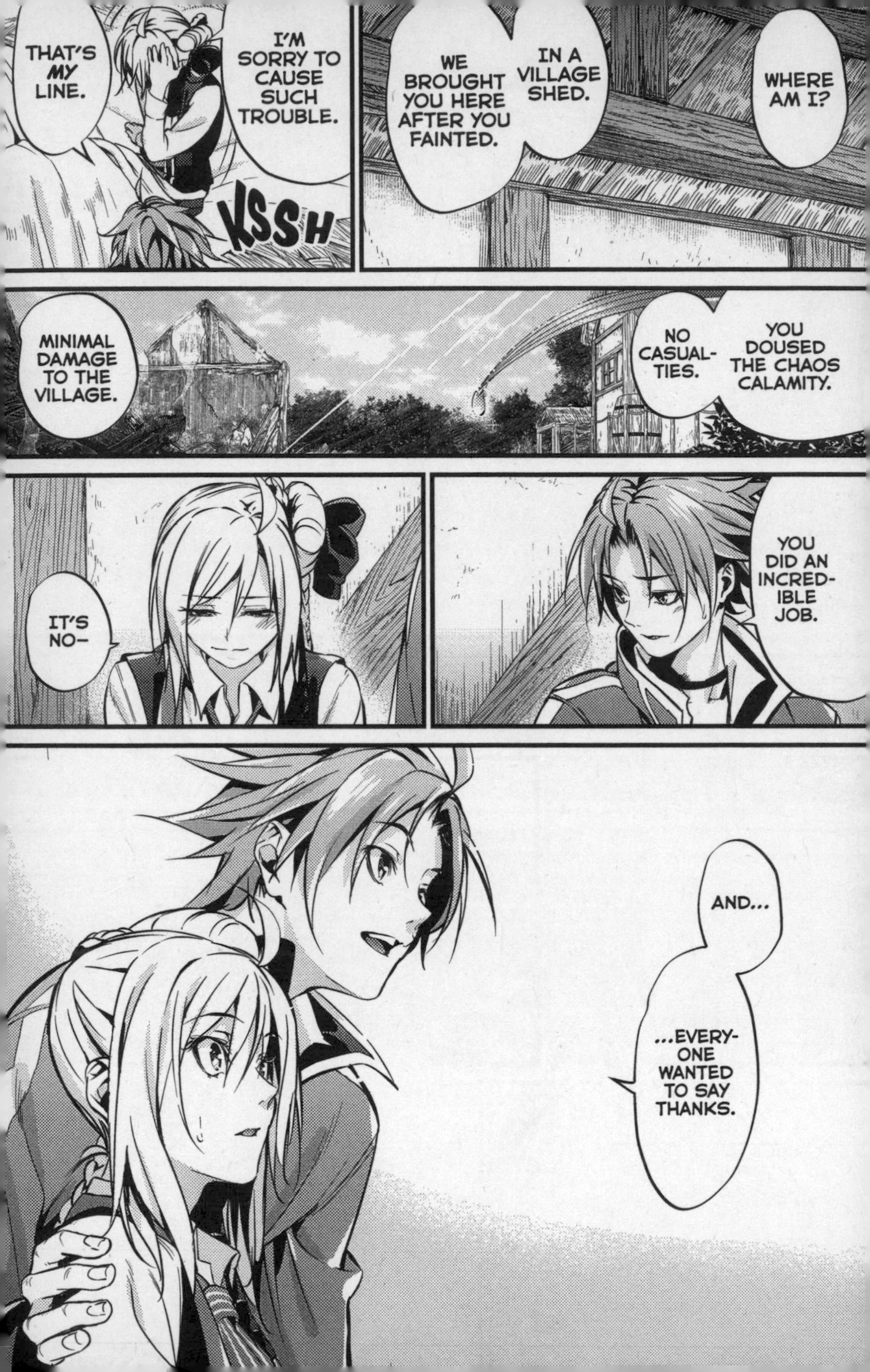
WHERE AM I?
IN A VILLAGE SHED.
WE BROUGHT YOU HERE AFTER YOU FAINTED.
I'M SORRY TO CAUSE SUCH TROUBLE.
KSSH
THAT'S *MY* LINE.
YOU DOUSED THE CHAOS CALAMITY.
NO CASUAL-TIES.
MINIMAL DAMAGE TO THE VILLAGE.
YOU DID AN INCRED-IBLE JOB.
IT'S NO–
AND...
...EVERY-ONE WANTED TO SAY THANKS.

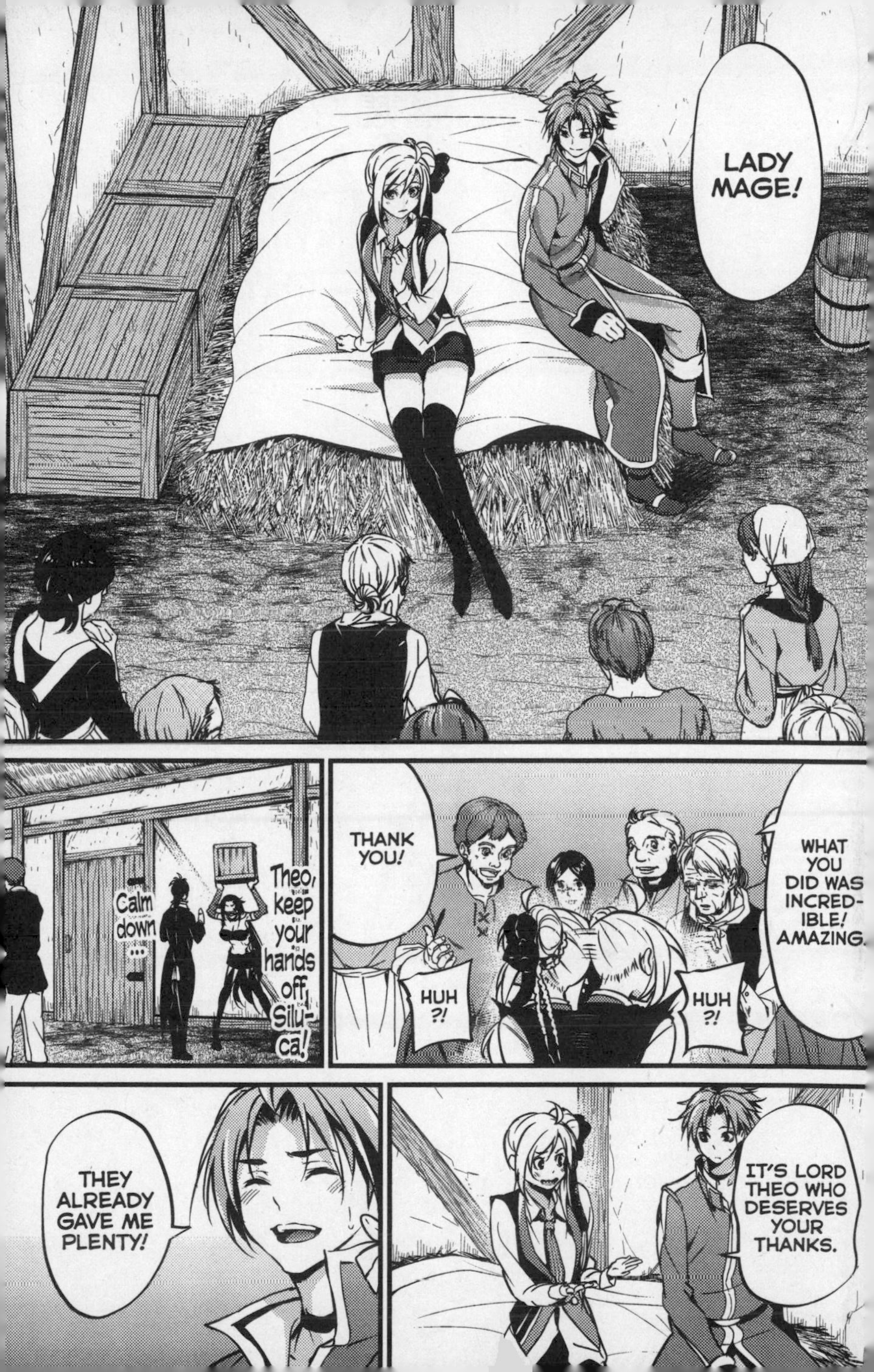
LADY MAGE!
WHAT YOU DID WAS INCREDIBLE! AMAZING.
THANK YOU!
HUH ?!
HUH ?!
Theo, keep your hands off, Siluca!
Calm down...
IT'S LORD THEO WHO DESERVES YOUR THANKS.
THEY ALREADY GAVE ME PLENTY!

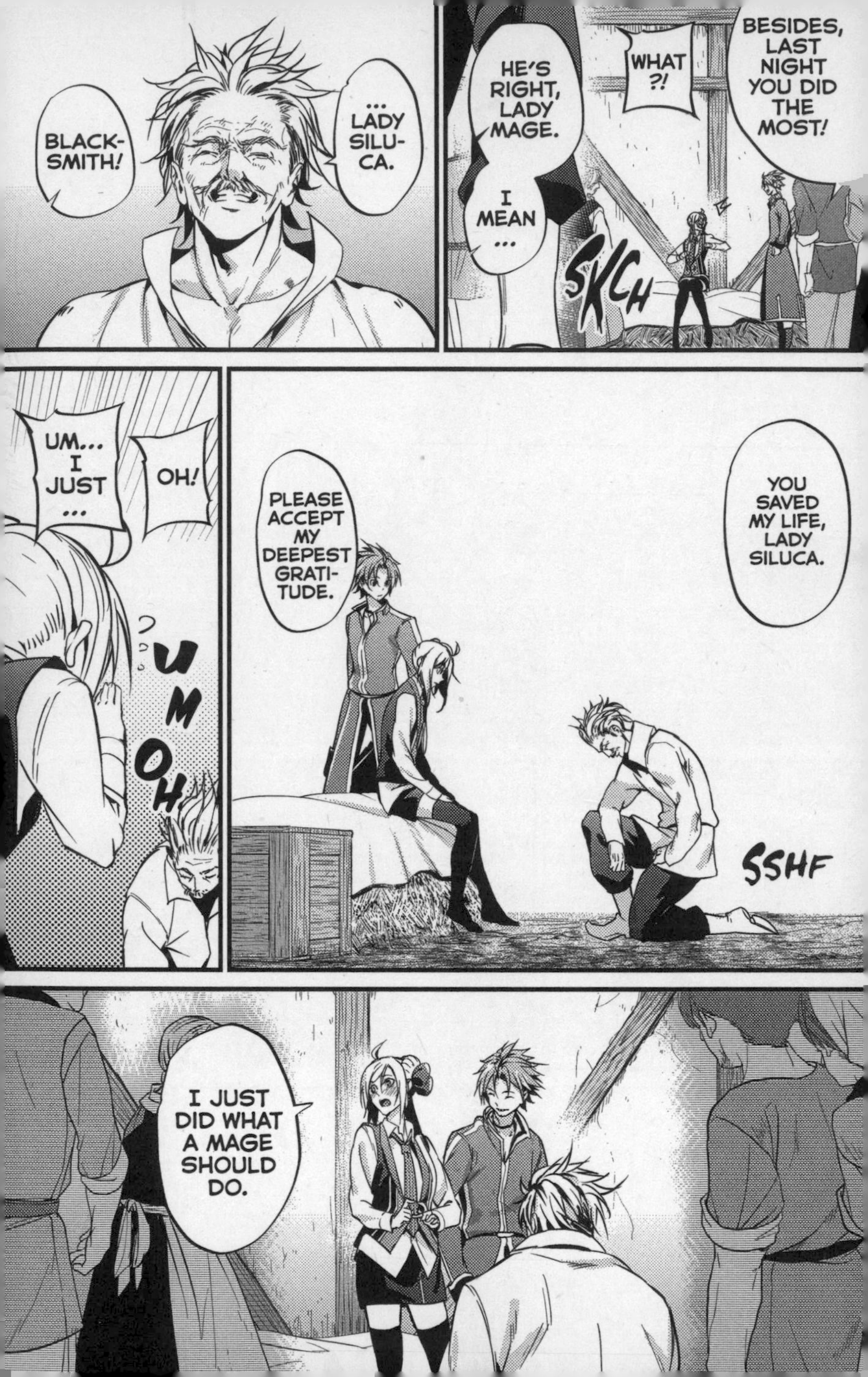
BESIDES, LAST NIGHT YOU DID THE MOST!
WHAT?!
HE'S RIGHT, LADY MAGE.
I MEAN ...
SKCH
... LADY SILUCA.
BLACKSMITH!
YOU SAVED MY LIFE, LADY SILUCA.
PLEASE ACCEPT MY DEEPEST GRATITUDE.
SSHF
OH!
UM... I JUST ...
UM OH
I JUST DID WHAT A MAGE SHOULD DO.

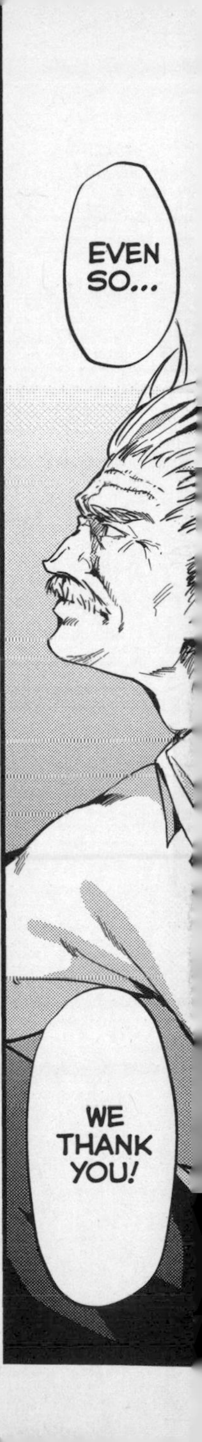
EVEN SO...
WE THANK YOU!
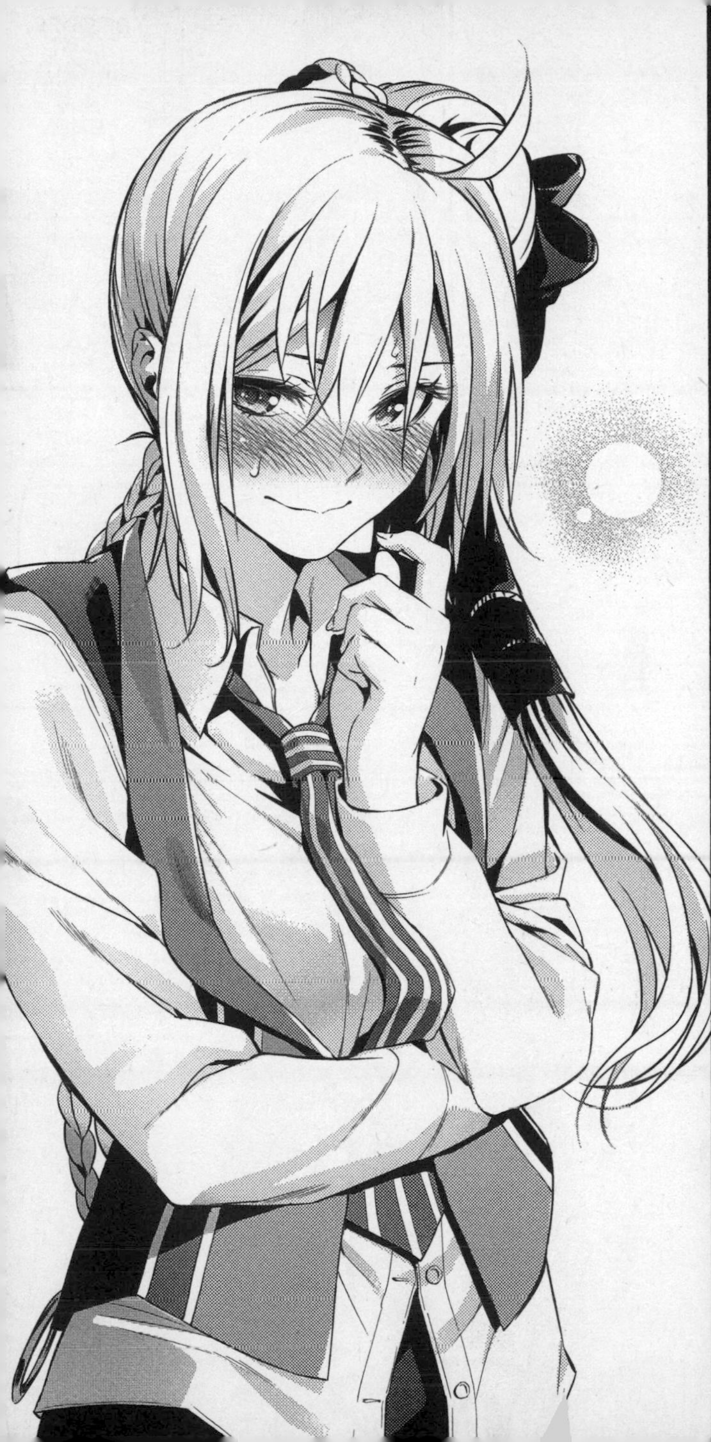

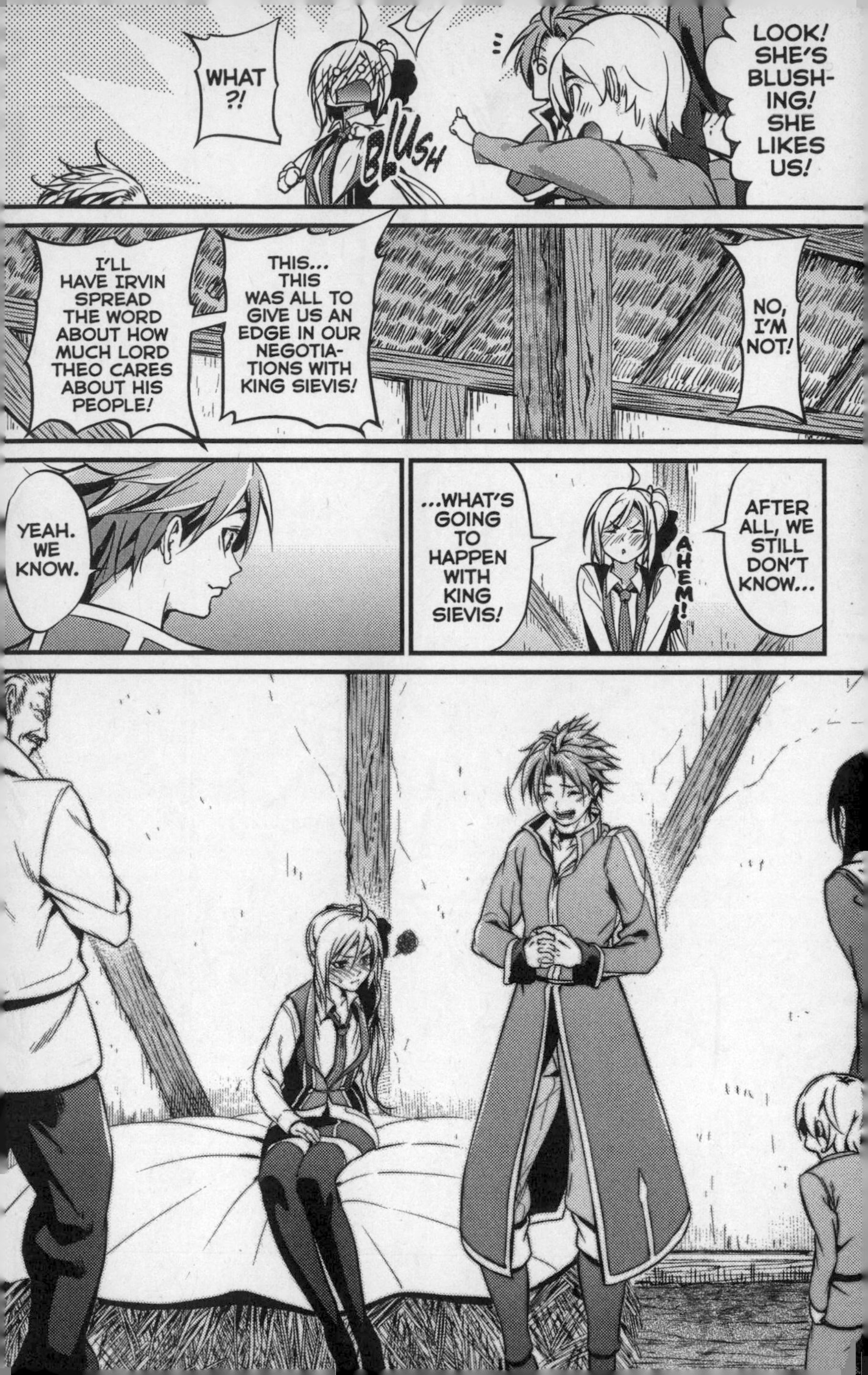
LOOK! SHE'S BLUSHING! SHE LIKES US!
WHAT?!
BLUSH
NO, I'M NOT!
THIS... THIS WAS ALL TO GIVE US AN EDGE IN OUR NEGOTIATIONS WITH KING SIEVIS!
I'LL HAVE IRVIN SPREAD THE WORD ABOUT HOW MUCH LORD THEO CARES ABOUT HIS PEOPLE!
AFTER ALL, WE STILL DON'T KNOW...
AHEM!
...WHAT'S GOING TO HAPPEN WITH KING SIEVIS!
YEAH. WE KNOW.

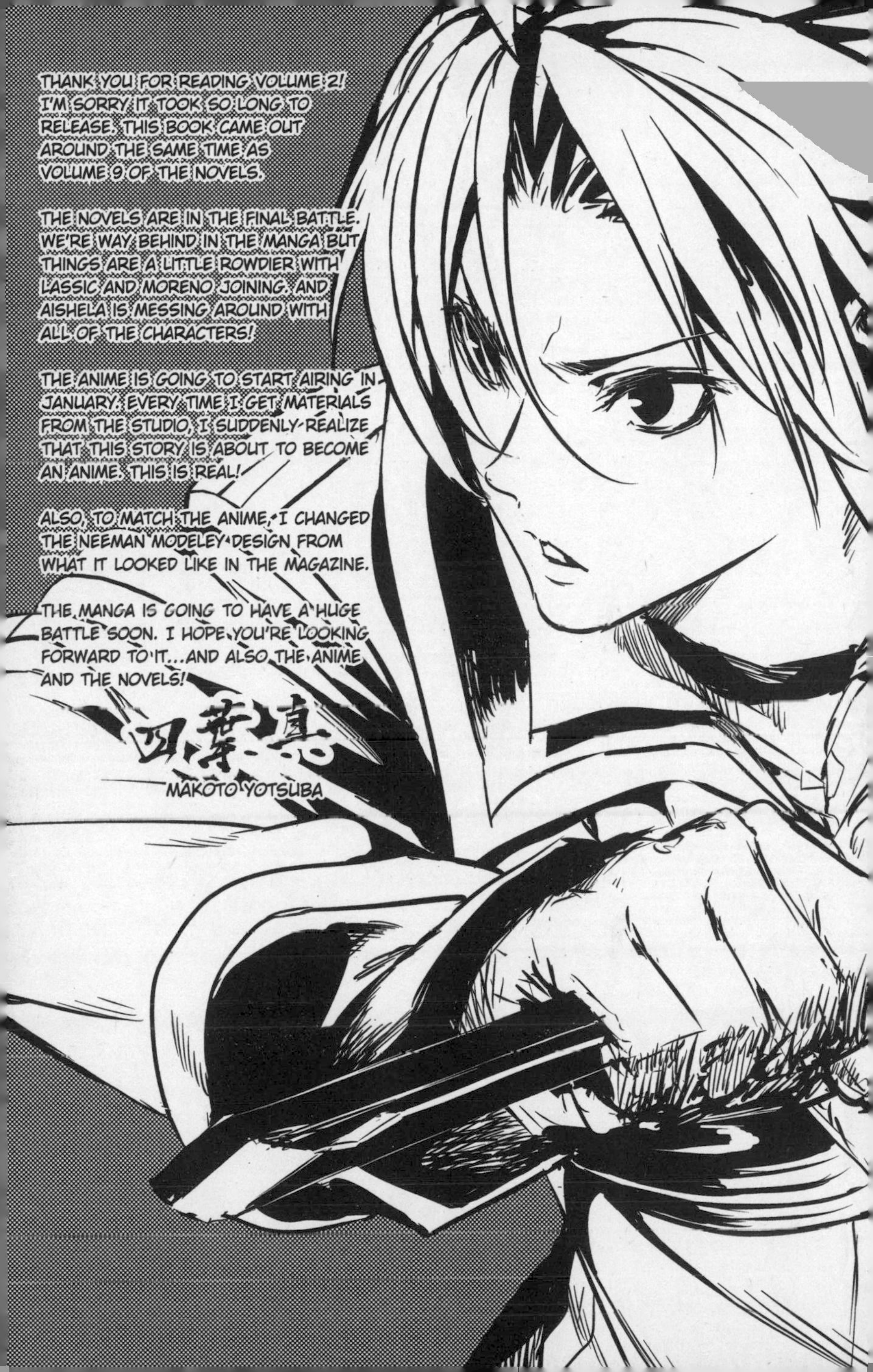

THANK YOU FOR READING VOLUME 2! I'M SORRY IT TOOK SO LONG TO RELEASE. THIS BOOK CAME OUT AROUND THE SAME TIME AS VOLUME 9 OF THE NOVELS.

THE NOVELS ARE IN THE FINAL BATTLE. WE'RE WAY BEHIND IN THE MANGA BUT THINGS ARE A LITTLE ROWDIER WITH LASSIC AND MORENO JOINING. AND AISHELA IS MESSING AROUND WITH ALL OF THE CHARACTERS!

THE ANIME IS GOING TO START AIRING IN JANUARY. EVERY TIME I GET MATERIALS FROM THE STUDIO, I SUDDENLY REALIZE THAT THIS STORY IS ABOUT TO BECOME AN ANIME. THIS IS REAL!

ALSO, TO MATCH THE ANIME, I CHANGED THE NEEMAN MODELEY DESIGN FROM WHAT IT LOOKED LIKE IN THE MAGAZINE.

THE MANGA IS GOING TO HAVE A HUGE BATTLE SOON. I HOPE YOU'RE LOOKING FORWARD TO IT...AND ALSO THE ANIME AND THE NOVELS!

四葉真

MAKOTO YOTSUBA

RECORD OF GRANCREST WAR

VOLUME 2

Original Story by **Ryo Mizuno**
Story & Art by **Makoto Yotsuba**
Character Design by **Miyuu**

Translation: **Satsuki Yamashita**
Touch-Up Art & Lettering: **James Gaubatz**
English Adaptation: **Steven "Stan!" Brown**
Design: **Julian [JR] Robinson**
Editor: **David Brothers**

GRANCREST SENKI by Ryo Mizuno,
Makoto Yotsuba, Miyuu
© 2016 Ryo Mizuno • Miyuu / KADOKAWA
© Makoto Yotsuba 2017
All rights reserved.
First published in Japan in 2017 by
HAKUSENSHA, Inc., Tokyo.
English language translation rights arranged with
HAKUSENSHA, Inc., Tokyo.

Printed in the U.S.A.

Published by VIZ Media, LLC
P.O. Box 77010
San Francisco, CA 94107

10 9 8 7 6 5 4 3 2 1
First printing, February 2019

PARENTAL ADVISORY
RECORD OF GRANCREST WAR is rated
M for Mature and is recommended for
Mature readers. This volume contains
graphic violence and sexual themes.

Ōoku

THE INNER CHAMBERS

by Eisner-Nominated creator
Fumi Yoshinaga

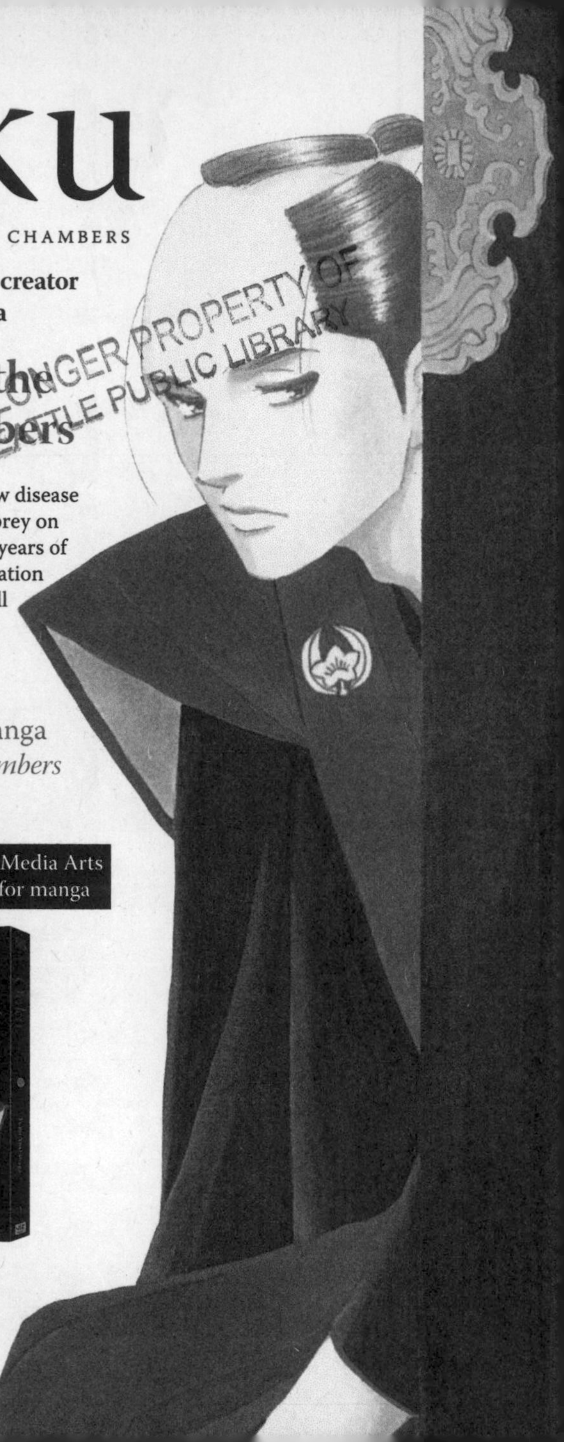

Tales from the Inner Chambers

In Edo period Japan, a strange new disease called the Redface Pox begins to prey on the country's men. Within eighty years of the first outbreak, the male population has fallen by 75 percent. What will the future hold in a world where men must be guarded as precious commodities?

Find out in the manga
Ōoku: The Inner Chambers
on sale now

Winner of the 2006 Japanese Media Arts Festival's Excellence Award for manga

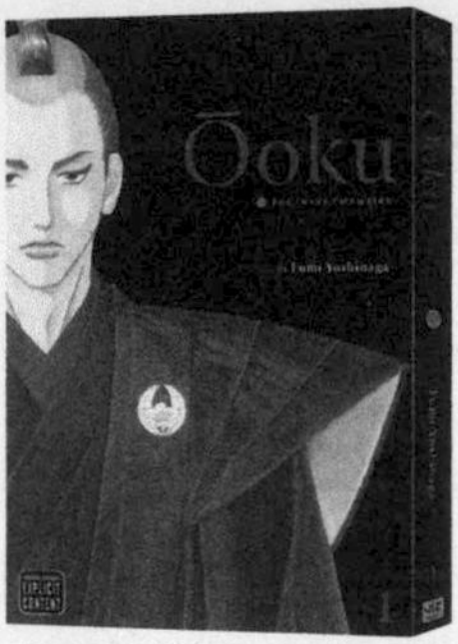
Ōoku
by Fumi Yoshinaga

VIZ media
www.viz.com

RATED M MATURE ratings.viz.com

PARENTAL ADVISORY EXPLICIT CONTENT

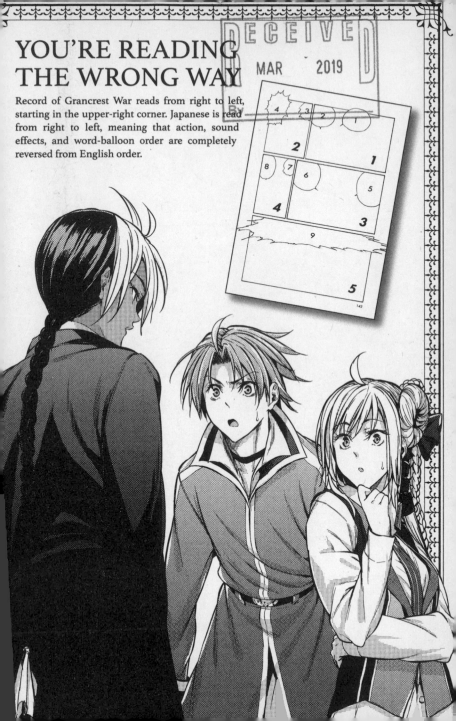

YOU'RE READING THE WRONG WAY

Record of Grancrest War reads from right to left, starting in the upper-right corner. Japanese is read from right to left, meaning that action, sound effects, and word-balloon order are completely reversed from English order.

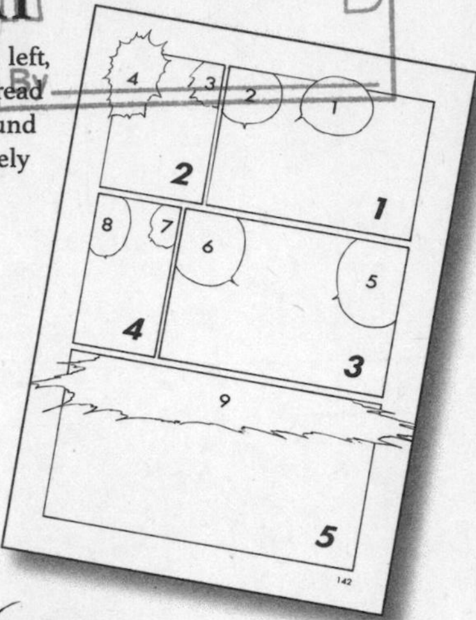
1
2
3
4
1
2
5
6
7
8
3
4
9
5
142

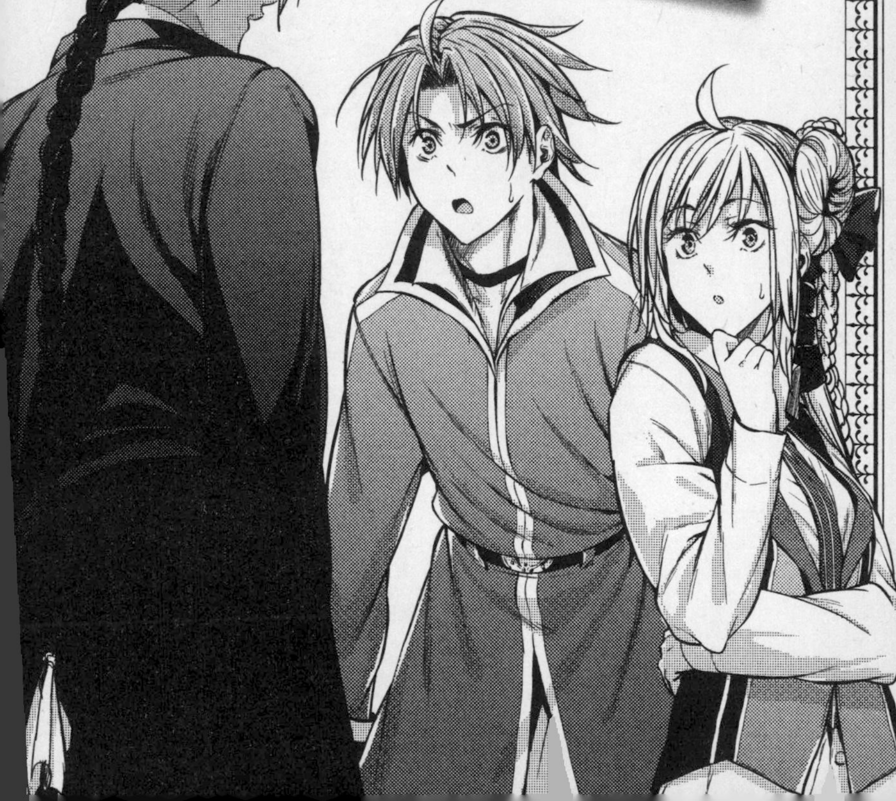